For Joseph T Comlet
Korean War Veteran
Enjoy in

W0007811

WAR, RELIGION AND THE PURSUIT OF SEX

Al Chamberlin

Al Chamberlin

8· 5· 02

ATHENA PRESS
MIAMI LONDON

WAR, RELIGION AND THE PURSUIT OF SEX
Copyright © Al Chamberlin 2002

All Rights Reserved

ISBN 1 930493 95 9

First Published 2002 by
ATHENA PRESS PUBLISHING CO.
1001 Brickell Bay Drive, Suite 2202
Miami, Florida 33131

Printed for Athena Press

WAR, RELIGION AND
THE PURSUIT OF SEX

To my heroes,
Bob Browne and Jack Neathery
of the Second Platoon of L Company,
179th Infantry, Forty-fifth Division.

Acknowledgments

I would like to thank my wife, Myrtle, for her loving patience and tolerance while I wrote this book.

I would also like to thank all the ladies who helped me in my pursuit. Without them this book would be much less.

May I also thank my daughter, Judy Joy Csicsatka, for her willing research efforts and my son, Rocky, for his constant inspiration.

Willard Chamberlin also deserves credit for valuable input into this book.

Foreword

I am prouder than words can say of my dad for having written this book. In a brilliant, candid, dynamic writing style he has told of a wild, dangerous, passionate time of his life from his eighteenth birthday through his return from the Korean War some ten years later. He has graciously given credit to many brave soldiers he fought with and exposed the villains and cowards for what they were. He does not glorify his own heroics in a war that twice decorated him, but rather focuses on the courage of others as well as the senseless horror, brutality, suffering and pain war inflicts. This is a book with a noble purpose and many moral messages.

But then I have always been proud of my dad. Simply put, for being who he is, a man of great courage, tremendous integrity and boundless compassion. In his life he has always been his honest self and treated those about him respectfully and generously, always a champion of the less fortunate, the underdog, never hesitating to assist, to offer a kind word, to lend what was needed, he was there for the simple asking. He was the benevolence that drew the soft, guileless hearts of children and animals like a magnet, as drawn was mine.

I am also grateful to my dad for letting me read this manuscript. But then again, I have always been grateful to my dad. Grateful for being the most wonderful father to me my entire life and for always believing in me.

I thank you for taking *War, Religion And The Pursuit Of Sex* in hand and hope you will enjoy it thoroughly.

Rocky Chamberlin

About The Author

Al Chamberlin was born in 1925 in Underhill, Vt. His family was poor and at thirteen he left home to work on local farms. He graduated from Underhill High School after serving in the Army in WWII. He graduated from Syracuse University in 1951. He served as an officer in the Korean War and was decorated for heroism. After leaving the service in 1953 he worked in a wide range of occupations including that of lumberjack, teacher, guidance counselor and social worker. He earned a masters in education from Suny at Buffalo in 1965 and a masters in Social work from Syracuse University in 1977.

He married his first wife, Josephine, in 1947. They have two children – Judy Joy Csicsatka and Rocky. He was divorced in 1974. He married his second wife, Dorothy, in 1983 after living with her for twelve years. Dorothy died in September 1993 of emphysema. She was an invalid for her last eight years during which Mr. Chamberlin was her sole caretaker. He married his current wife, Myrtle, in November 1994 in Chesapeake, Va. where they now live. He has two stepchildren from his second marriage – Chris and Teena, and two from his third marriage – Loretta and Pam. He has four grand children – Steve, Tony, Jennifer and David Alton.

When he became a teacher at the age of thirty-five he took up long-distance running and has completed over thirty marathons.

His first book, *Circle Of Courage* was published in 1991. It received excellent reviews and sold several thousand copies.

Chapter I

February 27, 1943 was my eighteenth birthday. WWII had been going on for over three years now, with no end in sight. We had been in it for nearly two years. I had to get home to register for the draft.

A two-day bus ride from Rumford, Maine, to Underhill, Vermont took me home. I pretended to be cool, casual and unemotional when I walked in through the front door of our house on the Raceway. But I was really happy and excited to be home again. Somehow it seemed important to me to go into the Army from my home town.

My mother hugged me and tears came to her eyes. "Oh Alton, where have you been?" she cried.

"I've been working in a lumber camp in Maine. I told you that was what I was going to do. I came home to sign up for the Army."

"Why didn't you write?" Mom continued. "I was worried about you."

"I just wanted to surprise you. I was all right. Nothing to worry about."

Being away from home for extended periods of time was not unusual for me or any of us four older brothers. We had all left home as soon as we could get jobs on local farms for board and room and a little spending money. We never got any spending money at home.

Conrow was five years older than me. He was now a Second Lieutenant in the Army Air Corps, flying B–17s. I was proud of him.

Kermit was twenty. He had a deferment to work on a farm. I was not very proud of him for avoiding the draft.

Willard was working on a local farm and was still in high school. He was sixteen months younger than me. We were close. We shared the same dream of becoming major league ball players.

Gerald and Olive were ten and eight. They were still in school and too young to leave home yet.

Anyhow, I wasn't very sensitive to my mother worrying about me. At least it appeared that way. Secretly, perhaps I wanted her to be concerned about me. Then when I did show up, I would be more important to her. I didn't know much about psychology then, but maybe that was why I did not always tell people what I was doing or where I was. The fear and trauma I put my mother through never entered my mind.

After I registered for the draft they ordered me to report to Burlington for a blood test. I guess they were checking for VD and to see how to classify us. Being in a long line of men, naked except for our shorts and shoes, made me feel very manly. I was happy and proud to be finally on my way to the Army.

But the big guy ahead of me didn't look so happy. He looked scared and pale. Though I wanted to be the strong, silent type, I didn't know enough to keep my mouth shut then.

"You don't look too good," I said.

Without a word he fainted and slumped to the floor. And he had not even had a needle stuck in his arm yet. That scared me, but fortunately I did not faint. I passed the blood test. One A became my classification.

Next they called me to Rutland for a physical. I packed all the stuff I thought I needed, including two baseball gloves and a baseball. My plan was to go right into the Army after I passed my physical. There was no need for me to return home for thirty days to take care of personal business.

The baseball equipment was in case I got a chance to play toss and catch with anybody or maybe even play in a team. My favorite pastime was playing baseball. Not only did I want to become a soldier and help fight the Germans and Japs, I also wanted to practice baseball as much as I could in my spare time. My dream of playing pro ball was still intact.

I was not into girls yet. Technically, I was still a virgin, unless some pre-puberty play in a haymow with some cousins would disqualify me.

In Rutland, they examined us from head to toe. They also weighed and measured us. They found nothing wrong with me.

But I was five feet nine inches and weighed only 118 pounds. For my height the minimum weight was 130 pounds. They told me I was too skinny for the Army.

Whereas many would have been happy to be classified 4F, unfit for the Army, I was devastated. My dreams were shattered. I had no alternate plans. I had boasted to the people in my home town of becoming a soldier and fighting for my country. Now how could I face them? Only like a dog with his tail between his legs.

In the summer of 1943, my brother Kermit and I worked on a farm in South Burlington for "Trick" Isham. We called him "Trick" behind his back because he said every task that had to be done had a "trick to it".

We ate well. Three big meals a day. Oatmeal every morning, but they wouldn't let us put cream on it. Only milk. So before we came into the house for breakfast, Kermit and I would drink a lot of cream from the top of a milk can which had been in the cooler all night. I tried to gain weight in case I got another chance to go into the Army. But I didn't gain much.

However, I did talk Kermit into giving up his farm deferment. I guess I shamed him into it.

Sometime in August we learned of a written examination for the Army Air Corps. Kermit and I took it along with a lot of other guys. Kermit had graduated from high school. I had finished only two years. But he flunked the test and I passed. Only one other person out of about thirty passed. That made me feel pretty smart, at least smarter than Kermit. I was elated. Now I would have a chance to be in the same branch of the service as Conrow. I might even become an officer, an accomplishment beyond my wildest dreams.

So back to Rutland for another physical. This time I was heavier, 128 pounds. But I was also taller, five feet ten inches tall. I failed again. I didn't even get past the scales.

Upon my return home there was nothing to look forward to. So for the want of anything better to do, I went back to school and started my junior year again. I was resigned to my fate of not amounting to anything, a prediction my father had pounded into my head as far back as I could remember.

Classes had barely started in early September, when I got another notice to report to Rutland for another physical on September 23. Kermit was also ordered to report on the same day.

On the bus ride down to Rutland we vowed to try to stay together as long as possible. We agreed to go right from the examination into military service without taking the thirty days personal business time. We also decided we would both go into the Army.

However, during the examination we were soon separated. But I trusted Kermit to live up to our agreement.

This time when they put me on the scales I was smarter. Instead of standing tall and proud, I slouched as much as I could. My weight was still only 128 pounds, but I was only five feet eight inches tall. This still was not up to standard but it was close enough to let me continue with the rest of the physical.

All went well until I got to a psychiatrist. He didn't think I was mature enough to be a soldier. Probably he noticed I didn't have much pubic hair yet or that I didn't need to shave. I begged him to give me a chance. He passed the buck to an Army captain to make the final decision.

The captain smiled and asked me, "What would you want to do if you saw a beautiful naked woman in front of you?"

Without hesitation I answered, "I'd want to fuck her."

"Okay, you passed," the Captain said. He looked at a companion and laughed. "He'll make a good soldier."

I was ecstatic. I rushed to find Kermit to tell him the good news. When I found him he said, "I joined the Navy."

"But we agreed to go into the Army together," I reminded him.

"I changed my mind. The Navy sounded like a better deal."

Out of that group two of us were put on a train for Fort Devens, Massachusetts. Finally I was in the Army.

Chapter II

The first morning at Fort Devens, I learned a new word: reveille. A sergeant came swaggering through the barracks hollering, "Reveille, rise and shine, huptadity. Get your lazy asses out of your fart sacks and fall in outside in five minutes for roll call."

It was six o'clock. No big deal for me. I was used to getting up at five on the farm to milk the cows. *This is great*, I thought. This is the way men talk to men in the Army, loud and dirty. I could do that.

Breakfast was at seven. That gave us an hour to stand in formation for roll call, do what we had to do in the latrine – another new word for bathroom – make our bunks and clean up our area. They told us we had to shave every day, but I didn't have anything to shave. That gave me an advantage.

At breakfast I tried out the Army way of talking. We ate at long tables with built-on benches. I wanted some sugar for my cereal. It was down at the other end of the table. So I hollered, "Pass the fucking sugar."

A fellow draftee sitting next to me said simply, "You don't have to use such foul language."

Maybe he thought I was mad about being in the Army, but I wasn't. I was just trying to talk like a soldier. He was older and more mature than me, but I figured he was not more of a man. I didn't bother to answer him.

After breakfast they lined us up for police call. We were told to pick up everything that didn't grow or wasn't nailed down. We walked slowly across the whole area around our barracks and picked up mostly cigarette butts and candy wrappers. Later, we were taught how to field strip a cigarette butt by tearing the paper off it, spreading the tobacco on the ground and wadding the paper into a small ball before discarding it. Then it would not be obvious enough to pick up. Other kinds of trash were not to be thrown on the ground. I didn't smoke so I didn't have to worry about field stripping cigarette butts, but I still had to police them up, whether I liked it or not.

At eight we started standing in lines. We lined up to get our uniforms. There was a line for personnel records. They gave us dog tags with our names, serial numbers and blood types on them. They were on chains to be worn at all times around our necks for identification. My number was 31340731 and my blood type was A. They told us to memorize our serial number because when we got paid we would have to state our name, rank and serial number to the pay officer. If we didn't know it, we would not get paid. That was no problem for me. I had always been good at memorizing stuff in school.

The Army paid privates fifty a month. That was about ten more than I was getting on the farm. I thought that was pretty good, on top of all the clothes, board and room they were giving us. I signed up to have $18.75 taken out of my pay for a $25 U.S. Savings Bond. That was the patriotic thing to do and a good way to save money. It was to be sent home to my mother. Later, I wrote her about it and told her to save it for me.

With great gravity they told us that name, rank and serial number were all we were supposed to tell the enemy if we were captured, no matter how much we were tortured. They told us the Germans and Japs were good at that. That made me hate the enemy even more and be even more patriotic. I guess I hated the Japs the most. Maybe because of Pearl Harbor. I thought they were more treacherous. I know I feared them more, I had heard they were very quick and good at jujitsu. I dreaded meeting one of them in hand-to-hand combat. My hope was to be sent to fight the Germans, not the Japs.

We each got a copy of the General Orders. These were orders a soldier on guard duty had to follow. They were sort of the military equivalent of The Ten Commandments. We were informed that we had to memorize them before we would be allowed to do guard duty. So that we wouldn't get the wrong idea, we were told there were plenty of other dirty details we could be put on, if we did not know them when our turn came up to pull guard duty, e.g., KP (Kitchen Police). One order went something like this: to walk my post in a military manner and take no orders except from my company commander. Some joker changed the last part of that to "take no shit from the company commander". I thought that was pretty funny.

Before the day was over we stood in another line to get shots for all kinds of immunizations. Shortly thereafter, some sergeant took us out to a big parade field and made us exercise. He told us it would make the shots spread through our bodies faster so it would not hurt so much. All it did for me was to make my arm hurt like hell.

During my brief stay at Fort Devens, I learned a few other things about the Army. Everybody had to dress the same. The uniform of the day was always posted on the company bulletin board. We were responsible to read it. No excuses were tolerated. We had to keep our shirts or jackets buttoned up, including pockets. Whenever we were outdoors we had to wear headgear. There were fatigue caps for our work uniforms and garrison caps for our dress uniforms. We learned to call them "cunt caps" because some wit thought the crease in their peak reminded him of his lover's genitals. Sounded good to me.

They taught us how to salute and told us we had to salute all the officers we met outdoors or those we had to report to indoors, e.g., the paymaster. The one exception which I remembered was, if you were double-timing – running twice as fast as a regular marching pace – you didn't have to salute. I never had the occasion to salute an officer at Fort Devens.

When we were not lined up for some sort of processing, an NCO (Non-commissioned Officer) would take us out to the parade field and try to teach us how to stand and march properly as soldiers. The Army called this close-order drill. Some of us were more clumsy than others. I, for example, always seemed to step on the heels of the man in front of me. I thought a step should be thirty-six inches but the Army wanted it to be only thirty inches. The guy ahead of me wanted me to stop stepping on him. I learned gradually. I don't think the NCOs cared whether we learned anything or not. They just had to keep us busy while we were there, which would not be long.

Every day, we had to check the bulletin board to see if our names were on a list to be shipped out. I bragged about wanting to be sent to an infantry outfit and going overseas into combat.

After about a week my name appeared on a list of men to be sent to an AAA (Antiaircraft Artillery) unit in Fort Bliss, Texas.

My disappointment was great. By now the allied forces had control of the air. The prospect of shooting down any enemy was remote. Being in an AAA outfit limited my chances of being in combat action to next to none. What could I tell the people back home I had done in the war, if I never saw any action? It was important to me to have a chance to prove I had the courage to fight. I was not like Kermit who always tried to avoid fighting. He was going into the Navy probably to get out of fighting. I was more like Conrow. He was now over in Italy flying bombing missions over German-held territory in Europe. To me, that made him a real man. Back home nobody, especially my father, ever thought of me as a man. Now my chance to prove it was gone.

But in the Army you do as you are told. So I was put on a troop train and sent to Fort Bliss, Texas.

Chapter III

When we got to Fort Bliss, they put us in some tents on the lower slopes of a mountain called Logan Heights, for a day or so before assigning us to a unit. It was there that I met the first officer outdoors. At first I panicked because I felt insecure about how to salute. I was scared he would chew me out if I didn't do it right. Then I remembered you did not have to salute if you were double-timing. So I broke into a run before I got to him. Saved by my memory!

We were moved to large, plush-looking, adobe-finished barracks down in the main part of Fort Bliss. I was assigned to C Battery of an AAA Battalion. The battery consisted of four 90-millimeter guns, four 0.50-caliber machine guns and fire control equipment – radar, rangefinder, stuff like that.

They put me in the machine-gun section. Except for the fact that I was not happy being in, what I considered, a non-combat outfit, things went fairly well for me for a while. Our section sergeant was good to us. He taught us all about the machine gun. We learned the names of all the parts and how they worked. We took the guns apart and put them back together so many times that we were able to do it blindfolded.

We were also issued more personal equipment like M1 rifles, shelter halves (half of a pup tent), leggings, steel helmets and helmet liners. We had classes on how to use our equipment. They called it supply economy. They told us if we lost any of our equipment, or if it were damaged, we would have to sign a statement of charges and pay for it by having it taken out of our pay.

Since our mission would be to shoot down enemy planes if we ever got into combat, we had to learn how to identify planes. They would take us to a theater and show us pictures of all the enemy and friendly planes. They also gave us cards for each plane to study in our free time. I found that I was pretty good at this. I kept getting better and better. On a final test we were given a quick glimpse of planes on the screen and asked to identify them. Another guy and I tied for the highest score in the battery. That made me feel good.

Soon thereafter, there was a list of promotions to PFC (Private First Class) put on the bulletin board. My name was not there. That made me feel bad. What good did it do to learn all about machine guns and airplanes faster than most of the other guys if they got promoted before I did?

The physical part of training was easy for me. We didn't spend much time on a regular basis doing calisthenics, but when we did, it was not hard for me. They did build us up gradually for long marches though. We started with a two-mile hike, then a five-miler, a ten-miler and finally a twenty-mile, all-day hike.

One guy didn't want to be in the Army. He was short and good-looking. He seemed very bright and articulate. Said he was from Hollywood and had played parts in some movies. Whenever we did close-order drill or PT (Physical Training) he would fuck up. He'd pretend he didn't know his right from his left and always turned the wrong way. He'd say he couldn't do the exercises or that he was sick. He went on sick call as often as they would let him. On the first two-mile hike he got a blister and dropped out from pain and fatigue. He volunteered for KP to get out of all the other hikes. In the evenings, when we were in our quarters, he would laugh about his gold-bricking. Then he would do one-arm push-ups to prove how strong he was. As far as I know, nobody ever squealed on him to the officers or cadre in charge of us. Maybe it was because he was always doing things for us, like giving us rubdowns after hikes. He gave me one after the twenty-mile hike and complimented me on the muscle structure of my legs. Maybe he was queer, but that never entered my head at that time. His rubdown felt good.

Another unhappy draftee used a different tactic to get out of the Army. He pissed in the bed every night.

Speaking of the twenty-mile hike, I did well on that. We started at eight in the morning and hiked until 1600 hours (military time for four o'clock in the evening), with ten-minute breaks every hour. At first it was easy for me. We were at rout step, which meant we did not have to stay in step or close to each other. That gave me a chance to take long strides like I used to back in Vermont. By about the third hour into the hike, the muscles inside my crotch started to hurt. I was scared I could not make it. Finally we stopped for a meal at noon. They gave us all the hot chow and coffee we wanted. I don't remember food ever tasting so good. Then we rested until one.

When we started walking again I decided to try a shorter, quicker stride. It worked! My inner thigh muscles didn't hurt anymore. I was pleased at how smart I was.

After lunch I was the second man from the lead, so when we came to an intersection it was my job to go ahead and be a road guard until the rest of the troops had cleared the intersection. Then the road guards were supposed to fall in at the end of the column. But not me. To show off, I ran past the others and took up the second spot so I would be the road guard again. The other guys didn't care because they didn't want to do it. I did this several times during the last three hours of the hike. The guy who had tied with me on the plane-identification test saw what I was doing and he did the some thing. It was like a competition.

When we got back to the barracks I boasted about how well I had done. I said, "I bet I could run ten miles."

A corporal, who was probably sick of my bragging, spoke up. "I'll bet you $50 you can't."

I just happened to have a little over $50 saved up. I couldn't back down after I had shot off my mouth. "Okay, you're on," I said. "I bet $50 I can."

So we set the date about two weeks from then, on a Sunday. We were arranging for a neutral party to hold the money when Sergeant Blum heard us. Sergeant Blum was in charge of the fire control section. He was from Boston and probably knew about the Boston Marathon. Anyhow, I guess he figured I didn't know what it took to run ten miles and that the corporal was taking advantage of me. So he came to my rescue.

"Gambling is against regulations, so your bet is off," he told us.

Gambling might have been against regulations, but I found out there was plenty of it going on in the day room in the evenings. One night I was watching a crap game. The shooter rolled a ten. Somebody said, "Ten to five no ten."

I had watched long enough to know that seven or eleven on the first roll were winners and seven on any roll after that was a loser. But I didn't know anything about the odds. I thought he could roll a ten as likely as a seven. I took the bet. I won. Two or three times I took similar bets that night and won. They told me it was beginner's luck.

Eventually, I got up enough courage to take my turn at rolling the dice. I usually broke even or a little ahead.

Later, I learned the game of Black Jack. At first I wasn't very smart, hitting 17s or even 18s sometimes. Once, when I was dealing, I hit an 18 with a 3 for 21. The number 21 is an automatic winner for the dealer. Luck seemed to favor me in this game too.

Then I tried my hand at poker. There I didn't do very well. Taking chances in poker didn't usually pay off.

Early in our training, they showed us a film on VD. We learned about clap, blue balls, and syphilis from graphic pictures. I guess they were trying to scare us away from having sex with prostitutes. But in case we did, the film explained how to put on a safety and how to use a pro kit after we were done. Most of us thought, the film was pretty funny. Old-timers in the service called it "Mickey Mouse".

El Paso was just outside of camp and Juarez, Mexico, was just across the border. I heard there were lots of whores there. I never went to town. Money was too precious to me to spend it on drinking or women. I did not even smoke. But many of my buddies would go to Juarez to get laid.

Della Bella was one of my friends He was a big, stocky fellow, built like a football player. He was not too bright. I thought he liked me because I caught on to things quickly and would explain things to him sometimes. But maybe it was because he found out I had some money saved up. Every chance he got he would go to Juarez for a piece. He told me it only cost him two dollars. He tried to get me to go with him but I wouldn't. He would always run out of money before payday. Then he would ask me to loan him enough to visit a whorehouse. I would loan it to him to keep his friendship. He always paid me back.

Hart was another good friend. We were about the same size and about equal when it came to learning things and doing physical stuff. He knew all about girls and also went to town frequently to pick up girls. He gave me the address of a girl from his home town in Pennsylvania, because I did not have a girlfriend. She was only sixteen but I was only eighteen, so I thought it was all right to write to her. She wrote back and we had a long, mushy correspondence.

One of my buddies from Texas (we called him Tex) got us in trouble. He let his dirty laundry pile up so we didn't pass inspection. I happened to find out he couldn't read well enough to make out a laundry slip. I felt sorry for him so I helped him fill out the slip.

But I didn't feel sorry enough for him not to be a party to a practical joke on him. He often went to town at night, after duty hours. We knew he was deathly afraid of snakes. So a couple of his other buddies and I, filled a condom with water, tied the end and put it in his bunk. Sure enough, when he came in and started to get in his bunk, he felt the rubber and thought it was a snake. He let out a frightened scream that woke everybody up. All hell broke loose. All the NCOs in the building converged on our section of the barracks. All the lights went on. Even Sergeant Tremont, our first sergeant, came. He chewed us out and told everybody to get back to bed.

Going through the infiltration course was a requirement of basic training. This was where you had to crawl about a hundred yards under machine-gun fire and barbed wire. To a couple of my buddies and me, it was exciting. After we went through once we ran back to the starting point and went through again. I guess we were bragging about how brave we were. While we were getting ready for our second crawl, we saw some of the guys cowering at the starting line. We laughed at their fear and felt superior.

At one point in our training we moved up to Logan Heights and lived in squad tents. They took us out into the field and taught us how to dig gun emplacements, set up our guns and camouflage them like we would in real combat.

One evening after supper, Sergeant Tremont came into our

tent. "I'm looking for volunteers to compete in a physical fitness contest against the other batteries," he said. "Chamberlin, you look like you're in pretty good shape. Want to try it?"

"Sure," I said eagerly. "What do I have to do?"

"Pull-ups, push-ups, sit-ups, squat jumps and run. How many push-ups can you do?"

"I don't know. How do you do a push-up?"

For some inexplicable reason I had spent about five months in the Army and had never been asked to do a push-up.

Sergeant Tremont showed me how. I tried. I couldn't do one push-up. I was totally embarrassed. Needless to say I did not compete in the physical fitness competition. I was beginning to realize reality can be a rough ruler.

After that rude awakening, I started getting up a few minutes early every morning and tried to do push-ups down behind the latrine, where nobody could see me. After a few days I managed to do one. Then I gradually got so I could do more and more.

It was at about this stage of our training that I learned some tragic news. My mother wrote that Conrow had been shot down while on a bombing mission over Yugoslavia. He was listed as MIA (Missing In Action).

Chapter IV

The news of Conrow, my oldest brother, being shot down by the Germans shook me. Conrow had been more of a father to me than my biological father. In my early years when I was ill, he took me to see Doctor Towne. When I was hungry he stole food from Kirby's store for me. He made me read books so I could do well in school. When I ran away from home he came to bring me back. He called me a "gem" he did not want to lose. Before he enlisted in the National Guard at the beginning of WWII, we worked together for Burr and Marion Gleason on their farm in Jericho, Vermont. He was always good to me. I loved him.

Even the time he shot a hole through the wall of our bedroom a couple of feet from my head did not make me think less of him. I remembered it well. We were rehearsing my eighth grade graduation speech. He wanted me to say it in a low, deep voice. I could not speak that way yet. So he picked up his 12-gauge shotgun, loaded it and aimed it at me.

"If you don't say it like you're supposed to, I'll blow your head off," he threatened.

"I can't," I whimpered and started bawling.

But I was not scared. My tears were more fake than real. I just wanted him to pity me, let me go downstairs, eat breakfast and go to school. I didn't think he was crazy enough to carry out his threat. I felt relieved when I noticed he pointed the gun a little to my right. I was even more relieved when the gun went off and the shot blew a six-inch hole in the wall instead of in me. I guess he needed to keep his promise to shoot and pretended he had missed.

When she heard the gun go off our mother hollered from the kitchen below us, "He has shot the smartest one in the family! Fordyce, do something,"

Our old man hurried up the stairs, but by the time he got there, Conrow had jumped out a window and run away. I was

25

glad he got away. He never came back to live at our house on the Raceway again. I think that was about the time he started working for Burr Gleason. Just before my graduation, Conrow bought me a nice gaberdine suit for the occasion from Sears Roebuck. It was the first suit I ever had.

Conrow's National Guard unit was called into active duty and became an Army unit soon after WWII started. He got a chance to go into the Army Air Corps and became a pilot. After he became a second lieutenant he married a pretty southern nurse named Mildred. I saw Conrow and his wife only once after he entered the Army. After their wedding they visited our place on the Raceway. Conrow looked so nice in his officer's green and pinks.

My brother Willard tackled him as soon as he saw him. Conrow landed on his back on the kitchen floor with Willard on top of him. Conrow's uniform got a little dusty. When we were growing up, Willard was always fighting Conrow and Conrow would beat the hell out of him. I guess Willard needed to prove that Conrow could no longer handle him. But this time Conrow did not fight back. Probably he did not want to embarrass his new bride.

Willard was now a Marine at Camp Lejeune. He had joined up in the fall of 1943 at the age of seventeen. I wondered how he felt about Conrow now that he had been shot down and maybe killed.

To me Conrow was already a war hero. Twice he had brought back his B–17 from bombing raids with only two of its four engines functioning. I knew he was in great danger and could be killed. But I never expected it to happen. I was devastated. I became despondent and bitter. Life lost its luster. I even stopped doing push-ups.

Was he killed? Was he wounded? Was he a prisoner of war and being tortured? Was he suffering? These kinds of questions would not leave my mind. Like lead weights they burdened me.

At about this time we went on bivouac near Waco, Texas. The big guns were set up and the machine guns were emplaced on the perimeter of the battery's position. We practiced firing our machine guns at long-sleeve targets towed behind airplanes. Sometimes we fired at radio-controlled planes. That was fun for the other guys. Nothing was fun for me anymore. Every fourth round in the machine-gun belt was a tracer bullet. These were coated with luminous paint that lit up, making the bullets look like a stream of fire in the air. That is how we aimed the machine-gun fire. In combat, our mission would be to protect the big guns and fire control section, by shooting down enemy planes before they got too close. Sometimes, when they were firing at make-believe tanks, the big guns would fire directly over our heads only a few feet above us. The shells whizzing over our heads made an awfully loud, cracking sound. It was much more scary than the infiltration course.

While in the field we lived in pup tents. There was no reveille. I shared a tent with Manning, one of my buddies. We decided one morning not to get up for breakfast when Sergeant Tremont came around to wake everybody up. We thought we'd get an extra hour of sleep by skipping breakfast. Sergeant Tremont had other ideas. When he came around the second time, not only did he yell, "Get your asses out of bed," he also pulled our tent down on top of us.

After we crawled out from under the torn-down tent, I noticed that my half of the tent had been ripped. My first thought was that I would have to pay for it. That made me mad.

I hollered at Sergeant Tremont, "Tremont, you dirty motherfucker, look what you did to my shelter half. Now I have to pay for it."

In a low, calm voice Sergeant Tremont replied, "Chamberlin, I'm going to court martial you."

Looking back at the situation, it is easy to see that he had no alternative. We were only a few feet behind the battery commander's tent, well within his earshot. He probably heard me. I didn't realize it then, but the Army will not tolerate that sort of insubordination.

Up to that point I had considered Sergeant Tremont a good guy, a friend, I thought that was the way friends in the Army talked to each other when they got a little pissed off. I still thought he was kidding.

In answer to his threat I added fuel to the fire by saying, "Tremont, go fuck yourself."

Chapter V

My summary court martial took place in the office of one of the battalion's staff officers. His name, if I ever did know it, did not linger long in my memory. But I do recall that he was a major. He sat tall, proud and intimidating behind his large, wooden desk. I sat humble and scared in a metal folding chair in front of him. We were both in our dress uniforms.

He read me some stuff from some papers and a book. Basically it consisted of the charges against me – insubordination and my rights. I could plead guilty and accept my punishment, I could plead innocent and take my chances with a summary court martial or I could request a special court martial in which the penalty could be more severe. I didn't think I had been insubordinate, so I chose to plead innocent and have a summary court martial. I did not expect any grave consequences.

The first witness was our battery commander, Captain whatever-his-name-was. His name escaped my memory also. (In later life I learned that people tend to forget unpleasant things.) The major asked him what happened.

The captain said, "I can't remember the exact words, but Private Chamberlin did refuse to get up when Sergeant Tremont ordered him to."

The next and last witness was Sergeant Tremont himself. He also said that I had been disobedient.

After that, the major gave me a little lecture on being a good soldier and then sentenced me to thirty days of hard labor and the loss of two-thirds of a month's pay.

Everything had been so formal and polite. To me it had all sounded like sickening sweet shit. Nobody had said anything about what I had actually said to Sergeant Tremont. It was like they were pretending soldiers didn't talk that way. Inside I was mad as hell, but I wisely kept my mouth shut.

To my total surprise, I was sent back to my own battery and

my first hard labor assignment was to dig up the sun-baked dirt around some shrubs by our barracks with a trowel. Sergeant Tremont told me how to do it and stood over me to supervise. By this time I hated him. But I tried to do what he told me to. For some reason he didn't like the way I was doing it and tried to make me do it the way he wanted it done.

I got pissed off and exploded, "Tremont, if you don't like the way I'm doing it, do it yourself." I was careful not to use any foul language.

With complete cool Sergeant Tremont warned me, "Chamberlin, I'm trying to make it easy on you. But if you won't take orders from me, I can make it a lot harder on you."

"I don't care," I said. "I'm not going to take any more orders from you."

I was immediately escorted back to the major's office. He asked me what happened.

I told him, "I don't think it's fair that I should have to do my hard labor under the man who pressed charges against me."

Apparently, he agreed with me or maybe he just didn't want to create a bigger stink. Anyhow, I didn't have to do anything more for Sergeant Tremont or C Battery during my thirty days of hard labor.

Arrangements were made for me to move my things to a private room in the barracks of another battery. I don't know why they didn't send me to the post stockade with other prisoners, but they didn't. Maybe you needed more than thirty days to qualify.

That evening at the changing of the guard, a new post was created – Private Chamberlin, I was to be escorted by an armed guard wherever I went for the next thirty days. At night the guard was stationed outside the door of my room. Apparently, I was a dangerous criminal. At least I was notorious in that little sphere of soldiers.

The irony of my having a private room did not escape me. It would have been a luxury to other GIs (soldiers in the U.S. Army) but it was my prison, my solitary confinement.

During the period of my imprisonment they still took me back to my battery for meals. I developed a cocky, happy-go-lucky attitude towards my battery peers. As much as I could I talked, joked and laughed with them. Somebody got me a fatigue hat with a brim all the way around it, like real prisoners wore. I wore it in a jaunty manner, cocked forward slightly on the left side of my head. It sort of matched my outward attitude. It was as if I were some kind of hero telling the authorities to kiss my ass.

I don't think my guards knew what they were supposed to do. Some would just follow me around and let me do whatever I wanted to, as long as I did whatever task was assigned to me. I think they were embarrassed with their assignment.

I cleaned every grease trap in the battalion, polished most of the latrines' faucets and mopped lots of floors while I was incarcerated. One time, a first sergeant was going to use my services to please his commanding officer. He furnished me with a GI brush, GI soap, hot water, rags and wax. He wanted me to wash and wax the floor of his captain's office.

"Chamberlin," (they all knew my name by now) "I want you to scrub the floor of this room with hot soapy water. Then let it dry. When it is dry, take a rag and wax it. Then do the same thing over again." He was very careful to show me exactly how to make the water soapy, use the scrub brush, dip the wax from the can with the rag and rub it on the floor – much like putting polish on our boots.

The guard was standing there and heard his orders as clearly as I did. So I did exactly as I was told. I got down on my hands and knees and scrubbed the floor clean, waited for it to dry and waxed it thoroughly. Then I did the same thing again – wash, wait and wax.

I knew it didn't make sense to wash off the first coat of wax, but I didn't give a shit. The stupid guard didn't say anything.

The captain came in about when I had the floor washed the second time. He was pissed off because he couldn't use his office.

The first sergeant showed up and chewed me out. I acted dumb and said, "I did exactly what you told me to do."

What could the sergeant do but call me "stupid" and go away mad? I was already being punished.

I laughed to myself as I finished waxing the floor, the second time. The captain was not able to use his office that day.

After supper each evening, the sergeant of the guard now had a special assignment to teach me close-order drill for about an hour. It must have looked silly as hell to any passers-by. I didn't care. I imagine the sergeants felt embarrassed though.

I was not supposed to be allowed to socialize with anybody or have any fun. They stopped me from talking to my friends when I went to eat at my battery and made me eat at a table by myself. But sometimes I would get a guard that I could manipulate a little. On one such occasion, the guard was following me through the building during the evening. We came to a bunch of guys shooting crap. I stopped to watch. Somebody offered a small side bet. I took it. The guard didn't know what to do so he did nothing. I won. I kept betting and winning. When it came my turn to roll the dice, I rolled them and won some more. I kept playing until the corporal of the guard showed up and stopped me. He chewed the guard out and made me go to my room. I kept my winnings and smiled at my luck.

Even though I maintained an outward appearance of carefree, light-hearted cockiness, on the inside I was not happy or proud. I was sad and ashamed. I didn't want any of my family or friends back home to know I had screwed up and got myself in trouble.

My mother and my brother Willard, were family members who wrote me quite often. Kermit wrote once in a while. My young pen pal from Pennsylvania wrote often, and was getting very mushy. When I wrote to them I pretended nothing was wrong.

My mail was censored. This didn't bother me too much except for correspondence with my female pen pal. I was careful what I wrote her, but she had no reason to be careful what she wrote to me. Not only did she write sweet, sentimental stuff, she would also put sweet-smelling powder in with her letters. One day the sergeant of the guard brought my mail to me. One of her letters was in it. It was heavily powdered and the pink powder had spilled over all the rest of my mail. The sergeant's face was red from embarrassment. I pretended not to care, but I was embarrassed too. I wrote and told her not to put powder in her letters anymore because the guys teased me about it. Our correspondence dried up after that and soon ended.

Finally, my thirty days were over. They were the longest thirty days of my life. I vowed to myself that I would never again be insubordinate.

Chapter VI

After my sentence had been completed they returned me to C Battery. A few days later a notice appeared on the bulletin board asking for volunteers for the Infantry. My heart leapt with joy! I rushed to the orderly room – the first sergeant's office – as fast as I could. Sergeant Tremont was only too happy to put my name on the list of volunteers. I was elated to finally be going to a combat outfit!

Three or four other malcontents, including my buddy Hart, also volunteered. We were sent to the Ninety-seventh Division which was training at Fort Leonardwood, Missouri. I was assigned to H Company, 303rd Infantry Regiment. They put me in the third squad of the second platoon. I learned that there were three regiments in our division. Each regiment had three battalions and each battalion had four companies. H Company was a heavy weapons company, made up of three platoons. The first and second platoons each had four squads. Each squad had a water-cooled 0.30-caliber machine gun. The third platoon was a heavy mortar platoon. It had four 81-millimeter mortar squads.

We were housed in two story wooden barracks. We were on the second floor and the first platoon was on the first floor. Our quarters were not as luxurious as the buildings we lived in at Fort Bliss, but I didn't mind. I was happy. I was in a fighting outfit at last.

They made me a second gunner and gave me a .45-caliber pistol as my TO&E (Table of Organization and Equipment) weapon.

The job of the second gunner was to carry and take care of the machine gun. The first gunner carried the tripod on which the gun was mounted when in position to fire. Boy, was I proud! I was the number three man in the squad, after the squad leader and the first gunner, and carried a .45. Somewhat different from my old outfit. There I had been considered a "yardbird", a misfit.

The 0.30-caliber machine gun was not much different from the 0.50-caliber machine gun that I had already learned all about. So my new job was easy for me.

I felt good. I knew what my job was. I was pretty sure we would get into combat if the war lasted long enough, and I would have a chance to fight for my country, to prove I was a man. On the one hand I wanted us to win the war as soon as possible. Everybody did. On the other hand I saw the war as a stepping stone into adulthood. At the time I did not see the paradox of my position. In fact, I doubt if I even knew the meaning of the word paradox.

To my surprise, not long after I joined my new outfit, they told me I was eligible for a ten-day furlough. But I didn't have enough money for the train ticket. So I wrote my mother and asked her if she would loan me the money. She didn't have it either. So she went to the Red Cross. They turned her down. Then she appealed to the Salvation Army and they loaned her the money. Since then I have never cared for the Red Cross. I never give them anything, but often donate to the Salvation Army.

My buddy Hart was assigned to another regiment. We visited back and forth. He had a sharp-looking pair of gaberdine, suntan pants. They looked a lot nicer than our regular cotton suntans. We were about the same size, so he let me borrow them to wear on my furlough, in case I met any girls I wanted to impress.

When I got on the train there were not many empty seats but I found one next to a young girl. She was quite good-looking and had an attractive figure. She was probably between sixteen and eighteen. I don't know because we never spoke. We just sat silently next to each other as the train traveled eastward. It wasn't so much that I was shy or bashful. I just didn't know what to say. I guess I was just dumb about girls. But the longer we sat quietly close, the more I liked her. I remembered that I had had a crush on a girl back home who was also shy and hardly ever spoke. Her name was Eva. We had never spoken to each other either.

When night fell and it became cool, blankets were brought to us for our comfort. We found ourselves under one blanket sharing the warmth of our bodies. Her body felt nice next to mine. We were covered up to our necks. The rest of us was invisible to the other passengers.

Slowly, so as not to be noticed by those near us and not to alarm her, I moved closer to her and turned slightly towards her. She did not seem to mind. She did not move away. Was she snuggling closer to me? I touched her arm. Still she did not move. My courage rose. I touched her chest. There was no resistance. Gently, so as not to startle her, I unbuttoned the top button of her blouse. Stealthily my right hand slid slowly inside the opened neck. It touched her left breast over her bra. She did not say anything. I accepted her silence as approval. My hand became bolder and maneuvered its way inside her bra and cupped the soft flesh of her bust. I had never touched a woman's breast before, except maybe my mother's as a baby. It felt good!

But that was as far as I went. I did not try to touch any other part of her body. I was more than satisfied to have got as far as I had. I did not even try to kiss her. That could have been seen by other passengers. That could ruin the moment. No one could see my right hand gently kneading her left breast. Throughout the night we remained in the same position. I did not sleep. My hand did not cease its gentle caressing. Did she sleep? I don't know. She didn't say.

Dawn came. I removed my hand. She buttoned her blouse. The blanket was removed. Soon the train pulled into Albany, N.Y. There I was to transfer to other transportation going north to Burlington, Vermont. She also got off the train there. We still did not speak until we were off the train.

Then as she hastily walked away, I said, "I don't even know your name."

She did not reply. She did not look back. I started to walk after her.

An MP (Military Police) stopped me. "Soldier," he said, "tuck in your shirt."

Sure enough, the back of my shirt tail was out of my pants. I set my luggage down and tucked it in. The pursuit of my silent partner ended in vain.

I boarded a bus for Burlington and continued on my way home. As the bus rolled northward, I dozed contentedly. I was not disappointed with myself. I could now tell friends at home that I was in a combat outfit and would probably have a chance to fight for my country. I didn't think I could tell them about what I had done last night. Not that I was ashamed. I just would not know how to explain it.

Chapter VII

Roy Keith was a long time friend from school days. He was about a year younger than I was. We had had a slight rivalry over a girl named Peggy, when we were in grade school. He had won because he had better clothes than I did and was more sophisticated. He also had more spending money so he could buy her stuff. I didn't have any spending money. For some reason he never went in the service. I guess he was 4F.

Roy and I buddied around a lot while I was home on my first furlough. We learned to drink together. We went to Burlington one day to look for girls. On the way we stopped at a state liquor store in Winooski and bought a bottle of cheap red wine. Winooski is a small city right next to Burlington. The drinking age in Vermont was twenty-one then. They must have sold me the wine because I was in uniform. I was only nineteen.

We went behind an abandoned factory building and drank the whole bottle, about a pint apiece, in a very short time. It made us half blind but happy as hell. We proceeded on to Burlington, laughing at everything and everybody, making passes at girls and just making fools of ourselves. That day we did not make out with any girls.

Across the street from the Keith house in the village of Underhill, lived Old Lady Cushion. She was an eccentric character. Her house was more run-down than most other houses in the village. In one room in the front part of the house she sold candy. When we were kids we would stop and buy some candy if we ever had a few pennies. She always acted sort of grouchy so we didn't like her very much.

As I was walking by her place one day, while on that first furlough, she came to the door and beckoned me in.

"Alton," she said, "let me look at your right hand."

I held out my hand to her and she took it in her hands. She studied it carefully. Finally she smiled and said, "You don't have to worry. You are not going to get hurt in the war."

"How do you know?" I asked.

"You have a long lifeline," she explained. "See," she said, as she pointed to a long line running down through the middle of the palm of my right hand.

I never forgot the prophecy of Old Lady Cushion.

Freddie Metcalf was another one of my friends from my high school days. He had a car so he would take Roy and me to barn dances in Williston, a small farming community a few miles east of Burlington. They had them once a week, so I guess we must have gone to two of them while I was home that time. We would get some wine and get to feeling good before the dance. Then Roy and I would dance and flirt with the girls. Freddie never paid any attention to the girls. He just hung around and waited for Roy and me. When we weren't dancing he would tell us a lot of dirty jokes. He never ran out of them. Freddie never went in the service either. I don't know why.

At one of the dances I met this gorgeous woman. I have forgotten her name but I'll call her Rose because of her beautiful rosy complexion. She had black hair and the most enticing bust I had ever seen. I danced with her most of the evening. Her beauty was so intimidating that I tried my best to act like a gentleman even though I was half drunk. I behaved well enough so she invited me to visit her at her home in North Underhill, a few miles north of where we lived.

I went to see her the next day. She was very nice to me. She was also interested in palm reading and she told me a lot about it. She agreed with Old Lady Cushion's assessment of my long life. As she held my hand she also showed me the love and money lines. I was going to be in love twice, have two or three children (she wasn't sure of the third one) and have plenty of money.

All very fascinating to me, but not what I wanted from her. I held her left hand – she told me you read a man's right hand and a woman's left – and tried to figure out her destiny. I wanted to do more than just read palms, but it was broad daylight and there were some young kids around. And I was trying to be even more of a gentleman than the night before at the dance. I was afraid she would send me home if she knew what I would like to do.

to report to him. After talking to me, I expect he gave up trying to cheat us out of getting an "early out".

I packed my stuff. I had acquired a metal footlocker while at Camp Drake. I put Bob Browne's Russian rifle, which he had entrusted to me to bring home to him, at the bottom of the footlocker and covered it with shirts and other clothing. The footlocker and my duffel bag had to be checked by a sergeant for contraband before being shipped home.

"Anything illegal in here?" the sergeant asked, as he opened the footlocker.

"I don't think so," I lied with a straight face. I knew we were not allowed to bring Russian rifles home. Why, I don't know. More military chickenshit, I guess.

The sergeant started lifting shirts one by one. I watched with bated breath as he neared the bottom. He stopped just short of the rifle.

Then he said, "I guess it's okay." Lady Luck had smiled on me again.

Whenever a soldier left a base he had to check out. A list of places he had to check out from was prepared for him, such as supply, personnel, etc. These checkout stations on his list had to be initialed before he was cleared to leave. My last checkout station was the officers' club in downtown Sasebo.

A nondescript looking WAC was there when I arrived to get my checkout list initialed.

"You have to pay your $15 membership dues before I can initial that," she informed me.

"But I'm not a member," I said. "I've never even been in the club."

"You still have to pay," she continued. "It's the rule."

"Some more goddamned chickenshit rules," I blurted out angrily. "That pisses me off."

A male sergeant was hovering in the background. He came to the WAC's rescue. "Watch your language, Lieutenant," he said.

"Pardon me all to hell," I snapped back at him.

I was almost tempted to stick to my guns and refuse to pay their measly dues. We were scheduled for another track meet in a few days and I weighed wanting to run in that and wanting to get the hell out of the Army. Plus maybe another night or two with Midori. In the end, wanting to get out of the Army and home to my family won. I paid their ill-gotten $15. She initialed my checkout list and I left.

A few days later, July 2, 1953, I opened the door at 114 Miles Avenue, Syracuse, New York, to surprise my family. My little bundle of joy, Judy Joy, was delighted to see me. I guess my wife Josephine was too. My son Rocky, whom I had not seen, was a little shy. I took him in my arms while Judy Joy clung to my legs. I vowed to myself that I would teach Rocky to be strong, tough, courageous and gentle. Jo gave me a passionate kiss. We were all happy to be together again as a family. I loved them all dearly.

Now we could get on with the rest of our lives.

She was a few years older than I was, much more sophisticated and a lot more well-to-do. She was a college girl, loved horses and said she planned to go to Australia and raise horses. I thought she was way out of my league.

Later in the evening, as we lay on the green grass of the lawn in front of her house she said, "Al, I like you a lot better when you are sober."

"You are very beautiful. I like you a lot, too," I replied.

She was on her back and her breasts pointed to the sky with alluring magnetism. It was becoming dark, the perfect time for a beautiful body to be touched, kissed and loved. I leaned on my elbow next to her and gazed at her twin mounds of living temptation, but did not touch.

Why did I act so differently towards Rose than I did with the girl on the train? I don't know. Maybe it was because she was in control and talked, or because I feared she would reject me. Soon I went home never to see her again.

I was supposed to be back in camp on a Sunday so I planned on leaving Saturday morning for the two-day trip. That gave me one more chance to go to the Friday night dance. An opportunity to possibly see Rose again. But she was not there. So we drank our wine, got drunk, flirted and danced the night away.

Towards the end of the evening I danced with this fairly attractive girl. She said she was a WAC (Women's Army Corps). When it was time to leave she asked me to button her coat for her. Then she offered me a ride to Burlington. I thought, *to hell with being back to camp on time.* This is a sure thing.

I told Roy and Freddie to go on home without me. I'd get home from Burlington somehow. On the way to Burlington, I sat close to her and put my arm around her shoulder. She didn't seem to mind. She pulled into a park on the north side of the city and stopped.

I moved closer, kissed her and ran my right hand up under her skirt. She stopped kissing me and said in no uncertain terms, "Stop! Let me get my legs around you first."

Quickly I did as I was told. She didn't even take her panties off, if she had any on. I did not stop to unbuckle my belt. I just unzipped the fly of the nice gaberdine trousers I had borrowed from my buddy Hart. I was as excited as a young virgin bull let loose with a heifer in heat. She lay on her back, wrapped her legs around me and directed me into her. I came almost immediately but did not stop. It felt so good I wanted it never to end. I kept thrusting and thrusting as she moved against me.

After many joyful minutes she suddenly pushed against me in wild passion and whispered loudly in my ear, "I love you!" as her orgasm shook her.

I responded with another ejaculation. Still I remained hard and being in her continued to be pleasant. So I kept on thrusting. Finally she asked, "When are you going to stop?"

"Just a little longer," I told her. Not much later my third orgasm left me spent and willing to let her up.

Then she drove me to a hotel, I guess she didn't love me enough to take me all the way to Underhill. I didn't ask her to and she didn't offer. While the car idled under a street light, she asked me for my name and address.

"Just in case," she said.

I knew what she meant but I was not worried. I had heard about WACs who wanted to get out of the service, by getting pregnant and who might want to latch on to some serviceman for an allotment and/or insurance if he got killed in the war. Sex with her had been so good that I thought it might not be a bad idea to marry her if I had to.

I asked her for her name and address also.

She said, "I'll write you."

I never heard from her again.

Chapter VIII

I walked into the hotel lobby a satisfied man. From behind the desk the eyes of the clerk focused on my genital area. I glanced down to see what he was looking at. A dark wet spot, about the size of a silver dollar, showed at the bottom end of the fly of the gaberdine suntans I had borrowed from my buddy Hart. Quickly, I took off my cunt cap and held it in front of the wet spot. It was embarrassing but did not lessen much the afterglow of losing my virginity. Hart's pants would just have to be dry cleaned before he saw them. I would not want him to know I had been too stupid to take them off before getting laid.

I registered for a room and spent the night. The next morning I caught the bus back to Underhill. It was too late to make bus and train connections back to camp on that Saturday. So I would be at least one day AWOL (Absent Without Leave). *What the hell, might as well make it two days,* I thought. I stayed one more day and started my return trip on Monday.

On the train, as it neared Springfield, Missouri, two MPs (Military Police) checked my papers. They noted that I was AWOL and wrote me up.

When I got into camp I had to report to our company commander. I think his name was Captain Hendrickson. That was the only time he ever spoke to me. I lied to him that my grandfather was on his deathbed. He bought my story, but restricted me to the post for two weeks. That didn't bother me because I didn't ever go anywhere, anyhow.

Not long after my return to camp, somebody from our platoon brought some beer in a jug from the PX (Post Exchange) to our barracks. Even though I had drunk wine while on furlough, I was still considered a non-drinker by my barrack mates and I wanted it to stay that way. My drinking on leave had been to give me courage to relate to girls. There were no girls in the barracks to relate to. But some of the guys who were bigger than I was insisted I have a drink with them. The first few swallows didn't taste very good, but after that it was easy to drink enough to get a little high.

I started bragging about how I could read palms. At that time Sergeant Janovich was our squad leader. He was one of those who insisted I drink with them. He asked me to read his palm. I looked at his palm. He had a short lifeline.

"Sergeant, you'd better be careful if we ever get into combat," I blurted out.

"Why?" he asked.

Immediately I realized I should not have said that.

"Well, you've got a short lifeline, but I'm not sure that means anything. I don't really know that much about palm reading. Besides, I don't believe in fortune-tellers." It was a vain effort to cover my tracks.

Not long after that Sergeant Janovich was transferred to company headquarters. (In March of 1945, Sergeant Janovich was the first man in our company to be killed on the battlefield in Germany. While on reconnaissance he was shot by a sniper.)

Corporal Pasqual Spano became our new squad leader. He was a well-built man with broad shoulders and curly, blond hair. I never got really close to Spano but he was a good squad leader and treated us fairly and well.

I liked Sergeant Bredl better than any of the NCOs in our platoon. He was the leader of the second squad. He was a very friendly, enthusiastic man from Buffalo, N.Y. Both he and I started taking a correspondence course in geometry. It had finally dawned on me that an education was useful even in the Army. I should not have quit school. I had already taken geometry in my second year of high school. But I had quit school just before the end of the year so I got no credit for the courses I took that year. I was very good at math so this course, which was a repeat of what I had already learned, was easy for me. Bredl had a little trouble with it and would ask me for help, which I gladly gave.

I made no secret of my wish to be in Bredl's squad. I also liked his first gunner, private first class Clarence Staten, very much. He was probably better at his job than anybody in the platoon. At least, I thought so. All the more reason for me to want to be in

Bredl's squad.

But my squad leader and my first gunner, private first class Roland, never treated me badly even though they knew I wanted to be in a different squad.

During the first part of the summer of 1944, while still training at Fort Leonardwood, we received more replacements to bring us closer to full strength. Our squad got Privates Knicely, Hajjar and Drake for ammo bearers. Knicely was a big, strong lad. Hajjar was also a big, strong fellow of Lebanese ancestry. He was very unhappy being in the Army. Drake was much smaller than the rest of us in our squad. He wasn't very tall and was quite skinny. He was a country boy from one of the Carolinas. Not well educated or articulate, he was rather sad, shy and fragile. I felt sorry for him and sort of took him under my wing.

Another sergeant joined our outfit while we were still in Missouri. I remember him for three reasons. Number one, his first name was Alton. Number two, he stank terribly from body odor, until some of the guys threatened to give him a GI shower with GI brushes and GI soap. Number three, he let me use his rifle on the firing range and I made expert. I had made sharp-shooter before at Fort Bliss. Expert was the best one could shoot. I had trouble zeroing in my rifle and his was zeroed in perfectly. I remember also that he wore the Expert Rifleman's Badge. I knew that you had to pass a very difficult test to get that. For some reason he was not in our unit long.

They promoted me to the rank of private first class a little while after I joined the infantry outfit. That was a surprise and a big boost to my morale. I was afraid my thirty days in the brig might be held against me.

About the same time I was asked by our platoon sergeant, Sergeant Papp, if I wanted to apply to go to OCS (Officers Candidate School). For the first time I learned, I had scored high enough on an IQ test (which we had taken when we first came in the service) to be smart enough to be an officer. The minimum score needed was 110. That made me feel really good and proud. But I still didn't think of myself as being officer material. So far I had never met an officer I liked. I couldn't see myself being one. I did not apply.

Somewhere it was decided our division should prepare itself for an amphibious landing. Perhaps the invasion of Japan? Little guys like me could only speculate. Anyhow, the Ninety-seventh Infantry was ordered to Camp San Luis Obispo, California, for amphibious training in the last part of the summer of 1944.

Chapter IX

In San Luis Obispo we lived in squad tents. The nights were quite chilly. Blankets were needed to keep us warm. Fog blanketed the ground in the morning and concealed the sun until midday. It remained cool until the sun burned off the fog. Then it became uncomfortably hot, especially for those wearing long johns to keep warm in the morning. Often we had to make a choice – suffer from the cold in the morning or the heat of the afternoon. Uniform-of-the-day orders did not cover underwear.

On the evening of our first payday in California, many of us gathered in the day room at the end of the company street. A crap game started on a pool table. All the big rollers surrounded the table. The first sergeant, mess sergeant, supply sergeant, and many other NCOs were present. There were also a few peons like me watching and taking a bet here and there, winning a little and losing a little.

A couple of hours into the game I suddenly got hot. I was rolling the dice. I kept throwing sevens, elevens or making my points. With each pot I won, my money pile in front of me got bigger. It got so big one of my friends became my banker. He pulled in the pots and sorted out the ones, fives, tens and twenties. He kept track of the bets and covered all side bets, while I concentrated on rolling the dice. At the peak of my luck there was so much money in my pile that we never did count it. It must have been over a thousand dollars, a huge fortune to me.

Gradually the crowd dwindled, as one after the other lost their pay to me. I finally lost the dice when there were only a few players left, mostly NCOs. Even though it was very late at night I could not quit. Gamblers who quit when they were ahead were not too well liked. I did not want to be one of them. As the night wore on into the wee hours of the morning, my pile of money slowly shrunk. Lady Luck left me. Joy turned to sadness.

When the game broke up just before reveille, I had just about the same as when I got paid the day before.

Was it worth it staying up all night, reaching an exciting high and then sinking to a sad low? I decided it was not. The pain exceeded the pleasure. I gambled no more.

One part of amphibious training, was learning how to disembark from a ship by going down rope ladders joined together in huge nets. We practiced this for some time out in the field on nets draped over a large wooden wall. We would climb up one side and down the other. I found that I was quite good at this and enjoyed this sort of physical challenge.

At the end of this phase of training we were tested. At the testing site we were given instructions by a tall, stiff Marine sergeant. We were to go up the ramp leading to the disembarking area and line up in waves of about a half dozen men behind the rail we were going to go over. As each wave went over the rail and down the net, we were supposed to stay lined up, all members moving down at the same speed. This was to prevent being stepped on by the guy above you.

I was in the first wave of my group. When the order came to go, I sprang over the rail like a monkey and with two or three giant strides was halfway down the net before the rest of the wave had taken their first step.

"Hey, Superman," hollered the Marine. "Where the hell do you think you're going? I told you to stay in line. Get your ass back up that net and stay in line or I'll personally relocate your ass up between your ears."

I did as I was told. On the inside I was overjoyed that I had found something I could do much better than most of the other guys and was called "Superman".

Later we were taken out on LSTs (Landing Ship Tanks) for the real thing. LSTs were flat-bottomed ships capable of carrying tanks. From these ships we disembarked over the side down into LCIs (Landing Craft Infantry), which took us to the beaches for mock invasions. We practiced hitting the beaches and running through the deep, loose sand with our heavy equipment. That was hard for me. We practiced unloading supplies from the LCIs, by passing five-gallon water cans filled with sand from man to man, as we stood in water up to our asses.

Then I was picked for a special crew which was to practice setting up supply depots on the beach. This crew had to get up at 0400 hours in order to be at the beach and get set up by 0700 hours to receive the supplies. While on this detail I no longer had to hit the beaches and run through the sand or do other dislikable details. The early hours didn't bother me.

We still enjoyed some free time on the weekends. My brother Willard had finished his training at Parris Island and Camp Lejeune. He wrote me that he would be passing through Camp Pendleton on his way to the Southwest Pacific. Camp Pendleton was about 250 miles south of San Luis Obispo, between Los Angeles and San Diego.

I loved my brother very much and wanted to see him before he was off to fight the Japs. So I got a weekend pass and set out by bus to Los Angeles. I took my baseball gloves and baseball in my little tote bag just in case we had a few minutes to play catch. Baseball was our bond. I thought I would have time to make it. At the bus station in Los Angeles, there was a delay before I could catch a bus to Pendleton. As I was having a bite to eat while waiting, it dawned on me that there would be just enough time to get there and hop on a bus to get back to camp. That would leave no time to find Willard, much less spend any time with him. I had no address to go by. I didn't want to be AWOL again. Sadly I returned to camp. When nobody was looking I put my baseball equipment back into the privacy of my duffel bag. Later, I was to learn that Willard had already shipped out. So I would have missed him anyway.

Towards the end of our amphibious training, we had to take a ten-day cruise on an LST, off the coast of California, to get us accustomed to living on a ship. We learned that you get seasick on flat-bottomed ships very quickly. Rough seas rock them more than they do normal ships.

Soon after setting sail, I was lined up with many others at the rail, puking my guts into the ocean. After everything was thrown up, dry heaves continued. I can recall nothing more painful or sickening.

During that whole cruise most of us were sick. The only place I could find partial relief was lying on my bunk below deck. I had trouble eating and could hold down only a little food.

Once at the height of my sickness I had to go to the head (the Navy's name for toilet). When I got there I was terribly sick and also had diarrhea. Which was I to do? Puke or shit in the toilet? Neither end would wait. I opted to shit in the bowl and puke on the floor. Somehow that seemed more dignified. I was too sick to clean up my puke. I've never wanted to die more than on that cruise. Never was I happier than when I got off that LST and back on solid ground.

One evening while we were sitting around in our squad tent, the talk turned to sex. Sergeant Roman, the leader of the fourth squad and a good friend of our squad leader, now Sergeant Spano, was there.

"Sex is no big deal," Roman opined. "Just about one second of pleasure when you shoot your wad."

"Don't you enjoy foreplay leading up to penetration and letting it soak a while before your orgasm?" I asked him, bluntly.

When I was about fourteen, even before reaching puberty, I had read *Married Love* by Dr. Marie Stopes. So I thought I knew a lot about sex. Also I felt somewhat expert after one successful experience with that unnamed WAC. That had certainly been more than one second of pleasure.

"That's all a waste of time," continued Roman.

"What about kissing? Isn't that exciting?" I asked.

"Not to me it isn't. A person's mouth is the dirtiest part of their body. I don't want to swap spit with any girl and get her germs. And who knows where her tongue has been," Roman explained.

"Oh, I love to kiss the girls and play with their tits. That really turns me on," I continued to hold forth.

"How many girls have you kissed? How many tits have you played with?" Roman questioned.

"I've kissed a lot of girls," I lied. I had barely kissed that WAC and perhaps one other girl, when we Underhill boys would go down to walk with the Jericho girls in the evening. That was when I was about fifteen. "And I've played with a few tits in my day," I lied even more. The only tit I had ever touched was the left one of the girl on the train. *But maybe you could count all the cows' teats I had pulled on the farms I had worked on*, I thought. Then I would not be lying so much. "That really turns them on. As a fellow says, get past the tits and you've got it made."

"That's all a waste of time," Roman repeated. "If a girl wants to fuck, she'll fuck."

"But girls don't like that slam, bang, thank you ma'am approach. They need more time to warm up. They like a lot of foreplay. That gets them all hot and bothered. It makes it harder for them to resist you. Then when you do fuck them, they like you to take your time. It usually takes them longer to climax than the man." Boy, did I remember what I had read in that book!

"I don't really care what a woman wants. Most of them don't even like to screw. They usually let you have it for money or if you buy them something." Roman held his position.

"Oh no, when a woman has an orgasm she enjoys it as much as a man does," I pressed my point.

"I don't think women have orgasms. They just pretend they do to get more out of you," Roman persisted.

"You probably never fucked one long enough to make her come," I challenged him.

"If the truth were known, I bet you never did either. You're probably still a virgin, still wet behind the ears," he scoffed at my pretense of great knowledge.

"Oh yes," I said. "Once I fucked this girl three times without uncunting. When I came the second time, she had a big climax and moaned with ecstasy as she whispered in my ear that she loved me. We must have fucked for forty minutes."

"Oh, you're full of bullshit. I doubt if you ever had a piece of ass in your life, except with mama thumb and her four daughters," he retorted.

"Why don't you guys knock it off so the rest of us can get some sleep?" Hajjar spoke up from his bunk. "Some of us have to go to church in the morning."

Sergeant Roman departed, our intellectual interlude over.

Chapter X

Allied troops landed in Normandy, France, at Omaha Beach on D-Day, June 6, 1944. They pushed on through France and into Germany during the summer and fall. Then, when their lines were spread thin, the Germans broke through in the Battle of the Bulge. Reinforcements were needed.

The Ninety-seventh Division was ordered to Camp Kilmer, New Jersey. We were there for a few days while being processed to ship overseas. Rumor had it that the decisive factor in determining our destination was the German breakthrough.

Part of the shipping-out process was a "short arm" inspection. These were done periodically anyhow, but especially at critical times like going overseas. You lined up naked in single file and a doctor looked at your penis to see if you had any venereal disease. He asked you to skin it back and milk it down. That way he could see if you had a discharge, a sign of the clap.

Eddie Hajjar was in line ahead of me. Some of us were a little embarrassed about the size of our penises, fearing we didn't measure up. I felt that way myself. Eddie was especially modest. He would hold his hands over it to hide its size and shape. He and I were uncircumcised, as were many others.

When the doctor told him to skin it back and milk it down, Eddie apparently had a little difficulty skinning it back. I couldn't see from behind him. It took longer than normal. The doctor waited patiently.

After Eddie had succeeded, the doctor advised, "You ought to practice stretching it by pulling on the foreskin. That would make it easier for you in the future." I could hear him clearly.

I identified with Eddie because my penis had a puckered up foreskin, much like his. But I didn't have any trouble skinning it back for the doctor. Eddie and I had become good friends so I never told any of the other guys what the doctor told him to do. I smiled to myself though, because it did amuse me.

Eddie lived in Brooklyn, which was not far from Camp Kilmer. He invited me to accompany him on a home visit. When we entered their modest flat I was amazed at the warmth and affection of the embrace and kisses between him and his mother. They kissed several times and their lips seemed to cling together as if bonded by glue. I loved my mother and she loved me, but we had never kissed like that.

Mrs. Hajjar was a short, sweet, lovely lady. She treated me with great hospitality and fine food.

During our short stay at Camp Kilmer, weekend passes were allowed to places within a certain distance. I think it was about a hundred miles. I guess this was so one could get back to camp quickly in case our ship was to leave on short notice, or to keep most of the men in camp to prevent temptations to go AWOL and get out of going overseas.

The wives of some of the guys lucky enough to have one, came to the metropolitan area around Camp Kilmer to have a last visit with their husbands before they shipped out. One of them was the wife of private first class Johnston. Johnston was the second gunner of the second squad, a position I wished I was in. I didn't like him. He was from one of the southern states. He had some education and was always using big words and bragging. He was a well-built man and had a large penis which he flaunted. He claimed he was married to a minister's daughter and that she loved him so much she would do anything for him. He was probably right. She came to see him off.

He told of one event that proved how much she loved him. He said they were lying on their backs in bed one morning after a night of lovemaking. As he held her so she could not move out of the way, he hacked up an oyster and spit it up into the air so that it would land in her face when it came down. Most of the guys who heard him laughed. I guess they thought it was funny. I didn't. I could not imagine myself doing that to someone I loved. But then, maybe he didn't love her.

One evening most of the men were gone, including all the NCOs. Many of them had lied about where they were going and ignored the hundred-mile limit. A few of us in the second platoon, were on the second floor of the typical wooden Army barracks. Some others from the first platoon were on the first floor. They were making a lot of noise. We wanted to sleep because it was late. We outnumbered them so we decided to go down and make them shut up.

After we made our demands one of their smaller men spoke up. His name was DeMarco. I think he was related to DeMarco, the boxer, from Boston who had several bloody bouts with Carmen Basillio.

He spoke slowly and calmly. "You guys could probably beat the shit out of us because there are a lot more of you than us. But let's have a fair fight, one of you against me." He paused. None of us volunteered. "How about you, Betts? You seem to be doing a lot of talking," he continued.

Betts was a skinny kid from the fourth squad. He was taller but about the same weight as DeMarco. I was also about as heavy as DeMarco. Boy, was I relieved he did not pick me to fight him. Fear prevented me from volunteering to take Betts' place.

Bunks were moved back to make room. They faced off. Before DeMarco could defend himself a wild left haymaker from Betts to his head knocked him across a bunk. As he was getting up Betts grabbed him in a headlock and started digging at his face.

"Let's square off and fight like men," DeMarco suggested from his vulnerable position.

Betts let him loose. Like the slugging DeMarco from Boston, DeMarco quickly landed a combination of punches to the head of Betts.

We saw that it was going to be a very uneven fight so a couple of us stepped in and stopped them.

We went back upstairs and to bed. They quieted down.

The next day Betts had a badly swollen black eye. DeMarco had several minor scratches on his face.

★

Soon we were on a troop ship heading for Europe. The voyage across the Atlantic was uneventful. They warned us about German U-boats, but we never saw any. Somewhere in the middle of the Atlantic, Eddie and I had a conversation. It was in the evening after dark. We were on the deck leaning against the rail looking out over the waves glimmering in the bright moonlight.

"I'm glad we're finally going overseas to fight," I said.

"I'm not," Eddie replied. "I admit it, Al. I'm a coward. I don't want to fight in this damn war."

"Well, I don't know if I'm a coward or not, Eddie, but I feel responsible to help win the war. The bastards killed my brother."

"The Germans never did anything to me, Al. I don't want to fight them."

"But Eddie, do you think we should just let them take over the world?"

"No, probably not. But let somebody else fight them. I don't want to. Besides, it's against my religion."

"What religion are you, Eddie?"

"Catholic. What religion are you, Al?"

"I don't belong to any church. I don't believe in religion."

"Why not? Didn't your parents take you to church when you were young?"

"My mother tried to. She's a staunch Methodist. But our old man didn't believe in religion. When we got old enough he made us help him in the woods on the weekends and vacations. So we couldn't have gone to church even if we wanted to."

"What does your father do, Al?"

"He's a woodcutter. Cuts cordwood."

"Didn't he go to church?"

"Yeah Eddie, he used to go to church all right; once a year – every Christmas – to get a box of candy. They gave them out to everybody." Sarcasm and hate dripped from my words.

"Wasn't he embarrassed?"

"No. He didn't give a shit what anybody thought. He was a mean, miserable old bastard. He didn't care about anybody but himself. Once when I was twelve he promised me and my brothers, Kermit and Willard, new bicycles if we would work hard for him that summer. He had a big job lined up. We agreed. Kermit was fourteen then and Willard was eleven. We had never had bikes before. Then one night we heard our old man arguing with our mother in their bedroom. He probably wanted some and she didn't. He told her he was going to buy her a new washing machine with the money he had promised to buy us bicycles with. The next day Kermit left home to work on a farm. Willard and I were too young to get jobs on farms yet, so we had to stay and cut wood with our old man that summer. But we went on a slow-down strike. So we didn't get much wood cut and he didn't save any money.

"Did he buy you bicycles?"

"No. And he didn't get our mother a new washing machine either. Speaking of church, Eddie, we did go to church twice that summer. Willard and I decided we were entitled to one day a week off – Sundays. So one Sunday we didn't put up our lunch to go to work. We went outside to play. He hollered at us to get into the house and put up our lunch. We told him that we wanted Sundays off. He came out and grabbed me by the arm and started pulling me into the house. Willard grabbed my other arm and tried to pull me the other way. Our mother split us up. She said we should have Sundays off so we could go to church. He said we wouldn't go to church anyway. We said we would. He finally gave in and we went to church a couple times and then quit."

★

We landed at Cherbourg, France. While we waited to move up to the front lines, we lived at Camp Chesterfield. The military camps in France were named after cigarettes. The food was terrible – mostly dried potatoes and vegetables soaked in water and boiled. One meal a day was usually C rations – a can of beans, hash or something and a can of soda crackers with some coffee or cocoa. We were not supposed to eat any of the natives' food, but we found a way to sneak out of camp and we would buy delicious French bread and bring it back to camp, hidden under our field jackets.

While outside of camp we were looking for French girls to have sex with, but we always seemed to wind up in the homes of some French families' eating snails and drinking cider. Then we would exchange cigarettes, candy bars or soap for long loaves of bread and sneak back to camp.

While at Camp Chesterfield I first became acquainted with our platoon leader, Lieutenant Murray. Somebody located some boxing gloves. A few of us put on the gloves and sparred with each other. Knicely and I boxed a little. I thought I was pretty good but Sergeant Papp, our platoon sergeant, remarked that Knicely had a nice left jab. He didn't say anything about me. Lieutenant Murray was watching us.

Papp said, "Want to put the gloves on with me, Lieutenant?"

"No, you're heavier than I am. But I wouldn't mind putting them on with Chamberlin. He's about my size and speed," Murray offered.

So I sparred a little with our platoon leader. We didn't hit each other very much or very hard. Most officers didn't mix with their men like that. I respected Lieutenant Murray a great deal after that.

Soon we were loaded into boxcars, with straw on the floor to sleep on, for a slow, long ride through France, the Netherlands and on into Germany. Then we were loaded onto trucks and moved up to just behind the front lines. It was now test time to see if I was a man.

Chapter XI

Most soldiers learn early on not to volunteer for anything. Volunteers are frowned on by their peers and are considered brown-noses. I had learned that lesson well. But now that we were near the front lines in Germany, I violated that unspoken rule.

It was pitch dark. No lights were allowed. We had unloaded from trucks and our duffel bags had been stacked in some sort of warehouse. In a low voice, as if the enemy might hear him, Sergeant Papp asked for two volunteers to guard the duffel bags.

I whispered to Drake, the little guy from the South that I sort of looked after, "Want to do it?"

"Okay," he whispered back.

So Drake and I spent our first night in what one might consider a combat area, huddled close together for warmth and security, on top of duffel bags. Fear and uncertainty kept us vigilant. I don't know where the rest of our company spent the night. Probably in nearby houses. It was the custom to commandeer civilian houses on short notice, for our troops.

We never saw our duffel bags again, until the war in Europe was over in May 1945. In combat, we carried only a combat pack made up of a sleeping bag, shelter half, a couple of changes of socks and underwear, toothbrush, toothpaste, soap, razor, towel and a minimum of personal items, maybe some pictures of loved ones, writing paper and pen or pencil. Attached to our pack was either an entrenching tool (a short-handled little shovel to dig foxholes) or a little hatchet. Other than that we had the clothes on our backs which included woolen long johns, woolen OD (Olive Drab) pants and shirt, woolen sweater, field jacket, steel helmet with liner, combat boots, gloves, our personal weapon (mine was a .45 side arm), cartridge belt with ammunition pouches, first aid pack, canteen and trench knife which could be used as a bayonet on a carbine. I also carried the 0.30-caliber, water-cooled machine gun. As first gunner, Roland carried the tripod upon which the machine gun was mounted. Knicely and Drake carried boxes of ammunition.

Now that we were in a war zone, far away from any dry cleaning services, the ODs, which were our winter dress uniforms, no longer had to be spotlessly clean and neatly pressed. We became a soiled, wrinkled lot.

The next night our company moved forward. The fourth squad of our platoon was leading. We were in a column of twos just a few feet apart so as to maintain contact in the dark. We moved as silently as possible. I had no idea how close we were to the enemy. Private first class Nemec was the point man. Nemec was the first gunner of the fourth squad. He was a tall, well-built, strong, handsome, intelligent man. He had excelled in training and was well liked and respected by his peers and leaders. I thought of him as an excellent soldier and looked up to him.

Suddenly a voice came out of the darkness in front of us. "Halt! Who goes there?"

We stopped. Nemec was supposed to give the password. He stood in frozen silence. Time stood still. A second became an eternity. Finally someone else gave the password.

The soldier who had halted us gave the countersign and then chewed us out for not speaking up faster. We could have easily been shot, he told us. He spoke and acted like an officer. But it was too dark to see. Even if we could see we would not have known what he was. Combat soldiers did not wear their rank on the front lines for fear of becoming targets.

I wondered about Nemec after that. I didn't look up to him anymore.

Our platoon moved into a house that night. The owners had been given very little time to move out. Whatever was left in the house was at the mercy of our men. Any items of value small enough to be carried in a pack were looted. Cameras, watches and jewelry were favorites.

I had not thought about looting anything, so when Sergeant Papp asked for a volunteer to stand the first two hour guard duty outside the front door and no one offered, I volunteered again – the second night in a row. My tour started at 2000 hours (military time for eight o'clock in the evening) and was to end at 2200 hours. But no relief came at 2200 hours. Midnight came and still no relief. I felt obligated not to leave my post. Somewhere around 0200 hours private first class Koenig, a member of the fourth squad, staggered out the front door to relieve me. It was obvious to me that he was drunk and in no condition to guard anything.

"I'm here to relieve you," Koenig said. "Go in and get something to drink. They got some good stuff in there."

"You're too drunk to stand guard," I replied. "Go back in and tell them to send somebody out who is sober."

"They're all drunk. Nobody's sober. We found a lot of good stuff in the wine cellar," he answered.

"Well, go back in and sober up then. Tell Papp I'll stay on guard until somebody is able to relieve me," I said.

So I guarded the front door until daybreak. I was not really angry. I was a little surprised nobody else felt responsible enough to stay sober when we were so close to the enemy lines. In fact I felt a bit smug about my own sense of responsibility. But I was only a private first class. What could I say?

The next night we moved up to the front lines. Our platoon was again quartered in a big house. There were two machine gun positions which we had to man. They were between the house and the German front lines. A river separated us from the Germans. Across the river was a large stone building big enough to be a hospital. There was a huge red cross painted on its roof, the sign of a hospital. Hospitals were supposed to be off limits for all fighting operations. They told us the Red Cross was just a disguise. The Germans used it as an observation post. So our artillery shelled it anyhow.

Two men were placed on each machine gun at night for four-hour watches, starting at dark. Again I volunteered to take the first watch. Why? I don't know. Maybe I figured I'd have to take my turn sometime anyway. Or perhaps, I was just anxious to test my true mettle under fire.

My partner for that first watch was Sergeant Roman, the fourth squad leader. As soon as we were positioned in the machine-gun emplacement, Roman behind the gun and I to his left as his assistant, we felt around to locate hand grenades and ammo boxes. It was pitch dark in the bunker. Roman was a smoker but he could not light up for fear of being detected. We sat on ammo boxes in complete silence for the same reason. The little sounds of wildlife in the nearby bushes were exaggerated by the eerie quiet.

Our position was relatively safe. The walls were well sandbagged and there was ample overhead cover. In the wall towards the enemy, was a firing aperture wide enough to allow the machine gun to cover its field of fire. The opening was about thirty inches wide and less than a foot high. Unless enemy fire came directly in that opening, or a mortar round scored a direct hit on top of our bunker, we would be okay. We were much more secure than we felt.

Suddenly, the area in front of us lit up with tracers flying through the air at us and resounded with the ripping burp sounds of rapid gunfire. (The Germans had developed machine guns and burp guns that fired at nearly a thousand rounds per minute – more than double the rate of ours.) Bullets sprayed our bunker, I could feel them thudding into the sandbags. Miraculously, none of them came through the firing aperture, or if they did, they did not hit either of us. I was scared. It was my baptism to enemy fire. The silence inside our bunker was broken by the sound of Roman's knees shaking. Did he hear mine too?

As quickly as it had started the firing ceased. All was darkness and silence again. We did not speak. We did not move. We sat in silent terror for the rest of the four hours. Our joy was great when it was over.

The next day we were to move forward. Lieutenant Murray went ahead to reconnoiter. He was wounded and evacuated. We were not to see him again until after the war was over and we were on occupation duty in Japan. Sergeant Papp took over as platoon leader.

On that same day Sergeant Janovich was killed by a sniper's bullet. I remembered how I had read his palm in the States and had warned him to be careful in combat. I felt sad and guilty. I wondered if he had been burdened by my foolish disclosure of his short lifeline. I hoped not. He was a good man.

We moved forward to a large building near the river. The Germans were in buildings and firing positions on the other side. Already rifle companies had crossed over and secured some areas on the other side. Now it was our turn to cross over. Our platoon was assembled in one area.

Sergeant Papp asked, "Whose gun is ready to go?"

No one spoke up. I guess nobody wanted to be first. I didn't either. But my gun was ready. I felt dishonest not saying anything. "My gun is ready," I volunteered.

"Okay, Sergeant Spano, your squad will go first," Papp ordered. "Load into the boat."

We crossed the river in a flat-bottomed boat barely large enough to hold our squad and the boat's crew. I was so scared and focused on caring for our machine gun that I don't remember whether we were rowed or powered by motor. Occasional enemy mortar rounds dove into the water around us.

Once on the other side, we ran forward and set up our machine gun in a gateway between a large stone building and a wooden barn. We were down to five men now – Sergeant Spano, Roland, myself, Knicely and Drake. Hajjar had been transferred to the motor pool as a jeep driver.

I had no idea where we were, except that we were in Germany and on the front lines. I didn't know what river we had crossed or what village or city we were in. Later on, we learned that we were cleaning up the Ruhr pocket which had been surrounded by the fast-moving Allied armies. Düsseldorf was its main city.

Before we could get our machine-gun loaded and ready to fire, a shell from a German 88-millimeter gun exploded exactly where we were. Roland and I would definitely have been killed, and the others probably wounded, had not Spano sensed the danger and ordered us to move to the cover of the barn a few seconds before the shell hit.

The urgency in Spano's command and the explosion of the shell made us hit the dirt face down next to the barn as quickly as we could. More shells followed but none of them hit us. The area of safety was a late pigpen. Pigs are very clean animals. They shit in only one end of their sty. Roland and Knicely sought cover in the shitty end of the pen while Drake and I went to the dry, clean end. I'm not sure where Spano was.

While lying there I felt something hit the seat of my pants. I reached around instinctively to brush it off. My right thumb contacted a hot metal pellet. It burned my thumb slightly.

When the shelling subsided Sergeant Spano ordered us to take cover in the nearby stone building. As we ran across the yard, my steel helmet bounced up and down on my head and came down over my eyes so I could barely see where I was going. We didn't fasten our chinstraps because we were told that the force of a close explosion could cause the chinstrap to rip our heads off. And I didn't have the headband in my helmet liner tight enough to keep the helmet from bouncing.

When we got into the safety and warmth of the stone building we were told to sit close together in a hall. That's when we learned that Roland and Knicely were covered with pig shit and stank terribly. We also discovered we were in the battalion CP (Command Post) with a lot of high-ranking officers. I don't think they wanted us there. Maybe we were in their way or they didn't like the smell of us.

Anyhow, we were soon ordered out. The next thing I remember is running across an open field with German 88s firing at us. I never knew I could run so fast. This time my helmet stayed put on my head because, fortunately, I had had time to adjust the headband of my helmet liner while in the stone building.

Soon we were in some woods with tall, dark fir trees. Spruce I think. I lost track of time so I don't remember if it was the same day or days later. However I do remember that the Germans lobbed a few mortar shells into our midst. Again we ran like hell. As one hit very close to me I hit the ground. The machine gun did a somersault off my shoulder and landed in the soft dirt of the forest. Luckily nothing was broken. Again, all five men of our squad were unharmed.

Later on, perhaps in the same woods on the same day or possibly under different trees at a later date, I remember being in our gun emplacement with Roland. It was at night and very dark. We were on guard while most of the other men were back having a rare hot meal. We were very hungry. Somebody brought us a hot meal. At least part of it was a little bit warm. It was all in one mess kit. We couldn't see what we were eating. We learned from the taste that it was turkey, mashed potatoes, dressing, gravy and ice cream. It was all mixed together. We took turns getting a spoonful. Whatever it was, it didn't matter. It was all delicious. I think it was the best and most memorable meal I ever had.

I remember another night in the forest. Again, I was on guard in our machine-gun emplacement. This time my buddy Drake was with me. It was cold. It was dark. We were alone. I think Drake was colder and more scared than I was. I felt protective towards him. We moved close together for warmth and security. I sat with my back against the dirt wall. He sat in front of me between my legs with his back against my belly. My arms encircled his waist to give him as much warmth and comfort as I could. His warm body felt good against mine.

Our forces captured a lot of German prisoners in the Ruhr pocket. Once we were in a large fenced-in area, perhaps a school yard. It was a collection point for the prisoners. From there large groups of defeated Germans were escorted by armed guards further back to other larger collection points. Sergeant Papp selected me and Pee Wee to take a large bunch back. I was sort of in charge because my date of rank was before his.

Pee Wee (I don't recall his last name) was a funny little guy from the second squad. He was the shortest man in our platoon, less than five feet tall. But he was a feisty little fellow. He was usually laughing and joking around. But today he was serious. I liked him.

We were told to make the prisoners put their hands on top of their heads where we could see them and not move them. If one did, we were to shoot him, no questions asked. One young prisoner had a shoulder wound and was crying. He complained that he could not keep his hands on top of his head. It hurt too badly. At first we made him do it. We were afraid of what he might do if we didn't. Pee Wee showed no mercy. He wanted to make the poor prisoner do as he was told. But, as my fear wore off, I began to feel sorry for him and eventually we let him put his hands down.

It took us about a month to overcome all the German

resistance in the Ruhr pocket. By then we had become dirty, hardened combat soldiers. We had earned a battle star for our campaign ribbon and a Combat Infantryman Badge. Along the way some of us made some adaptations to our equipment. The leather holster of the Colt .45 had a flap over the top to keep the pistol from falling out. On mine I cut this flap off so I could draw my gun quicker if I needed to. I also tied the leather thong at the bottom of the holster around my leg so it wouldn't flop around, sort of like some cowboys in movies I had seen. Being in combat, there was no worry about paying for damaged equipment. I also picked up a broad-bladed, non-military hatchet somewhere. I would carry this in my right hand as we hiked along roads and throw it at trees so the blade would stick in the tree, I got pretty good at this.

All during this campaign I never shot an enemy with our machine gun or my .45, or tomahawked anyone with my hatchet.

Chapter XII

In the spring of 1945 we moved into Czechoslovakia. I can't recall many details except that we walked for days through light snow, rain, cold and mud. It was difficult to keep our feet dry and warm in our leather combat boots. We had a buddy system. Each one of us was responsible for the care of the feet of a buddy. Roland and I were feet buddies. When we had a chance we would take off our footwear and rub our feet or the feet of our buddy to get them warm and stimulate circulation.

There must have been good days with sunshine too. But I don't remember them. The bad ones left an indelible impression.

The machine gun weighed heavy on my shoulders. When one side ached I would shift it to the other until they both ached. Then we just kept moving. At night we bedded down wherever we were. We tried to keep as dry, warm and comfortable as we could. It was not easy. I remember one night, sleeping on solid rock with only my shelter half, sleeping bag and my clothes between me and the cold stone. Weariness demanded sleep.

We ate cold K or C rations. There was no time for our kitchen to set up and cook us a hot meal. We were in a hurry to catch up with the Germans, defeat them, end the war and go home.

I don't know how close we were to the retreating Germans. Nobody told us much about where we were or what the situation was. Our company made very little contact with them until we got near Pilsen, Czechoslovakia. Even then the major task was rounding up prisoners. There was little or no resistance.

The farm buildings in rural Czechoslovakia, were built in a circle with an open area in the middle. You could go from the living area to the cow stable, to the hay barn, to the tool shed and back around to the living area without going outside. Good planning for bad weather. In the open space surrounded by the buildings the farmers piled their cow manure in the winter to be spread on their fields for fertilizer in the spring. These shit piles created a distinct household aroma and perhaps, also added some warmth as well. I remember spending a night in one of these homes outside of Pilsen. The smell was not uncommon to me. It reminded me of my shit-spreading days when I worked for Burr Gleason on his farm in Jericho, Vermont, with my brother Conrow before the war.

Conrow was dead now. He had been shot down by enemy antiaircraft fire somewhere over Yugoslavia, as I mentioned previously. But not before he had bombed the hell out of the Germans in B–17 raids over northern Italy and other German-held territory, sometimes bringing his four-engine flying fortress home with only half the engines functioning. He was now officially listed as KIA. I was now resigned to his loss. The military does not allow any grief time. Many GIs lost family members. I was not alone. Somehow we all carried on. But I would never forget Conrow. He was my war hero and big brother who had always been good to me.

When we got to a village, a little west of Pilsen, we were ordered to stop and set up billets in local houses. We had been anxious to get to Pilsen and meet up with Russian troops coming in from the east. We thought of the Russians as our friends fighting against a common enemy. We hoped to celebrate victory with them and exchange souvenirs and tales of the war. But that was not to be. For political reasons we did not understand, we were not allowed to meet the Russians at that point.

One day, while Pee Wee and I were walking down a street in the village looking for girls who might be willing sex partners, we turned the corner around a tall building and came face to face with two German soldiers. Each had a pistol drawn and could have easily shot us. Instead they extended their guns towards us as a gift of surrender. So Pee Wee and I each had a souvenir pistol to take home. Mine was a 9-millimeter Spanish make.

We were obligated to take charge of the prisoners so our search for sex was frustrated for the day.

Private first class Johnston was always bragging about his sexual exploits. He would boast about the German women he screwed. They ranged from the young to the old, good-looking to ugly. It didn't seem to matter to him. To hear him tell it, you'd think that whenever he met a woman in Germany, time permitting, he would simply pull his gun on her and demand sex from her, either normal or oral. He never took no for an answer. Did he rape any of them? I never knew for sure. I expect he did. But he was never charged with rape.

In a way I envied Johnston. I wished I had as large a penis as he did. I felt inferior to him. It seemed to me that Sergeant Papp liked him better than he did me. Papp didn't make fun of Johnston like he did me. He called me "Corn feed". At the time I thought he was making fun of my small penis. Later on in life I realized he was probably only referring to how skinny I was. Eventually, I also came to accept my penis as adequately average.

I also thought Johnston was smarter than I was. I considered him better looking, better built, more well liked by our peers and more attractive to females. At least he was getting more sex than I was. I had not had any since I lost my virginity to that WAC. I figured he was stronger, braver and a better second gunner than I was. But I hated him for his meanness and lack of respect for women. I never confronted him, though. I staved clear of him as much as possible.

Private first class Malek was one of my friends. He was Polish and could communicate with the Czech people. I guess their languages are similar. One day Malek and I were walking around looking for girls as usual. We came to this farm and wandered into the barn where the cows were being milked.

Sitting on a milking stool with a pail between her knees was a very attractive young woman milking a cow. She had a pretty face with big brown eyes, brown hair and round, rosy cheeks. But it was her breasts that were most alluring. They were large, round, firm and milky-white. We could not help but notice them due to the loose-fitting, low-cut shirt she was wearing. As she leaned forward to squeeze the cow's tits the deep, seductive cleavage between them came into full view of my greedy eyes.

A nervous, perhaps scared, smile swept across her face as she looked up at us, perhaps pleading that we not hurt her.

I had no intentions of hurting her. I just wanted her. Thoughts of her beautiful breasts pressing against my chest as we embraced in mutually satisfying sex, flashed lustfully across my mental screen.

Fortunately, Malek did not choose to compete for her affection. He talked to her in Polish and learned she was Polish and had been brought from Poland, as a young girl in the early part of the war as slave labor. I guessed she was now around seventeen.

"Ask her if I can come back to see her tonight," I asked Malek.

He did and she apparently approved.

We left. The rest of the day I could hardly wait, the anticipation was so great.

When I returned after dark she was already in bed. But she was in the same bedroom as the old couple with whom she lived, in a sort of parent-daughter relationship. By virtue of gestures and a few words mutually comprehensible, I let them know I wanted to sleep with her. At least I thought I did. She led me upstairs to a garret bedroom and fixed a bed.

Now she was clad in a long gown and was braless. As she bent forward to make the bed, the loose top of her gown revealed great expanses of beautiful, milky-white breasts with their brown nipples free to see. My passion rose.

While she fixed our bed I took off my cartridge belt and started stripping for action. She finished the bed making when my pants were halfway to the floor. I thought I had it made and my erection indicated my intentions. I thought she was equally ready. But she hurried towards the stairs. I tried to ask her where she was going and I thought she indicated she would be right back.

I finished undressing and got into our freshly made love nest, eager for her return. I waited for several minutes, my erection throbbing. She did not come back.

I got out of the bed, dressed, buckled on my cartridge belt and went downstairs determined to make her go to bed with me. After all, this is what Johnston did and got away with it. Why couldn't I?

She had retreated to the sanctuary of the family bedroom again, probably hoping I merely wanted to spend the night there in a soft bed and that I would now leave her alone.

She stood there near the old couple who were also in their nightclothes. I became angry. I took her by the hand and tried to lead her back up to the attic. She started to cry and huddled close to the old couple for protection, sensing, perhaps for the first time, that I wanted to have sex with her, for I had not touched her before. She folded her arms over her bosom in an attempt to hide her charm from my lusting eyes. This merely pushed her busts together and accentuated their loveliness.

The old couple were jabbering excitedly. To hell with all this stupid fooling around. *They all knew what I wanted*, I thought. I felt entitled. So I acted the way Johnston, the man I disliked but envied, would. I pulled out my .45 and pointed towards the door. They all started wailing like mad, but did not cooperate.

Two thoughts crossed my mind then; I sure as hell could get into a lot of trouble over this and I suddenly felt sorry for the girl. I wanted to love her, not rape her or force her to have sex with me. I reholstered my .45 and went back to our lonely living quarters. I guess I wasn't the same caliber as Johnston after all.

Chapter XIII

On May 7, 1945 the Germans surrendered. Our disappointment at not being allowed to meet the Russian troops was soon softened. Almost immediately after the surrender we were ordered back to the States. Rumor had it that, since we had not seen a lot of action in Europe, we were destined to take part in the invasion of Japan. But we were happy to return home, even if only for a little while. The Statue of Liberty was a joyous sight as we neared the American shore. We were given thirty-day furloughs with orders to report to Fort Bragg, North Carolina, when our leave was up.

As the war was winding down in Europe, my brother Willard was with the Marines who invaded Okinawa in April 1945. Although I cannot write about his experiences with the same intimacy as I can my own, I'm sure he underwent as much, or more, combat hell and danger as I did in Europe. He wrote me that during a terrible typhoon he was in his mess tent. (He was a mess sergeant.) The wind blew the tent down and the ridge pole hit him on his back. He woke up in a hospital. Later on he would write me about all the good baseball he was playing. This was after the war, while he was still on occupation duty. Apparently the blow from the tent pole did not permanently injure him.

Meanwhile, my brother Kermit was sailing the high seas in relative safety, although he did tell me later of the dangers of submarine-infested waters in the Atlantic Ocean. He spent time in England, Hawaii and other exotic places. He had been engaged to a girl in Burlington, Vermont, when he went into the Navy. She wrote him a "Dear John" letter. So he became engaged to a girl in England. He had always been a ladies' man, and had been engaged to one girl or another since his high school days. He liked girls more than he did sports. He was different than Willard and I were, although Willard was also engaged to his childhood sweetheart, Becky Corliss. I was still looking, not so much for a girl to become engaged to, but at least one to have sex with.

Typically, I did not warn anyone of my homecoming. Mom was elated to see me. My old man couldn't care less. Gerald and Geraldine seemed proud and pleased.

When they learned I was home the three Delaire girls came to see me. Rose Mary, the oldest one, used to write me before I went overseas. She was very pretty, intelligent and wrote nice letters. I have forgotten which one of us first signed our letters "with love". Anyhow, for a brief, exciting period I thought we were in love. When my love letters became too serious, she wrote me a "Dear John" letter.

I have forgotten the name of the second oldest Delaire girl. She was not as pretty or intelligent as Rose Mary, but I think she liked me more. I probably should have written to her. Janet was the youngest. She was also very pretty but I thought she was too young for me.

While they visited, I pretended to be very war-weary and reluctant to say much about my combat experiences. I was flattered that they came to see me but a little embarrassed and confused. I couldn't understand how Rose Mary could make so much of my homecoming after she had written me the "Dear John" letter.

Soon after my arrival home, I met a very attractive young lady about my age. She was sitting on the porch of Kirby's store. I think there was another girl with her but I don't remember anything about her.

Ever searching, I stopped to test the possibilities. She was very friendly and happy to talk to me. It turned out she was also on a mission, but one much different from mine. She was doing religious work with the youth the Methodist church in Underhill that summer. She was a college student and was spending her summer vacation in the service of her Lord.

Anyhow, she invited me to a weeny roast that the church youth were having on the hill, in the cow pasture of the old Fowler place. Since I was a soldier who had been in the war, she asked me if I would read a letter-from-a-soldier to the group. I don't recall just how the letter went, but it was something to the effect that this soldier had got "foxhole religion" due to his fear of death while under fire. He did not want to go to hell. I don't know if it was a real or phony letter.

I had not become a believer in any of my foxholes but for the sake of my mission I accepted her invitation and agreed to read the letter. For the time being I kept my mission – to get into her panties – a secret.

The letter reading went well. I read it from behind the group so it would seem to come from any combat soldier, either a live one or a dead one from heaven. My new lady friend was impressed. She asked me to do another reading at a church in a nearby village the next Sunday. I did, forever focusing on my mission.

It came about that we went to many religious group meetings in the evenings. We would ride in someone's car, usually Mr. Smith's. He was the pastor of the Underhill Methodist Church. We would sit in the back seat with other passengers, sometimes Mr. Smith's son, Vernon, and some other girl. It was not long into our relationship that I kissed her. Then in the darkness of the back seat during the night drives my hand found her breast, first on the outside of her clothing and then inside, underneath her bra.

She was not a buxom woman. Probably about 110 pounds on a five-foot-four-inch frame. Her tits were soft and saggy, not firm and fleshy. But they felt good to me. I played with them diligently. She didn't seem to mind. In fact, she snuggled close to me, leading me to believe she enjoyed being fondled. The presence of Pastor Smith driving the vehicle did not seem to deter her. Nor did the pastor's son. He was usually making out with the girl next to him.

One day, I lured her into taking a walk back up into the cow pasture where we had had our weeny roast. We brought along a picnic lunch and a blanket. After eating we were soon stretched out horizontally on the blanket. While kissing her my hand groped for her breast. She yielded to my passion willingly. This was it. D-day. Time for the invasion. I reached down and caressed her inner thighs under her skirt. As I touched her genital area she gently moved my hand away and said softly, "No, please don't."

I had heard from male friends that a woman's "no" often means "yes". So I moved my free right hand – her head was resting on my left arm – to my fly and exposed my eager organ.

Again she protested demurely. "We must obey the commandment, 'Thou shall not commit adultery'. This is not right. We should go."

Probably I could have held her down, forced myself on top of her and penetrated her privates. But she frustrated my mission by sitting up and slowly getting to her feet. She straightened her clothes. I buttoned my fly and let my passion soften. Much like I had done with the big-busted polish girl in Czechoslovakia, I chose not to let my pecker control my brain. Raping was not my style.

We walked slowly back down the hill to the village. She hung onto my arm but words between us were few.

I had wasted most of my thirty days trying to score with her and had struck out. But I had a few days left. I called my buddies, Roy Keith and Freddie Metcalf, and we arranged to go to a barn dance in Westford. Being in uniform it was easy to get girls to dance with me.

Soon I found myself dancing with a woman who eagerly ground her genitals against mine. She willingly went outside with me.

"I like to fuck servicemen," she admitted. "I know they're clean."

We looked for a place to do it. There was a garage between the dance hall and a nearby house. We went in there but it was too dark to see where we were going and I didn't want to bang into something and make a lot of noise. So we went outside again.

Finally we chose to do it standing up next to a big tree. Probably a maple. It was difficult to make the entrance, but by bending my knees a little to lower myself to her, I finally succeeded. Whether it was the awkwardness of the position or the wine I had drunk, it took me a long time. She didn't seem to be getting much satisfaction.

"Hurry up," she said. "This is getting boring."

Finally my climax came. We returned to the dance hall. We did not exchange addresses or phone numbers.

One of our distant cousins, Marjorie Chamberlin, had started writing to me while I was in Europe. Writing to a soldier in the war, especially if he was a relative, was the patriotic thing to do – a contribution to the war effort by keeping up the morale of the troops. For a female teenager it was also romantic, if he did not have a girlfriend.

Marjorie lived up in Jeffersonville, Vermont, with her aged grandparents, her unwed mother and a couple of younger brothers in a ramshackle old farmhouse, about ten miles from the Raceway where we lived.

With only a couple of days left of my furlough I decided to visit her. Her letters had been rather childish but also a bit seductive. So I borrowed my father's bicycle and rode up to see her.

Everybody in the house was happy to see me. A visit from a soldier returning from the war was a real honor to them.

Soon after my arrival on a warm summer day Marjorie, her two little brothers and I were down in a pasture fishing in a small brook. Marjorie had no difficulty taking charge. After her brothers had spent enough time with us to satisfy their visitation rights, she sent them back to the house. When they were out of sight and we were alone together, we lay down on the soft, green grass beside the trickling brook. We held each other and kissed.

Marjorie was a very pretty, dark-haired, slim young girl. She was probably about sixteen. Her breasts were small and firm but not fully developed.

She wasted no time. "Do you want to do it?" she asked eagerly.

"Sure," I agreed with all my heart.

We did not take off all our clothes in case the kids came back. But we bared enough so we could do it. She was very small and seemed completely inexperienced. It was extremely difficult to make the initial penetration. But after several minutes of maneuvering and probing I finally made the invasion. She was very tight and did not lubricate well. She did not know how to move. But it was good. As usual I came quickly and stayed on for seconds. She seemed very appreciative that I was doing it to her.

"You're the first one," she whispered softly in my ear. "I love you."

In the heat of the moment I responded, "I love you too."

That night, I was supposed to sleep with her two younger brothers in a bedroom, adjoining the one in which Marjorie was sleeping. I left our bed to go into her bedroom to kiss her goodnight. I chose to do it under the covers and soon we were doing it again. This time the entrance was easier. Things went more smoothly. It took longer and the satisfaction was greater. I asked her to move a little. She did. There seemed to be some lubrication. Midway between my first and second climax she suddenly asked me to stop.

"I've got to pee," she said.

I didn't want to stop but I did. I thought it was a peculiar time to have to pee.

She got up and tried to pee in a potty. (Back in those days most poor country people did not have bathrooms. They had outhouses. We called ours on the Raceway the backhouse. Piss pots under the foot of the bed were the norm.) Pee did not come so she returned to my arms and I finished what I was up to.

Since then I've often wondered if her sensation of wanting to pee was her first orgasmic feeling. Maybe an almost-but-not-quite sensation.

To keep things looking right I went back to my assigned bed with the boys.

The night passed swiftly. Daybreak comes early in the summer. I slept well and was still asleep when Marjorie came into our room and slipped silently under the covers with us. Since space was scarce she got on top of me. As usual I had a piss hard. So it was my turn to say I had to pee. After that was done we assumed our positions again with her on top. She seemed happy to be in this position. We kissed. The commotion had apparently awakened her brothers. They giggled. Angrily she shooed them downstairs so we could have some privacy. Then with little or no foreplay she lowered herself down onto me. I grasped her small, tight buttocks and pulled her against me. The third session was even better than the first two. Again I ejaculated twice before going downstairs for breakfast.

Later that day we parted with promises to write, to love and wait for each other and all that sweet stuff. I felt good on my bicycle ride home. Marjorie was a nice girl. She made me feel big and satisfied with myself. I was not sure I really loved her, but maybe...

Chapter XIV

The switch from combat soldier to garrison soldier was difficult for me. In combat there was no reveille in the morning. We did not march in formation to a cadence. There were no police calls, no Saturday morning inspections. The military class system was not so obvious. Combat leveled the playing field. Courage rated more than rank.

To me most of the things we had to do at Fort Bragg, North Carolina, did not make sense. It was mostly a repeat of what we had already done in basic training, e.g., requalifying with the M1 rifle. I couldn't see the point in that for me since my personal weapon was a .45. I couldn't see why combat soldiers had to go through the same old chickenshit again.

Fort Bragg is hotter than hell in the summer. We had to keep our fatigue jackets on and buttoned up and our helmet liners on all the time. So we were always sweaty and smelly. Even though we were no longer in danger, I was not a happy soldier there. But we were not there long.

On July 16, 1945 the first atomic bomb was tested at Alamogordo, New Mexico. I read about it and how the scientists had not been sure the chain reaction of the splitting atoms would stop before destroying the world. I explained this to some of the less literate of our platoon and they thought I was very intellectual.

On August 6, an atomic bomb was dropped from a B–29 on Hiroshima, Japan. The destruction was devastating to Japan. We were elated. That evening we celebrated on PX beer.

Three days later, before Japan could make their intent to surrender known to General MacArthur, Nagasaki became the second victim of the destructive power of the atomic bomb.

On August 14, the Japanese surrendered. The war was over. We no longer had to worry about invading Japan. We were ready to go home. But that was not to be yet.

However, the end of the war did put an end to our misery at Fort Bragg. It was rumored that MacArthur refused to put troops on Japanese soil until there were two infantry divisions on their way for reinforcements. Whether that was true or not, the Ninety-seventh Division was soon on its way across the country and across the Pacific Ocean to Japan.

We did not really want to go to Japan. Every mile towards Japan was a mile farther away from home and our loved ones. I missed Marjorie. So we were a hard bunch to discipline on the troop ship. That job was given to the Marines. We called them "Salt Water Cowboys". We did not have much respect for them. Marines had a reputation of being bragging glory hounds. We resented taking orders from them.

One day a Marine guard met my friend, Pee Wee in a passage-way. Pee Wee's fatigue jacket was unbuttoned.

The Marine barked, "Button up your jacket, soldier."

"Kiss my ass," Pee Wee snapped back.

The Marine brought his M1 down to Port Arms as if to emphasize his authority. This was rather ridiculous since it was not loaded.

"I'm arresting you for being out of uniform and disobeying an order," he informed Pee Wee.

Unfortunately for the Marine there were several of Pee Wee's friends including myself, within earshot. Before the Marine could carry out his arrest he was surrounded by angry soldiers.

"Throw the bastard overboard," was the cry.

If it had not been broad daylight that might well have happened. But cooler heads prevailed and the Marine was allowed to leave.

Word soon spread all over the ship that we were not going to take any more orders from Marines and that any Marine caught on deck after dark was apt to be thrown overboard. We heard that the big brass had a meeting and it was decided that, for their safety, the Marines would no longer patrol the ship. They would stay in their quarters below deck. This meant that soldiers would have to take over the routine guard details. But we didn't mind. We no longer had to put up with Marine chickenshit. Things became more relaxed and Pee Wee didn't get arrested or disciplined.

Sometime in September we pulled into Yokohama, Japan. I was amazed as I looked down from the ship's rail at the Japanese workers on the pier. They were so tiny! They reminded me of monkeys scurrying around at their assigned tasks. Later, when I was to witness them working on high scaffolding, I was even more convinced they had monkey-like skills of balance and agility, as they would scamper along horizontal poles which were no more than four inches in diameter. The dock workers seemed to be all dressed in black. They never appeared to walk. They moved quickly in a sort of short-stridden jog. I couldn't imagine ever being a friend to one of them or having an intimate relationship with a Japanese woman. We had been taught to hate them. We were told not to trust them for fear they would stick a knife in our backs or cut our throats.

Our first living area was in an open airfield. We pitched our pup tents in neat rows. While living in our tents torrential rainfall dampened our gear, clothes and bedding, as well as our spirits. We all dug little ditches around our tents to try to keep the water out. Our success was limited. But we were soon moved into large buildings that had housed Japanese warplanes. There we set up bunks and life took on a regular barrack's quality.

As usual, Saturday morning inspections became the norm. As our executive officer looked at me standing at attention in the ranks one morning, he said, "Soldier, looks like you need a shave."

My heart leapt with joy. Finally I had whiskers visible on my face. Another evidence of manhood, even though it was only light peach fuzz. As a young lad I had constantly looked at my forearms and genital area for signs of manly hair growth.

Immediately after the formation I got out my unused safety razor and shaved with glee.

My turn for KP (Kitchen Police) came up one day. During the noon meal, my job was to serve cake to the men as they passed through the chow line. For some of my buddies I gave extra pieces. The mess sergeant caught me.

"Oh," he said, "Chamberlin, you like KP so much, we'll put you on KP again tomorrow."

So I did KP the next day. After two days of hard work and long hours I slept soundly. To my surprise, I was awakened the next morning by the corporal of the day.

"Time to get up for KP," he said.

Apparently he got the bunks mixed up and it was the turn of one of my buddies for KP. I started to protest and then decided not to. I did my buddy a favor and did KP for the third day in a row.

While on KP that third day, the company had a draw for some Japanese souvenirs, one of which was a Japanese Luger pistol. Guess whose name was pulled out of the helmet – mine. So now I had souvenir pistols from both of our WWII foes.

The people of Japan were desperate for everything, after the war. In the black market GIs sold all kinds of stuff. A pack of cigarettes brought two dollars worth of Japanese yen (I think fifteen yen equaled one dollar), or a session with a geisha girl. A cake of soap or a candy bar would bring the same. Blankets were worth a lot more. At first our men could buy as many money orders as they wanted to and send them home. I remember one man in our company bragging about sending enough money home to buy a Cadillac. But soon orders came out limiting the amount one could send home.

I was too naive to take advantage of the black market in the beginning. But I didn't smoke, so when we got our cigarette rations I agreed to go to town with my friends, Pee Wee and Malek, to sell a few packs. I had no thoughts of going to a geisha house to get laid. But our first sergeant made us take prophylactic kits (we called them pro kits), just in case. I heard that the Japanese liked to play baseball. So I took along a glove and ball, which I still kept in my duffel bag.

Despite my pure intentions and for whatever reason I don't know, we soon found ourselves entering a Japanese abode which turned out to be one of ill repute. Perhaps we were selling our wares from house to house.

We were met at the door by a little old Japanese lady who smiled and bowed politely and then knelt down before us and started unlacing our boots. We got the message and took our boots off.

Then we were led into a room where there were several very cute young Japanese girls, all dolled out in pretty kimonos and attractive make-up. We offered to sell them cigarettes for thirty yen a pack.

The little old lady, who we were later to learn was called mama-san, started jabbering rapidly and pointing her hands towards the girls. Not being versed in Japanese I can't quote her verbatim. But she got her message across. The cigarettes were for the girls. One pack per piece.

Pee Wee was hot to trot. Malek was agreeable. I didn't want to be a killjoy. So we followed the mama-san's directions and each picked a girl and went into small private rooms. The floor covering was of straw mat material. The room was clean and bare. There was no bed. On the floor was a cotton-quilted pad. A box of Kleenex completed the furnishings.

There was no foreplay. This was strictly business to them. My girl helped me undress and quickly slipped out of her kimono. We did not kiss. There was no fondling except for her taking my already ready penis in her little hand to guide it into her. She moved deftly in unison with my thrusts as if she were enjoying it. I came quickly as usual. Our racial differences dissolved in the liquid passion of my sperm. Being in her felt good so I continued thrusting until I came again.

When I was done I unwrapped the pro kit. As directed by the film we had seen on VD, I squired some of the ointment from a tube into my urethra and smeared the rest all around my genital area. Then I wrapped them with the toilet paper (which came in the kit for that purpose) so as not to soil my underwear and uniform. Then I lost no time in dressing and going outside, not knowing exactly what to do with myself.

While I waited for my buddies I saw some kids near by tossing a baseball. Using sign language I offered to play with them. As I was playing catch with the young Japanese boys a military jeep drove down the narrow street. In it were two MPs. They stopped and asked me what I was doing in an off-limits area.

"I'm just out sightseeing and playing ball with Japanese kids," I half lied.

"You'd better get back to camp before you get in trouble," I was told.

So when Pee Wee and Malek were finished we returned to camp with smiles on our faces. We had broken the cultural barrier.

Chapter XV

Marjorie wrote me often after our short, sweet encounter. At first I welcomed her letters and answered them faithfully. They remained rather childish and silly. They were no longer seductive. She had already done that. They became a little controlling, demanding and somewhat boring. I recall one letter that said something about her looking forward to us setting up housekeeping and her having me mop the kitchen floor for her. For some reason that turned me off. Maybe, because of an unconscious fear of being told what to do by a woman. She had seemed to enjoy the top position. Anyhow, I soon stopped writing her. Now that I had found Japanese girls were nice and readily available, the need for a girlfriend back home was less. And I did not want to lie about being faithful. I could also rationalize that we were cousins. Screwing a cousin was one thing, marrying one was something else.

We were soon moved to a campsite in the hills a few miles outside of Nagasaki. We moved into wooden barracks that probably housed Japanese soldiers before the end of the war.

Not long after we arrived, a couple of Japanese men rode into the compound on bicycles. They had gifts for our leaders – two large bottles of sake. Roland, Malek, Pee Wee and I met them and told them we would gladly deliver their offerings to our leaders. But before delivery we decided to sample the liquid for poison. We laughed, "We don't want our leaders to drink something that was not good for them."

It was good. It went down easily so we sampled a little more. Before we knew it, between the four of us, we had drunk all two quarts of the libation for our leaders. And we became drunk out of our heads. To hell with our leaders and to hell with everything else. We decided to head for town to get laid.

When we got out on the road we met four Japanese riding bicycles. We stopped them and took their bikes. This was the first time that I noticed the mean streak in Roland when he was drunk. Ordinarily, he was a very easygoing, mild-mannered, pleasant person. But now he acted really mean.

"Give me your goddamned bike," he yelled angrily as he grabbed a bike from a little Japanese man.

We rode the bikes down the hill on a sandy road. The loose sand and our drunken state caused us to take many flops on the bikes. We blamed the bikes. We met some more natives on bicycles. We decided their bikes were better than the ones we had already stolen. So we made them swap with us.

We rode the newly stolen bikes on down the hill for a few miles until we came to some houses. We went to the houses in search of women. But these were not geisha houses. The people did not understand what we wanted. We were so drunk that the details of what we did are foggy. But I can remember seductively rubbing the back of a little old blind lady. She had probably been blinded by the Nagasaki blast. And I recall that Roland acted so mean to the people there, that Malek and I sort of had to intervene and talk him into leaving before he raped or otherwise hurt somebody.

By now we had sobered up enough to realize that we had better get back to camp. We had no permission to leave. So we rode our stolen bikes back to camp. It was now after dark and the lights were out, so we sneaked into the barracks and slipped silently into bed.

The next morning our section leader, Sergeant Dobson, came looking for us. "Did you boys bring those bikes into camp last night?" he demanded to know.

Sheepishly, we admitted we did.

There were some Japanese looking for their bikes. So we graciously offered them the bikes. They excitedly waved their hands around and shook their heads. "*Dami, dami*," they cried, pointing at the bikes and some numbers on them.

We finally figured out that these were not their bikes and they would accept nothing other than their own bikes.

Lieutenant Murray, who had been wounded in Germany and was now back with us, was brought into the picture. The sake had been meant for him but we didn't say anything about that.

"You men have until noon today, to return these bikes to their rightful owners and bring back the bikes you stole from these people," he ordered. "Otherwise you will be court-martialed."

I sure as hell didn't want to go through that again.

So we set out up the road in the direction the natives were going when we took their bikes. We took along the second set of stolen bikes. We stopped at each house along the way. We felt it was a hopeless task, like finding a needle in a haystack. We were four unhappy troopers facing time in the stockade. But Lady Luck was with us. Miraculously, we found the owners of the bikes we had and they gladly gave us the ones we had forced them to trade for. They were happy to get their own bikes back and we were happy to be able to return the first stolen four to their rightful owners. This episode gave me a better appreciation of the honesty of the ordinary Japanese people. They did not want property that did not belong to them. Rather different than how their leaders and the military had acted during the war.

It was not long before we got passes to go to town. Lieutenant Murray was very good to his men and we were to learn later that he also enjoyed frolics in geisha houses. He understood the needs of young soldiers far away from home. So, as long as we did our job of guarding a large number of oil drums, he let us go to town as often as we wanted to.

I'm not sure, but I don't think we were supposed to go to Nagasaki. I don't know if our government was worried about us being exposed to radiation or not. Anyhow, in the little village near the camp we found a cab driver who took us to Nagasaki. We were shocked at the devastation. A large portion of the city was flattened, either from the blast of the atom bomb or the fires that followed. But we did not dwell upon sightseeing. Our driver knew what we wanted and where to get it.

In the midst of the leveled city, was a tiny structure about six feet high and maybe three feet wide with the backside sloping towards the ground. It was an entranceway to an underground geisha house. I'm not sure who was with me on that first trip. I know Pee Wee was there and probably Malek. We screwed around a lot together. I don't think Roland was there. After that drinking episode he didn't socialize much with us. Maybe he was embarrassed or thought we were a bad influence. Anyhow, we had our cabbie wait for us while we went in to get laid.

The underground geisha house was a beehive of activity. Soldiers from many outfits were lined up with cigarettes, soap, candy bars, Japanese yen, military scrip or whatever, to pay for a piece of ass. The girl I got that evening was not so hot. She seemed tired and in a hurry to get on with her next customer. But she flopped her legs together in rhythm with my moves. After I came she wanted me to quit but I pretended I had not come yet and continued screwing her until I came again.

We visited that whorehouse on a regular basis while we were on that occupational assignment. We used the same cabbie all the time and became close friends with him. He picked up a little English and we learned a few Japanese expressions so we could communicate.

On our second visit, I got a nice little girl who seemed to enjoy sex with me. She smiled, giggled and was playful. She was warm and cuddly. Sex with her was more like making love to a girl than fucking a prostitute. We kissed. I fondled her breasts. She rubbed my back and caressed my body. She became my steady, number one geisha girl.

After each session with a Japanese girl I faithfully used a pro kit to protect myself from VD. I think most of the other guys did too. So after we would get up the next morning we would have to unwrap the toilet paper from our genitals and wash off the protective ointment. After being in the Army for a while, pissing, shitting and showering next to naked men, I had lost all sense of embarrassment. So I would get some warm water in my steel helmet and wash my not-so-private genitals, out near the open latrine area, in plain sight of anyone interested in watching. Sometimes there would be Japanese cleaning ladies in the area. They would look at me and giggle. It didn't bother me. I let it all hang out.

One evening, our cabbie took us a few miles up into the hills to another geisha house. On the way we stopped at a place and had some Japanese food and beer. Their beer was not as potent as their sake but it was strong enough so that I got pretty drunk. I wound up in a room with a rather unattractive, overweight geisha.

While we were having intercourse, she reacted to my up and down movements with her own up and down, round and round motions. It was fantastically pleasurable. Never before and never after have I experienced the same sexual dexterity in a woman.

But, as my sperm spurted up into the innermost sanctum of her body, vomit erupted from my mouth towards her face and pillow. She proved equally dexterous with her hands as with her ass as she quickly caught the puke and cupped my mouth with one hand and grabbed tissues with the other. Her swift, timely reaction prevented what could have been a far greater mess.

I was in a very foggy state of drunkenness. I remember some of my buddies came into the room to help me. My mind focused on two very important things – guarding my wallet and the proper application of my pro kit. In my drunken blindness I was capable of little else. With the help of my friends and our cabbie I got dressed and we made it back to camp.

Several times after that, we went back to the same village but I could never find that geisha with her sensuous swivel. She had been my first and last rotary ride.

Not long after that sensational sex in the hills, I awoke one morning and discovered a sore on the bottom side of the head of my penis. I was filled with fear. Had I used the pro kit properly the night I was so drunk? I had had sex several times since then. I wondered about the incubation period, trying to pinpoint where I went wrong. I went on sick call. The examining medic confirmed my fears.

"Looks like you've got VD all right," he said. "Probably syphilis."

Chapter XVI

On the train to a military hospital in Tokyo I was one sad lad. I resolved not to ever again be bad. It was much like being born again. I vowed to myself to never again commit the sin of fornication with a geisha girl. That was the closest I ever came to praying.

At the hospital, blood was taken and tests were done. Having American nurses tend to me was embarrassing. They knew why I was there. I thought they must think it was pretty low of an American soldier to have sex with a Jap whore. I could not look them in the eye, much less flirt with them. I might never be able to make love to a woman again, so dark were my thoughts.

Several days passed while I waited for the test results. Each day I washed my genitals carefully and inspected the sore on my penis. It seemed to be healing. On rounds an MD perfunctorily looked at it. On about the third or fourth day the sore seemed to be gone. About that time the doctor told me the tests had come back negative. I did not have VD!

"Probably rubbing on your underwear caused an irritation," the doctor said with a mischievous smile.

The hospital discharged me and sent me back to my unit. By then, the second platoon had rejoined the rest of H Company and the company had been moved to a new position closer to Tokyo. I can't remember the name of the city. Nor can I recall the details of my transportation back to my outfit. Probably train, bus and perhaps taxi. But I do recall vividly what I did during some free time during the trip. By now I was horny as hell, not having had sex for over a week. Since I did not have VD all resolutions were off.

A geisha house was not hard for me to find. By this time I felt like an old pro at it. Soon I was in a nice, clean place with a mama-san and a couple of cute girls, I paid for the service and made my choice from among the ladies. We went into the privacy of her boudoir and were about to consummate our relationship when the sound of two American voices entered our ears.

Quickly she put her finger to my lips for me to be quiet. She opened the sliding door of a sort of large linen closet built in along one wall. She motioned for me to get in. Then she put my clothes in with me and closed the door, again signaling for me to be still.

As I lay there naked on top of clean sheets and towels in a space about six feet long, two feet deep and three feet high, I figured out that the American voices were from MPs checking whorehouses for GIs who were not supposed to be there. All geisha houses were still off-limits. I wondered if they had spotted my boots and would then search the house for me. The tone of their voices was very friendly. They indicated they did not have time to stay long but would be back later when they had more time.

Soon after they left, my crime-abetting little lady returned and let me out of my hiding place. She confirmed my suspicions about the MPs. We made love for quite some time. It was in the middle of the day, a slow time for their business, so she was in no hurry. Being almost caught seemed to enhance the fun of it. We giggled, caressed, held each other close, wiggled, enjoyed and relaxed.

My earlier resolve to never again have sex with a Japanese woman, had not been strong enough for me to discard my protection. I still had pro kits with me. I applied one religiously. My faith in them had been restored.

H Company had received some new replacements while I was gone. Jimmy Mansour was one who was assigned to our platoon. He was a nice young lad of about nineteen, rather good-looking with dark, curly hair, short and of small frame, very intelligent, quite friendly and very religious. To my knowledge he never swore or spoke badly of anyone. He didn't smoke or drink and, of course, was a virgin and intended to stay that way until he married. He followed the teachings of his Catholic faith.

For some reason, religious people and I seem to be magnetically drawn together. I like them because they are almost always good people. Why they like me, I'm not sure. It is not for me to judge. Perhaps, they think I need to be saved and am a challenge to them. Anyhow, Jimmy and I became close friends.

But our friendship did not deter me from being part of a cruel trick on him. On Christmas Eve, 1945, while Jimmy was attending church services at the chapel, there was a Christmas party going on in our company day room. There was food, drink and girls to be had. After a drink or two some of the jokers from our platoon, including myself, felt sorry for Jimmy in his lonely virginity. We all liked him so we decided to help him out. We procured one of the prettiest girls at the party. We took her to his bunk, had her undress, get under the covers and wait for him. She was delighted to be part of a pleasant Christmas surprise. Then we dimmed the lights and retired to our nearby bunks to await Jimmy's return.

When he got back from church Jimmy stripped down to his underwear before he noticed the naked girl in his bed. When he saw her, he was mortified. He wanted nothing to do with our Christmas gift. He turned on the lights and covered himself with his hands.

In no uncertain terms, he gave orders to whom it may concern:

"Get her out of here!"

From us there was a spontaneous roar of laughter. For the poor girl it was a huge embarrassment to be unwanted and rejected. It was a cruel hoax on her as well as on Jimmy.

I felt sorry for her and, since I was in part responsible for her plight and her services were already paid for, I volunteered to take her home. While there I made her feel desirable and wanted again.

Steve Malek was one of my closest friends in our platoon. He was a dark-haired, good-looking, friendly young soldier about the same age as I was. He was of average build, about five feet ten inches tall and probably weighed around 160 pounds. He was a nice guy. I liked him. By this time I had grown to a little over six feet and weighed about 140 pounds. We had one thing in common which made our friendship stronger. We both loved Japanese pussy. He was ever ready to let me lead him astray. Perhaps I had more leadership qualities than I thought when I had previously turned down a chance to apply for Officer Candidate School.

Be that as it may, one evening Steve and I went to a geisha house together. I think it was sort of a family business – a mama-san and her two daughters trying to make a living the best way they could. Probably Papa-san had been killed in the war. This was often the case. The women left behind did whatever they could to survive. Pleasing men was what they knew best. It was part of their culture – their education. U.S. soldiers were a ready market. Steve and I were more than willing to do our bit to keep food on the table for hungry Japanese ladies.

Anyhow, after we had taken off our boots and entered a brightly lit living area, the mama-san stood in front of me with a big smile on her face. Seems like she was only about half as tall as I was, her face about level with my belt buckle. With no preliminary negotiations she unbuttoned my fly. With each button undone my joystick swelled with anticipation. Her nimble fingers reached in, parted the pee hole in my shorts, and grasped the full measure of my erection. Her face was so close. She glued her eyes on me. Her mouth so available and open. Her lips puckered. I really thought she was going to kiss me. Her head would hardly have had to bend. She had maneuvered me so my back was towards the others. They would not have known. But, somewhat to my disappointment, she put it back inside my underwear carefully so as not to bend it, buttoned me up, smiled and went to Steve for the same purpose.

Later, though she could not tell us due to the language barrier, it dawned on us that she had measured us to find out which daughter each of us would best fit. She had two lovely girls. One was taller and a little slimmer than the other. Mama-san paired me with the taller. She gave us no choice. Not that it mattered. The girls were equally charming. To myself, I wondered if maybe mama-san gave me the taller girl because she felt I had a longer tool than Steve. I had never looked at it that way before.

The girls were good. We stayed a long time. It was not a house with a lot of business. We visited there several times after that, becoming almost part of the family. We were very satisfied with the way mama-san had bedded us. We never thought of swapping.

I don't think mama-san would have allowed it.

Guarding a large ammunition dump was one of the missions of H Company at this occupational site. I was a member of that guard detail. This was not bad duty. Even though guard duty is a boring activity and unpleasant if the weather is bad, I usually managed to find a comfortable spot out of the weather where I could relax, and sometimes even snooze a little. Guards are supposed to be alert at all times and take their duty seriously. I was alert all right – alert enough not to get caught off guard. Since the war was over, I no longer took any military duty seriously. I guess I was not a very good soldier, I just wanted to put in my time, earn my points and go home. Most of us felt that way.

One nice thing about this assignment was that I found a large supply of ammo that fit my seven-millimeter Japanese Luger, which I had previously won. I took several hundred rounds and put them in a large cloth bag with draw strings, and hid them in my duffel bag. We were supposed to guard the ammo, not steal it, but that did not stop me.

The ammo dump was a short walk from our quarters. In between was a large river spanned by a long bridge. There were also many Japanese houses on the way.

One stormy night in January 1946, another member of the guard detail and I were crossing the bridge on our way to our assignment. A strong wind was blowing snow into our faces. We bent forward against the cold blast. In the middle of the bridge we met two small, shadowy figures. They were ladies. We were gentlemen. They seemed to be in distress. Since we had a little time on our hands, we offered to help them through the storm to their house near by.

After entering a small entranceway, the ladies quickly knelt before us and took off our boots. What better way to invite us into their quarters for something warm for our chilled bones? They led us into a dimly lit room. On the floor were two sleeping pads with comforters to ward off the chill of winter. Then they helped us out of the rest of our uniforms and slid under the comforters with us, each pair to its own pad.

From the feel of her body and the texture of her vaginal muscles I could tell my pad pal was not a young gal. Her flesh did not have the firmness of youth. Her breasts were flat and saggy. Her vaginal walls were dry and leathery. But she was warm and willing so we went at it. It wasn't too bad. After we were all finished and our eyes had become adjusted to the dim light, I could see that my partner's woman was much younger and prettier than mine. I envied him.

We paid the standard fee, made an appointment for the next service and went on to report to the sergeant of the guard. We were a little late. The sergeant was madder than hell. The next day he called me into his office and demanded an explanation.

I lied. "It was such a bad storm that it took longer to get there than we calculated."

"I don't believe you, Chamberlin," he retorted. "I think you were fucking off."

"No, we weren't," I continued to lie unconvincingly.

"I've a good mind to court martial you," the sergeant threatened.

"I wouldn't if I were you," I warned him. "Unless you want me to tell about you handing out souvenir sabers to your friends."

I didn't like tattle-tales. It was not my nature to be one. But it was the only defense I could think of at the time.

The sergeant had been doing just that, so he knew I had him. "Okay, Chamberlin, I'll let it go this time," he conceded. "But don't ever let it happen again."

As I was leaving, perhaps to make me an equal partner in his guilt, the sergeant said, "By the way, Chamberlin, do you want one of those sabers?"

"No thanks," I responded self-righteously.

Thinking about it, I thought I had got screwed the first time by being selected by the older and less sexually attractive lady of the night. So on our way to our next meeting with them, with an ulterior motive in my mind, our conversation went something like this.

"Buddy, how was your girl last night?" I asked.

"She was okay," he replied, "How was yours?"

"She was good," I stretched the truth a bit. "Hey, just for the hell of it, let's swap tonight," I continued.

"Okay," he agreed.

The ladies objected a little due to a strong Japanese sense of loyalty. But the switch was made.

Underneath the covers with my new girl I learned something about myself I never knew before. My new sex partner reached down and gently stroked my inner thighs. No one had ever done that to me. It was the most erotic foreplay I had ever experienced. I returned her tantalizing touch in the same way and added this new knowledge to my repertoire of sexual stimulants. When we joined, she seemed as aroused as I was. She was warm and wet. I felt comfortable and snug within her. In a leisurely manner and lovingly we moved to a climax, as if we did not want it to end. At that point it did not end. With ever longer periods of soaking in between, I came again, and again. It was my first triple-header in Japan. She smiled with happiness and fulfillment.

What happened to my buddy and the other lady I have no idea. My new sex mate let me know where she lived. From then on, while still stationed at this site, I went to her house every night I could and we would make passionate love. I no longer considered her a prostitute. She did not wear the fancy kimonos of the geisha girls, nor did she use pretty make-up to enhance her charm. No longer was our relationship on a paid-for-piece basis. Sometimes I brought her food, candy, soap, cigarettes, etc., stuff she could use or sell, but not always. I considered her my girlfriend. I was faithful to her and I thought she was faithful to me. I loved the feel of her fingers caressing me. She loved to have me suck her breast during long periods of foreplay.

Unfortunately, she did not speak much English and I knew little Japanese. So our communication was mostly by body language. I loved her and each encounter was an expression of that love. If I could, I would have married her and brought her home with me, taught her English and taken care of her. But that was unheard of then and it was not to be.

Chapter XVII

Sometime during the winter of 1946, the Ninety-seventh Division set up a school for those of us who wished to further our education. There were plenty of educated personnel in the division able to teach. Many of us wanted to earn credits to be used in our future schooling. I, for one, had learned early on that education helped you get ahead in the Army. I figured that was why I was still only a private first class. I had already decided to return to school after I was discharged.

So I signed up for the school. I hated to part from my new love. But I vowed to be true to her and, in a sense, I almost felt I would be improving myself for the good of both of us. Romantic were my thoughts. But my romanticism stopped short of considering how she would take care of herself while I was away.

At the school we were housed in some old military barracks. On the second floor of the building I was assigned to, was a small private room which had probably been for non-commissioned officers. We were allowed to pick our own sleeping area, so I chose the private room, perhaps thinking I could study better there. No one challenged my choice.

I signed up for Public Speaking, Psychology 101, Typing and Geometry. This was my third time around for Geometry. I had not quite finished the correspondence course I was taking in Geometry, so had not yet earned credit for it. It was getting pretty easy for me, Psychology turned out to be a basic course in Anatomical Psychology which was far too scientific for my taste, and I didn't like the teacher. So I switched to Applied Psychology. These were all good subjects and were very helpful in my future education and life. Academically, I did well at the thirty-day school.

In a way I kept my promise to my girlfriend. I did not visit a geisha house while at the school. But one dark, gloomy night, after my homework was done, I went for a walk in the streets around the school. I had long lost my fear of being attacked by Japanese civilians. The dimly lit streets were almost totally empty of people and traffic. But I came upon a small, hooded figure. As I was about to pass, a tiny arm reached out and tugged at the sleeve of my jacket. A wee voice begged for a cigarette. I recognized it to be a woman's. My heart reached out to her. I had some cigarettes in my room that I could sell to her.

"Come with me," I offered. "It will get you some cigarettes."

I led her to our barracks. I'm not sure what the rules were about having women in the barracks. I don't think we were supposed to. Anyhow, I did not want anybody to know I was taking a woman up to my room. So it was a challenge to me to sneak her in. But it was after lights-out so the entranceway was barely lit. We sneaked in silently.

Once in my room, she removed her hood. I saw that she was an elderly lady. Her face was thin and wrinkled, her body skinny, small and slightly stooped. I felt sorry for her. She was probably suffering from the deprivation and depravity of the war. My tender feelings for her translated into lust for her body. She was woman. I was man. I had not had any for several days. I was horny. Age and appearance didn't matter.

We did not take off all our clothes for fear of being caught, just enough to be unhindered. We moved to my bunk. There was no foreplay. I entered her quickly. She was not yet wet but she was well broken in and large enough for easy penetration. Her dryness created ample friction for me to come quickly. As I came, her vaginal muscles tightened around my penis in a vice-like grip. I could not move. It scared me a little. It felt like she was sucking out my sperm to the last drop. But despite the tightness I did not soften. A pack of Camels was worth more than one brief quickie.

Suddenly she opened up to the extent that I felt lost within her. She was now wet. She thrust her little body up hard against mine. We humped together. At first there was no friction. It was like probing empty space.

Then gradually this phase of her performance changed and her love tunnel closed snugly around me again. For some time we moved up and down against each other. It was good. She knew how to please a man. She was more than earning her cigarettes.

I came again. Again, like the steel jaws of a bear trap, she clamped down around me. This time I was not afraid. I knew what was coming. I relaxed and enjoyed her. Soon she relaxed and the wide, open, bottomless chasm returned. I pumped a little and wiggled from side to side, searching for the walls. But only she controlled the shape of her inner self. Again things came back to normal. We stayed together for a while longer, but I was drained.

We parted. I gave her two packs of Camels. She slipped silently back into the darkness of the night, I conscientiously applied a pro kit to my limp member.

Many nights after that I roamed the nearby streets in search of her. I never found her. Nor would I ever find another so gifted.

However, I did meet another young lady while at the school. This one was about my age. She spoke good English and was well educated. She took me to her humble house to meet her mother. They served me tea and we talked a lot. But they were not in the sex business. That did not dissuade me from my pursuit of the fruits of the flesh.

I invited her to my room. Innocently she came. I expected that once she was in my room the rest would be easy. My hopes soared high. We talked a bit, sat on my bunk, held hands, looked lovingly into each other's eyes, kissed and lay down together. We held one another close. My right hand found her breasts. They were nice. I fondled them. She seemed to enjoy my attention. My lust leaped upright. She was wearing the typical Japanese slacks. I reached down and tried to pull them down. She grabbed them to hold them up. I finally succeeded in getting them halfway down to her knees. Then I tugged at her underpants. She did her best to keep them up. All the while I was kissing her so she could not protest. I got her panties down a little. I took out my throbbing tool, rolled on top of her and tried to put it in. It rubbed against the elastic band of her panties but did not enter her. The friction on the underside of its head, coupled with my eagerness, caused an explosive discharge upon her belly. I was through for the night.

As sort of an apology for my selfish behavior, I kissed her tenderly on her eyelids, caressed her cheek softly with my hand and said, "I'm sorry." Then, like a gentleman, I walked her home.

We remained friends and I saw her several more times, but I never again tried to soil her.

At the end of school I returned to my unit. The first night back I went to see my true love. As I was about to take off my boots a pair of GI boots already there startled my eyes. I was shocked! Even though I had not been, I had expected her to be faithful. I sat on her doorstep sad and dejected. How could she do this to me? She came out, put her arms around me and begged me to come in. At first I resisted. Then a tall, slim soldier appeared at the door. Lo and behold, it was none other than Brazil, one of my best friends from H Company.

"Come on in Chamberlin," he said, "I'm done."

Was the girl I thought I loved and who I thought loved me nothing more than a prostitute, I wondered. Gradually reality sank in. I put sex with Japanese women in its proper perspective. It was no big deal. With a little more coaxing I took off my boots and entered her house. Brazil put on his boots and left. We had sex. It was as good as before. But love was now only lust. I emptied my sperm into her on top of Brazil's.

Within days both Brazil and I were ordered to Yokohama to be processed to go home for discharge. We were in Yokohama for a day or two before leaving. The night before we left, another dogface and I were roaming the streets in search of a final piece of Japanese culture. We ran across this young female with thick glasses. She seemed sad and lost. We wanted to cheer her up. We spoke to her. She did not answer. Maybe she was mute – a victim of the horrors of Allied bombings during the war. We had no way of knowing. We felt sorry for her. It was very late at night. We asked her if she had a place to stay. Still no answer. So we decided to take her to a hotel and put her up for the night. She offered no objection. The hotel clerk took our money and took us to a large dimly lit room which was already occupied by several people sleeping on pads on the floor. The three of us were allotted a small sleeping space. We lay down with her in the middle facing me. He entered her first doggy fashion from behind. She did not resist. He didn't take long. Then I entered her from the front. She was warm, wet and felt good. Sorrow for her plight made me want to make it better for her. I kissed her brow tenderly as my passion spilled within her. I did not consider what we were doing to her as abuse. It was just one of the depraved realities of war and its aftermath, not much different than lining up at a whorehouse. None of us made much noise for fear of disturbing the others in the room. We each had seconds before the night was over. Then we men shared a pro kit. He didn't have one but I did. We took the still silent soul back to the streets and gave her $10 in military script, which was actually worth much more on the black market than the official rate of exchange of one dollar to fifteen yen. Then we returned to our military station. The next day we sailed for home.

Chapter XVIII

On March 18, 1946 I received my "ruptured duck", a lapel pin symbolizing that you were now a veteran, a civilian, a free man once again. I went home to our house on the Raceway in Jericho, Vermont. As usual I didn't tell anybody I was coming. My mother and my younger siblings were surprised and pleased. My father may have been surprised too, but he didn't care. I doubt if he even cared when Conrow was killed in action. Ironically, he received a pension from Conrow's government insurance for the rest of his life. But the others were glad to see me safely home and I was happy to be home.

While I was gone my mother had used the money I sent home to put running water and a bathroom in the house. I had not intended for her to do that but I did not make an issue of it. I stayed at home for the next fifteen months. My room and board for that period more than offset my money she had used.

Within days of my return Kermit came home from the Navy. For a few days we were together and slept in the same bed again. He told me about the English girl he was engaged to when he was in England. He would take her out on dates but she was too proper to have sex with him. After he would bring her home and kiss her goodnight, her not-so-proper sixteen-year-old sister would sneak out of their house and meet him to have sex. For some reason that engagement ended, as had the two he had before he entered the Navy. Kermit needed a woman. He was lonely without one.

"Remember June, the cashier in the grocery store in Perkinsville, where you and I lived when we worked in Springfield before we were drafted?" he asked me.

"Yes, I remember her," I said. "She was a nice girl."

"She was awful homely and kind of fat," he continued. "But I think she liked me. She used to talk to me when I bought things in that store. I bet she would make a good wife. I think I'll go down there and ask her for a date. What do you think?"

I thought about some of the homely ones I had screwed in Japan. "Homely ones sometimes are better than the pretty ones," I said sagely. "Might be a good idea."

We talked for some time about our war experiences. He had become a storekeeper, which is like a supply sergeant in the Army. He had the three stripes to go with it. He didn't have any combat stories to share with me, except that when they sailed through submarine-infested waters it was scary. I couldn't brag much about my rank of private first class but I did tell him about some of my other experiences.

Soon thereafter Kermit headed for Perkinsville to see June.

A few days later, Willard came home from the Marines. We were happy to be reunited. We talked mostly about baseball and his great love for Becky. He repeated his accounts of great games he had played at Camp Lejeune and in Okinawa. Unlike Kermit he had some combat tales to tell.

Among other things he told me about being in a foxhole one night. It was pitch dark. He heard this Jap sneaking up on him. When he got close enough so Willard could see his eyes, Willard shot him. The next morning, on the very edge of his foxhole with a bullet hole right between his eyes was a billy goat. To this day I don't know if that really happened or if Willard was joking.

Willard had done much better than I had, not only in baseball but also in promotions. He had become a mess sergeant with the stripes to go with the job.

As I recall Willard did not stay at our house long, if at all.

After I was home a few days I went back to Underhill High School and finished my junior year. I don't think I really studied or learned much those last few months of the school year, but Mrs. Ellsworth, who was now the principal, gave me credits for being in the service, my correspondence courses and those courses I took in Japan. The next fall I went back to high school to finish my senior year.

Gerald was now thirteen and in the sixth grade. His best friend was Arnold Machia. They were not very good students and raised a lot of hell. Maybe that's why their male teacher invited them to his room up over Effie's Lunch. Whatever his reason, after he got them up to his room, he tried to have sex with them. The boys resisted and Gerald told me that he only got as far as sticking his pecker between Gerald's legs, but he did not get it into him.

I became highly pissed off. I loved my little brother and I didn't want any grown man trying to fuck him up the ass. But I kept my cool and tried to act responsibly. At the time I did not know anything about pedophilia. I had never seen or heard the word. But I knew that trying to screw young boys was a perversion and against the law. I thought something should be done about it. So I went down to talk to Frank Machia, the father of Arnold. We made sure the authorities, including Sheriff Howard Davis, knew that the boys had been molested, but for some reason it was covered up. Nothing was ever done except that the teacher lost his job at the end of the year. He was a very good friend of the Catholic priest in Underhill Center and a regular churchgoer. I suspect the said priest helped in the cover-up. Today we hear more and more about pedophiles in the priesthood.

During my talks with the Machias I became better acquainted with Lorraine, Frank's oldest daughter. She was five or six years older than I was, not very attractive, and had been married to an itinerant heavyweight boxer. I had known her before the war but she was too old to be a sex object for me then. But now when I met her at the dance at the "Chicken Coop" in Underhill Center on Saturday night, I asked her to dance. She ground her genitals against mine in a slow dance. I got the message. Soon we were in the back seat of a car. She made me use a rubber, which I just happened to have for just such an emergency. We did it. It was okay but I didn't care much for the rubber. It took away much of the warmth. It had a sort of separating quality. She was rather loose which led me to believe her former husband was much larger than I was. But she was good enough for seconds. Not long after that I went down to her house for an evening visit. After her elderly parents went upstairs to bed, we sat on a sofa in their living room, kissed and petted for a while. I was going to screw her on the couch but she whispered "no" and pointed to a heat register in the ceiling through which we were visible from the bedroom above. So we moved over near a piano where we could not be seen. Again I donned a condom and we went at it, standing close to the piano. Too close, for when I came, it drove her ass against the ivories which added a loud, discordant musical note to my climax.

I don't think she really enjoyed sex with me. I doubt if I satisfied her. We did not become an item. I still had one safety left of the three-pack I had bought. I kept it in my wallet.

★

My mother had a car which she parked in a driveway on the northeast side of our house. There was a garage at the end of the driveway which she could not use because it was full of junk, mostly my father's. Without telling anybody I decided to clean it out so my mother could put her car under cover. After cleaning out a huge heap of junk I called up Ralph Russin, who had a dump truck, to come get it and take it to a dump. Mother was pleased, but when Dad got home from the woods he was mad as hell.

"How dare you throw out my stuff?" he hollered at me.

"I did it so Mama could put her car in the garage," I explained calmly. "It was only junk."

"It may have been junk to you," "Dad continued angrily. "But it was worth something to me."

His pale blue eyes stared at me threateningly. I stared back at him defiantly. I was now over six feet tall, probably four inches taller than he was, and outweighed him by several pounds. I was ready to beat the shit out of him if he laid a hand on me.

"I've got a .45 upstairs," he warned me. "If you ever touch anything of mine again I'll put a bullet right between your eyes."

From the time he had first started beating us when we were kids, I had looked forward to the day when I was big enough to whip his ass. Now I knew I could do it.

My voice remained low and cool as I responded to his threat. "If you ever shoot at me you'd better be damn sure you don't miss. If you do it'll be the last fucking shot you ever make."

Never again did he ever threaten me. Nor did I ever have to whip his ass.

Chapter XIX

During the spring of 1946, it was decided to have an Underhill Town baseball team. I tried out for the team and made it. We played in the Northern Vermont League. Our home games were in Carpenter's cow pasture. Before every game someone would have to clean up the field of any cow shit. The field was rough. Balls took bad hops in the infield and it was hard to chase down fly balls in the outfield.

Three Bolio boys – Bob, Babe and Honey – were on the team. Mom didn't like the Bolios. They drank beer, smoked, were Catholic and were reputed to have been sexually promiscuous. All of which Mom frowned upon. Mom was a hard-working, wonderful mother, but tolerance was not one of her virtues.

Also on the team were the two Littner brothers, George and Max. Willard and I never liked George. When he was in high school he used to pick on little kids. We were little then. We used to call him "Muckle Chops" because of his facial features. He was a southpaw and usually pitched. Like most pitchers he was not a good hitter. Max was not a very good hitter either and didn't always play. Sometimes he played right field. He was also a southpaw.

Others on the team were Foster Paige, who usually caught. He was the best hitter on the team. Len Lamphere played first base. He also hit well. He would not use a first baseman's mitt. He used a small fielder's glove and would complain if we threw the ball to him too hard. Don Langlois, who now ran the farm next to our house for the owner, Mr. Wheeler, played with us when he had time. He was a good short stop but didn't hit too well. Freddie Metcalf and Shrimp Carpenter, my friends who had cars and would give us rides to dances and girl hunting, were also team members, but didn't play much. Freddie could never hit the ball in batting practice so they would not let him play in the games.

Willard also played with us in two or three games that year. He pitched and had a really good fastball and curve. His fastball would ride up a little and was not only hard to hit but also hard to catch.

I started out playing second base. I was not very good. I usually made one or two errors every game and didn't hit very well. But for some reason they kept me on the team. We didn't have a regular coach. Sometimes Parker Rice would manage us during games. I caught one game that Willard pitched up in Jeffersonville. We won the game but I did not catch well.

After the game Willard said to me, "I didn't know you had to wind up to throw down to second base."

I did not have a good arm. That's why I preferred to play second base. But I wound up playing third base. I started catching another game Willard pitched at Carpenter's field. We got behind and Willard got a little wild. I could not catch his fastball when it was too far away from where I expected it. Bob Bolio relieved me behind the plate. He could not hold Willard either. Then Foster Paige took over as catcher and, if my memory is correct, George Littner relieved Willard on the mound. We lost that game.

Despite all this, Underhill won the northern half of the league and played in the championship game against Vergennes at Centennial Field in Burlington. This was a well-groomed semi-pro ball field. I played third base. Ground balls did not take bad hops and I made several plays without an error. I also had two hits. It was the best game I ever played.

But we lost the game by a wide margin. "Muckle Chops" didn't want to pitch. He wanted his brother Max to pitch. Max gave up a lot of runs. Then Honey Bolio came in to pitch. He was not effective either, but he had a hell of a good time. Every time the opposing pitcher came to bat, Honey struck him out with big, sweeping curve balls. Then he laughed.

In desperation, Parker put Freddie Metcalf in the game. To everybody's surprise he got two hits and played well in the outfield. I felt good for my buddy.

After the game Parker said, "Chamberlin and Metcalf were the only ones who played good."

On July 10, 1946 Willard and Becky were married in a Protestant church in Jericho, Vermont. I was the best man. Wilma Tribe, Becky's niece, was the bridesmaid. It was a small wedding with only family members present. In those days none of us had enough money for a big gala affair. After the wedding they went to live in Massachusetts and he played baseball for a team there.

At one of the dances at the "Chicken Coop", I spotted this nice-looking, tall, slender, brown-haired woman sitting on the sidelines. She had large, strikingly bright brown eyes that said, "Come dance with me". Bedroom eyes would aptly describe them.

She was sitting with another fairly good-looking woman. They turned out to be sisters. One of my friends, Don, was with me. We asked them to dance. I took the one with bedroom eyes. Her name was Viola, Vi for short. Her sister's name was Beverly. We danced together the whole evening. We fit well together and I enjoyed her company. Don and Beverly got along well too.

After the dance they offered to give Don and me a ride home in Beverly's car. Vi and I sat in the back seat. We parked on a short crossroad by Sweeney's sawmill. Probably Don and Beverly kissed and petted in the front seat. I don't know. I was too busy in the back seat kissing and fondling Vi to notice. Vi was not a novice at necking. Our lips met and our tongues tasted each other in lustful desire. I fondled her breasts. They were not large but they were soft and nice. She unbuckled my belt and reached inside my pants to inspect my hardware. It was already upright. But, of course, we did not have the privacy necessary to consummate our lust. She massaged my peter with loving tenderness. A few strokes were all that were needed for me to spill my sperm in my shorts.

My little veteran of foreign wars must have passed inspection. When I called her (we now had a phone in our house) the next day, she was more than willing to borrow her sister's car and pick me up for a joyride. Again we used the relative privacy of Sweeney's convenient sawmill and the darkness of night to make out. We climbed into the back seat. We had a mutual mission.

There was no need for coaxing or foreplay. We were two completely uninhibited adults. She took one leg out of her panties and I lowered my trousers enough for full genital contact. She guided me in with expert fingers. She was damp with desire. We fit well. Our lips locked in lust. Our tongues twisted around each other and thrust deep into our oral cavities. Like we had danced the night before we moved fluently together. I came quickly and she pushed hard up against my throbbing thrust. She was good. I stayed hard and we were soon moving again. My second climax came about the same time as her first. Then she graciously let me continue for a third coming. I think she felt fulfilled.

Now that we were both satisfied and spent, we sat and talked for some time. We told each other about ourselves. She lived on the old Jimmo farm in Underhill Center about two and a half miles from our place on the Raceway. She was separated from her husband whose name was Camera. She had a baby boy whom she called. "Bozo". He was about one and a half years old. They lived with her two sisters, Beverly and one who was only four years old (I forget her name), and her father, Mr. French, who was also separated from his wife. They were from Massachusetts.

Vi and I became an item. We made love often for the rest of 1946 and into the next year. Many times, I would walk the two and a half miles to her place to see her. When Beverly's car was available we used it. One night when there seemed to be no place to do it, she led me into their woodshed. It was pitch dark, but she knew the layout. She led me to a block of wood and directed me to sit on it. Then she exposed me and sat on me. She was in control. It was fantastic and I exploded upward into her with great enthusiasm. She galloped her way to ecstasy.

After her father cut his first crop of hay and put it in the barn, we decided to do it in his haymow. That was fun. The hay smelled nice and was soft and cozy. We could lie there together as long as we wanted with no fear of being caught. Especially in the rain or when it was a little chilly outside, it was cozy and secure. We did it several times in the hay after the dances at the "Chicken Coop". Usually I would walk home after the lay in the hay.

One time after we did it in the hay and were outside the barn kissing good night, I noticed my wallet was missing from my left rear pants pocket. We went back in the barn and pawed around in the hay on our hands and knees seeking it. But in the dark we could not find it. We worried that her father would find it and know that we were fucking in his newly mown hay.

Vi said, "I'll get up early and come out and look for it in the morning while Dad is milking the cows, before he throws hay down to them."

She kept her promise and found my wallet. When we were together again she gave it to me.

"I see you have a rubber in your wallet," she said. "How come you never use a rubber when we do it?"

"You didn't ask me to," I replied, "I don't like them."

"Did you use them with other girls?" she asked with a hint of jealousy in her voice.

"Yes," I confessed. "But that was before I met you. They were just quickies. Not like what we have."

I guess my explanation satisfied her. She never brought the subject up again.

One night, I slept the night at her house in a guest room. In the morning, after her father got up and while he was out in the barn milking, I slipped into her bedroom and under the covers next to her warm body. We took off whatever we had on and lay naked full length against each other. It was the most pleasant feeling I had ever had. We kissed, caressed and made love. I was on top of the world. We were two unconventional, uninhibited, loving adults who satisfied each other completely.

From that time on we started thinking of a lifetime together. I thought how wonderful it would be to lie next to her warm, willing body every night.

She asked me once, "What would you do if I said 'no' some time?"

"I would try again the next night," I assured her.

For some reason that answer increased her tender feelings for me. "That's what I was hoping you would say," she said and hugged me tightly.

We agreed that I should finish high school and go to college if I could. In the meantime she would try to get a job to save up some money. I didn't have much left of the $1,200 I had when I was discharged from the service. After she and her husband were apart for two years and she had enough money, she would get a divorce from him. Her husband was a musician and now lived in California. After they were divorced we would marry. We planned, partied and fornicated happily together.

Chapter XX

In the fall of 1946, I returned to Underhill High School for my senior year. I found myself competing with June Cook for valedictorian of the class of 1947. In the end she won and I was salutatorian. Mrs. Ellsworth, the principal, sort of apologized to me for not being able to manipulate my grades so I would win. She seemed to have taken a liking to me. I guess she was proud of me for coming back to school. She arranged for June and me to take a scholastic achievement test sponsored by Pepsi-Cola. The top ten per cent in the state won a fifty-dollar college scholarship. I won one. June did not.

Mrs. Ellsworth asked me what I wanted to study in college. I told her I wanted to be a writer. She helped me fill out an application to Syracuse University which was noted for its School of Journalism.

In my last year of high school I took English, Algebra II, French II and Latin I. My French and Latin teacher was a petite, dark-haired, nice-looking young lady. She had some sort of deformity in one of her legs. She walked with a pronounced limp. She was probably a year or two older than I was. There were three students in the Latin class; Jean Wooley, Ted Weatherbee and myself. Jean was a young, pleasantly plump, blond freshman. Ted was a WWII Navy veteran who had returned to finish high school also. He wanted to go to dental school. Neither of them was a very good Latin student but I had no trouble getting "A"s in it. I was the only student in French II, so my pretty little teacher and I were alone in the classroom. We sat close together as she tutored me and gave me her undivided attention for forty minutes a day. My Algebra teacher was also a nice-looking young lady who wore short, provocative skirts to go with her nice body. I did well in her class and we had good rapport. But neither of those lovely teachers kept me after school for extra-curricular activities. Nor did I make any seductive suggestions to either of them. I was faithful to Vi.

Kermit brought June Hunter home and they were married November 28, 1946 in the living room of our house on the Raceway. Our mother's sister, Aunt Bertha, and her husband, Maurice, stood up with them. They went to live with her parents in the South. He later told me that June helped her parents in their family-owned eating place. Kermit cut hair as an apprentice barber. In his spare time, he tried to save money by digging a cellar by hand for their future home.

Sometime in the fall of 1946, Vi got a job caring for Mrs. Jimmo. Mrs. Jimmo was wheelchair-bound and needed someone to watch her during the day while her husband worked. After they sold their farm to Mr. French, the Jimmo bought the house right next to the Underhill School. Often I would spend my noon hours with Vi. Sometimes she would take me down to the cellar where there were blocks of wood for the furnace and we would do it like she had taught me in their woodshed. Other times we would do it leaning against the sink in the kitchen if Mrs. Jimmo was out of sight in her bedroom.

On New Year's Eve of 1946, I decided to impress Vi by putting on my Army uniform bedecked with my Combat Infantry Badge and campaign ribbons, and walking the two and a half miles to her house in the cold Vermont winter to see her. I thought I looked nice in my ODs with my Ike jacket and polished combat boots. We didn't have a date. I wanted to surprise her.

Much to my surprise she was angry at me for showing up in my uniform.

"I wanted to go out tonight," she said. "You can't go out with me dressed like that."

"I'm sorry," I said. "I didn't know you wanted to go out. I can go home and change."

"Okay," she agreed. "We're all dressed and ready to go. Bev will pick up Ken and we'll drop by your house on the way so you can change."

Ken was the owner of a garage in Underhill Center. He was a married man. Don and I had learned that he and a married cattle dealer named Fred had been fucking Beverly and Vi before we met them. One night, when we went up to see Beverly and Vi soon after we first met and found they were not home, we spotted Fred's cattle truck at Ken's garage. It was after dark and no one was around. Don boldly opened up the hood of the truck and pulled the wires off the distributor cap.

"There, that'll fix his ass," Don laughed.

I don't think I would have done it. But I was glad he did.

Now I was surprised that Beverly was still seeing Ken. But it did not dawn on me that Vi may have been planning to go out with Fred. I thought I was her one and only. Love is blinding.

The four of us went to a nightclub in Burlington, had a few drinks, danced and watched the New Year in. It was not a good time for me. I was glad when the date was over. I knew that Ken thought Don and I had sabotaged Fred's truck. I felt ill at ease. I don't know if Ken got in that night or not. I didn't. They dropped me off at my house on their way home. But a few more loving sessions with Vi restored my faith in her.

Later that year, Vi got a job as a waitress at the Arcadia restaurant on Main Street in Burlington. Due to lack of transportation she rented a room in the city. Arrangements were made for her son Bozo to stay at our house. My mother cared for him while I was at school and I took care of him when I was home. On her days off, Vi would sometimes take the morning bus from Burlington, which passed through Underhill, to see Bozo and me. Then she would take the evening bus back to Burlington. We often made love in our house when we were alone.

I became very attached to Bozo. A strong bond developed between us. I loved him like a son. I think he loved me like a father. I taught him things, like brushing his teeth. Nobody had taught me to brush mine until I was in the Army. Probably we didn't have enough money to buy toothbrushes and toothpaste. I was determined to treat him better than our father had treated us. So I was kind to him and protected him. Vi gave my mother $10 a week for his care.

Sometime during the middle of that school year I ran out of money and was not doing anything to earn any. What with school, taking care of Bozo and traveling back and forth to Burlington to see Vi, I didn't have time to work. So I applied for the GI Bill educational benefits. I was not positive yet that I would go to college and I did not want my benefits to go completely to waste. For the rest of that school year I got $65 a month from Uncle Sam.

One day Beverly came to our house with a strange man. He was very well dressed, neat and clean. Fairly short with brown, well-groomed curly hair.

"Mrs. Chamberlin, Al," Beverly said. "I would like you to meet Mr. Camera, Bozo's father."

Bozo had run to me at their arrival and I was now holding him in my arms. To my knowledge he had never seen his father. At least he did not now know him.

"Bozo, this is your Daddy," Beverly continued. "He has come to visit you."

"That's nice," my mother said.

I did not know what to say.

"We were wondering if we could take Bozo for a ride and do some shopping for him?" Beverly asked.

I liked Beverly and trusted her completely. She and Vi were very close. I could not conceive of her doing anything behind Vi's back. So I said, "Okay."

But Bozo did not want to go. He clung to me. Beverly finally took him and they left. They never returned.

Vi appeared to be heartbroken when I told her what happened.

"As soon as I get enough money I'll get a lawyer and go get him," she promised.

The days wore on. Nothing happened. Vi told me she had contacted a lawyer who was willing to go to California with her for nothing. But she thought he just wanted her body for payment. She didn't want that. She said she was not that kind of a girl.

I continued visiting her every weekend. Before Easter we bought coordinated cocoa-brown suits. Getting Bozo back was put on the back burner. We went to a Catholic church on Easter in all our finery. We did not have much money and figured on putting only a dollar in the collection plate. That would leave us just enough for lunch. I don't know what the priest's sermon was about. It was all in Latin. Every once in a while we would have to kneel down on a kneeling board in front of the pew to pray. The money collectors made their rounds not just once, but several times. Each time Vi would nudge me to put in another dollar. Before the service was over our lunch money was gone. And I was hungry. On top of that, when we stepped out of the gloom of the church into the bright sunlight, I noticed the knees of my new brown suit were covered with ash-colored dust. I made no bones about reaching down and brushing them off. I wondered what the hell they did with all the money they collected. They certainly did not use it to keep the church clean. None of this endeared me to Catholicism.

Having sex with Vi was the most enjoyable part of my life. I was completely committed to her. I hoped she would eventually get Bozo back, divorce her husband and we would get married. I assumed that having sex with me was equally enjoyable to her. But one Sunday morning, when I went down to see her, she sat in her landlady's living room reading the Sunday paper while I waited in her bedroom for her to join me in lovemaking. I waited and waited. She read and read. By the time she came in I was in a sulking mood. Now she wanted sex and started making love to me.

"If you can make me wait," I said, "I can make you wait."

"You can't hold out on me," she challenged.

"I can hold out just as long as you can," I replied.

"I bet you can't," she continued.

"I bet I can," I answered.

By now she was lying on her bed with little on. I was kneeling on the floor next to her bed. She hugged me and pulled my head down so she could kiss me. I put my hand on her crotch.

"I can make you want me more than you can make me want you," she whispered in my ear.

"No you can't," I whispered back.

She stuck her tongue down my throat. I stuck my middle finger up her vagina.

"Where did you learn how to do that?" she asked.

"I read it in a book," I told her.

She moved against my finger. She became wet. She was ready. I became hard involuntarily. Physically I was ready. She reached into my pants and exposed my maleness. She skinned back its uncircumcised head. She leaned forward and put her lips around it. Her tongue twisted tantalizingly around it. It was a sensational feeling, but my will power was stronger than my lust of the flesh. I pulled away and rose to my feet. A look of sheer surprise and shock came over her face. She seemed crestfallen. Her power was shattered.

"Are you going to leave me like this?" she complained.

"That's right," I said. "If you can make it hard for me, I can make it hard for you too."

Slowly she got herself together and I walked her the few blocks down Church Street to Main Street where she worked. We did not talk.

A thought stuck in my mind. Was she a ferry? I had run across a couple of them in my travels. In fact I had had a blow job in Japan by an old lady trying to make an honest living. But I had been taught that ferries were queers and criminals. It was hard for me to lump her in that group. What was I to think? How could something so bad feel so good? I didn't know what to say. I had never read about oral sex in a book. I thought about the time a queer had peeked in a window at me peeing in the toilet in the rest room in the Ten Eyke Diner in Springfield, Vermont, when I worked there as a dishwasher at the age of seventeen. It had scared me. I told a local cop about it when he came in to eat there.

"I know about him," the cop said. "He's harmless. He has a wife and kids at home. He's like that when he has a few beers."

Then there was the time when I was hitchhiking through Kentucky after I had left Springfield. An old guy gave me a ride in a pickup. He reached into my pants and encircled my soft cock with his thumb and index finger. It got hard quickly against my will. He skinned it back and it spewed sperm immediately into my shorts. It was a warm but scary feeling. He wanted to take me to his house and give me fried chicken. I knew that was not all he wanted to give me. I summoned up the courage to ask him to let me out and he did.

When Vi and I parted in front of the Arcadia she gave me a warm, lingering kiss and then said, "Did you know that I'm pregnant?"

Chapter XXI

Shortly after we first met Vi had given me a cute little puppy. I named her "Tippy". She was mostly black and white with a white tip on her tail. By the spring of 1947 she was about a year old. She was a nice little dog and I loved her very much.

During the school spring vacation I worked for Russell Hunt. He had purchased Burr Gleason's farm on the Jericho Center road. Conrow and I had worked for Burr Gleason for a couple of years when I was a teenager. Burr's lovely wife Marion had been like a second mother to me.

Vermont is famous for its maple syrup. Maple trees are tapped in the spring, when the frost starts to leave the ground and the sap of the maples moves up from their roots to the branches in the warm daytime and back down in the cold nights. The sap drips out of the spouts into buckets and is collected and brought to a sugar house. There it is boiled down into syrup.

There was a large sugar bush on the farm. Russell hired me to help him sugar. It was my job to collect the sap with a team of horses pulling a sled with a big gathering tank on it. Russell did the boiling in the sugar house.

Russell also had a dog which was a lot bigger than Tippy. The dogs would follow us to work. One morning when we arrived at the sugar house the dogs scared up a porcupine. Russell's dog took after it, with Tippy following, and got a mouthful of sharp, barb-tipped quills for his troubles. Tippy also ended up with a face full of quills and some in her paws.

I quickly dropped what I was doing, grabbed a pair of pliers from a handy toolbox and went to Tippy's rescue. I had heard that porcupine quills could work their way through a body to a vital organ and cause great misery or even death. I held my little dog with one hand and pulled out the quills one by one with the pliers in the other. I thought Russell would do the same for his dog. There were more pliers in the toolbox. But no, he didn't. I guess he didn't have the stomach for it. Every quill I pulled out hurt Tippy and she would yelp in pain. But I just thought it had to be done, so I did it. It took me several minutes to get them all out of Tippy. Meanwhile the quills were working their way deeper into the flesh of Russell's dog. When I finished with Tippy I went to work on his dog. He was harder to hold but I managed. It was also harder to yank the quills out of him. There were more of them and they were more imbedded. I expect the pain was greater too. Finally I got them all out of the outside of his face and paws. But he was still in pain and by the way his jaws moved I could tell there were some inside of his mouth. I tried to extract them with pliers but I could not hold his mouth open with one hand. So I grabbed a jaw in each hand and pried his mouth open. But I did not have a third hand to use the pliers to pull them out.

"Russell," I hollered. "Come here and help me."

"I can't," he answered meekly. "I'm busy."

I did not take the time to argue with him or tell him what I thought of him. I could think of no other way, so I stuck my mouth inside his and bit onto one quill at a time and yanked them out with my teeth.

I'm not sure how much Russell appreciated what I had done for our dogs. He never said. Maybe they did not mean that much to him. But the dogs looked at me with love and respect in their eyes. They seemed to understand that they were as important to me as any human.

★

The news of Vi's pregnancy did not make me unhappy. I loved her even more. I was a proud father-to-be. I continued my weekend visits with her. Our sex life remained very satisfying. Vi seemed happy too. We never held out on each other again. Nor did she ever try oral sex on me again. We never spoke of it. Perhaps she realized how it had shocked me.

One Saturday afternoon, after I had walked her to work from her rooming house on Church Street, I was sitting in a booth in the restaurant where she worked. I was doing a crossword puzzle to pass the time until the bus left for Underhill. A total stranger joined me.

"You're the boyfriend of that waitress, aren't you?" He nodded towards Vi.

"Yes, I am," I admitted proudly.

"You seem like a good kid," he continued. "So I thought somebody ought to tell you. She's been messing around with the bartender. Last weekend they went to Massachusetts together."

I was surprised, shocked, shaken and sad.

"How do you know?" I asked.

"I come in here a lot in the evening and I've seen them rubbing up against each other behind the bar," he told me. "Last weekend neither one of them was here. I asked the other bartender where they were and he told me. Just thought you ought to know."

As he left I said, "Thanks."

I left the Arcadia without saying goodby to Vi. The night was long and sleepless for me. I had to find out for sure from Vi. Sunday morning I took the bus back to Burlington. Before going to see Vi I spent an hour in a nearby church. Not to pray, not to be born again. I think I had already done that when I was trying to make out with that Christian girl, not that it had amounted to anything. Perhaps I needed to find something; the truth, peace, myself – I don't know.

When I got to Vi's room she was still in bed and not expecting me.

"What's this I hear about you fooling around with the bartender?" I got right to the point.

"Where did you hear that?" She appeared surprised at my question.

"A guy told me yesterday," I continued. "He said you spent last weekend with him in Massachusetts."

"Oh, why don't you grow up?" she answered angrily. She turned her head away so as not to look me in the eye. She did not deny anything, say she was sorry, or ask my forgiveness. All of which confirmed what the stranger had told me.

"Okay," I said and left, never to return to her bedroom.

Later that evening on the bus ride home I met this girl who I had known the previous year in school. She was a short, dark-haired, dark-eyed, pretty girl with a nice body. I had liked her before but thought she was somebody else's girlfriend. She sat with me in the back of the bus. There were not many other passengers. I was sad, lonely and vulnerable. We talked. She admired my class ring. I gave it to her. Nothing meant anything to me anymore. She put her arms around me and kissed me. We held each other close like teenage lovers for the fifteen-mile ride to Underhill.

Sometime later, when Freddie Metcalf and I were at a barn dance one night, I ran across her again. We danced. Freddie and I offered her a ride home. She was then living with her sister and brother-in-law at Fort Ethan Allen, in old Army barracks that had been turned into civilian housing. I walked her up to their second floor flat while Freddie waited for me in his car.

When I kissed her goodnight at the top of the stairs, she said, "Why don't you stay with me tonight? You can sleep on the couch with me."

It was an offer I could not turn down. I was instantly horny. "Okay," I said. "Wait until I go tell Freddie."

Once on the couch we went into action. I exposed her breasts and sucked on one of them while I squeezed the other one with my hand. They were nice and firm and well rounded. Around their nipples were little black hairs, something new to me. We did not undress completely in case somebody should enter the room while we were doing it. I entered her easily. She was already wet. She wrapped her legs around my back, a new experience for me. It drew me closer and deeper within her. She moved up hard against me and I planted my seeds into her garden of love. As was my wont I stayed hard and continued jabbing away at her.

Soon she moaned, "I'm coming. I love you."

My sperm spilled again. Her legs relaxed and we lay together for a few more pleasant moments. She was good.

She got up to go to the bathroom. When she returned to my arms she said, "I've got my period, I don't have any napkins so I'm just using an old rag."

"That's okay," I assured her.

We lay close together, rested and slept a little. When I awoke a little later I was hard again. She was more than willing to put the rag aside and do it some more. She seemed to enjoy it even more this time and got her cookies a second time as I pumped my warm juices deeply into her soft belly.

The next morning, after a nice, pleasant family breakfast, she walked me the few hundred yards to the bus stop. Never had I been so close to a woman who stank so badly. Maybe from her bloody rag or sweaty body odor, or both, I don't know. It reminded me of my stinking father who never took a bath until our mother had a bathroom put in our house with my money. However, her stink had a personality all its own. I kissed her goodby at the bus stop and never saw her again.

Somewhere about this time Kermit came home. It was very late at night and everybody was in bed. He climbed in bed with me. We talked. He told me his troubles and I told him mine. He had left his wife, June.

"She used to work all day and late at night in the diner," he said. "Whenever I wanted a little she was either too tired or had a headache."

"That's too bad," I commiserated with him. "Was she always like that."

"No, but at first I had a hard time getting it in," he continued. "Finally we found I could do it if she rubbed my back."

"Vi and I broke up too," I told him. "We had lots of good sex, but I found out she cheated on me. Now she's pregnant and I don't know whether I'm the father or not."

"We thought June was pregnant too," he said. "But her doctor told her it was a tumor. After that she didn't want sex anymore. I got lonely and horny. You know, a man needs a little once in a while."

"I know what you mean," I agreed.

Kermit did not stay home long. Soon he was involved in barbering in Essex Junction, a railroad village about six miles north of Burlington. To my knowledge he made no contact with June after he left her. Our mother stayed in touch with her. A few months after Kermit deserted her. June gave birth to her tumor. It was a healthy baby boy.

Chapter XXII

Later on Kermit divorced June. He then married Elizabeth Buckland in Georgia, Vermont, in November of 1949. He built a small house on a small parcel of land in Jericho, Vermont. Together they raised a family of four boys and one girl while he barbered in Essex Junction.

Some twenty odd years after June's son (whom she named John) was born, he came north to see his biological father. Kermit never told me what their meeting amounted to.

For me life was much different after saying goodby to Vi. I spent more time with school activities, e.g., playing baseball in the school yard at noon and playing the lead role in the senior play.

Christine also had a part in the senior play. She was a dark-haired, fairly pretty girl with a well-shaped body. Her family was very poor, so she did not have nice clothes and things. She was meek and shy, as if accepting her humble social status. She sat in front of me in school. Sometimes I would touch her hair just to let her know I did not think badly of her. She would turn and give me a sheepish smile.

Play practice was in the evening. When we would finish it would be dusk. Christine lived with her family in a small house on Route 15. It was located at the entrance to the ball field on Carpenter's farm and belonged to Carpenter. It was about one mile south of where we lived on the Raceway. To go home after practice Christine had to walk down Route 15 to the Raceway, then down the Raceway almost to where it rejoined Route 15 and then cut across a field to her house.

I started walking with her as far as our house on the Raceway. We never said much to each other, but one evening I asked her if I could walk her home.

"Sure," she said eagerly.

When we got to the Browns River bridge just below the Fitzgerald's place, I asked her if she would like to walk along a path by the river.

"Sure," she replied and looked up at me with a happy smile.

She took my hand and let me lead her into the meadow next to the flowing water. Her hand was warm and sweaty. Mine was too. When we were far enough away from the road to ensure privacy, I asked her if she would like to sit on the sweet-scented green grass.

"Sure," she agreed without hesitation.

We sat down. I kissed her. We lay down. We kissed some more. I put my hand on her breasts. They were nice but it was late at night, so I didn't take the time to go inside her blouse and bra to feel their bare beauty. Instead I reached up under her skirt and put my hand on her crotch. She was completely passive. There was no complaint. I stroked her inner thighs as I had been taught by my Japanese lover. Slowly and methodically I removed her panties. She cooperated much like a willing child. I lowered my pants enough for full genital exposure and contact. I was ready. She was willing. There was no coyness. Entering her was easy. I was obviously not the first. But we fit together well. I was horny. I had not had any for quite a while. So I came quite quickly after a few fast thrusts. Then we lay in the warmth and sweet serenity of our bodies letting our organs soak in warm wetness. In a little while I started moving slowly again. She lay there motionless letting me do whatever I wanted to with her as long as I wanted. The second time took much longer, perhaps due to the lack of reciprocal movement on her part, and I was spent. She was not as good an active partner as Vi and many others had been, but I had no complaints. We lay together until I was no longer hard. Then we put ourselves back together. I walked her a little way further down the Raceway to where she climbed over a barbed wire fence and cut across the field to her house. I walked back home. It was well worth the walk.

After that first time we walked that same walk to the same spot many times after play practice. It was always the same. Very little talk, a long walk and sex on the grass beside the river.

One time I asked her, "Do you love me?"

"What do you think?" she replied without committing herself, but implying that the answer was obvious.

I did not follow up on her response. I liked her, enjoyed the fruits of her young body, but I did not love her.

Mrs. Ellsworth was the director of our senior play. She coached us much like a football coach would coach his team. After a lot of scolding and badgering she was finally able to get us to learn our lines and put on a decent performance. The audience, made up of parents and friends, was greatly appreciative and made us feel proud with their applause.

In fact, we were so pleased with ourselves that a few of us boys in the play played hooky from school the next day. We spent part of the day in the village park across from Clark's garage playing baseball.

The next day in school, Mrs. Ellsworth donned her football coach's hat and spent most of the day scolding and lecturing us on morality, responsibility and everything else that has to do with doing what we were supposed to. Since she knew I was the ringleader, she asked me to stay after school. I expected to get reamed out some more on a one-to-one basis.

After all the other students had left she approached me. She handed me an envelope. "Here, this is for you."

Inside was a letter of acceptance from Syracuse University.

"Thank you," I said with little emotion.

"Congratulations," she said and shook my hand.

As I walked home I felt deep gratitude towards Mrs. Ellsworth. I had always liked her as a teacher. Her scoldings never bothered me much. I was used to them. I had heard her rant and rave about doing the right thing many times. She taught more than textbook subject matter. She also taught values. Sometimes when we did not have our homework done, we would bring up some topic we knew she would spout off about so she would not find out we had not done our lesson. Before she married she would often lecture us about sexual morality. Then when we would see her and Raymond Ellsworth drive past our house, we would laugh. We thought they were going down our road to park and make out. I still have fond memories of her. When I was a freshman at thirteen and she was then Miss Kilgallon, I had outbid her boyfriend, Raymond Ellsworth, by one penny for her box lunch at a box lunch social. I think I paid thirty-three cents for it. Then she, Raymond and I shared her lunch. I was sort of her pet after that. Then while I was in the service I used to write to her occasionally. She always answered promptly and was very supportive of me in whatever adversities I wrote about.

This was not the end of her scoldings. Both the valedictorian and salutatorian had to give graduation speeches at our graduation ceremonies. We had to write our own speeches. I decided to write mine about a soldier who had learned the value of an education in the Army. It was about my own experiences. But I kept procrastinating.

When it became close to graduation time, Mrs. Ellsworth started getting after me to finish writing my speech because she had to read it to make sure it was all right and then rehearse me to make sure I knew it.

I finally wrote it about two days before graduation day. Maybe I needed stress to do my best. She was pleased with it and added only a few words about wise old King Soloman. On graduation night I delivered it easily and, remarkably for me, with little or no stage fright.

After the formal ritual was over Miss Ester Hayden, an old maid whom Parker Rice had once tried to seduce by getting her drunk on wine, came up to me and told me in a naively seductive manner that my speech was the nicest one she had ever heard. By the way, I don't think Parker was successful.

The class of 1947 was the last class to graduate from Underhill High School. Shortly after graduating at the age of twenty-two, five years late, I boarded a bus for Syracuse, New York.

Chapter XXIII

I arrived in Syracuse with just enough money to rent a room and to eat on for about a week. I was confident I could get a job and earn a living during the summer before school started. Then my GI check would start coming again. I carried with me a large suitcase full of clothes and a portable typewriter. I bought a newspaper and found a room on Avery Avenue for seven dollars a week. The next day I reported in to the registrar at Syracuse University. A young lady told me all I had to do was show up on orientation day in September.

Using the newspaper ads again I landed a job selling Real Silk. With a sample kit of female and male hosiery and ordering information I was to go from door to door to try to make a living selling. I was not a very good salesman but Real Silk was a good product, so I managed to eke out enough to pay the rent and buy cheap meals. We were allowed to take out our commission from the down payment so I could live from day to day, sale to sale. That would have been fine and I might have been able to even save a few bucks if I had not run into Bill Mead. Bill was from Underhill.

One day when I was having a small meal by myself in a place where they served food and alcoholic beverages. Bill walked in. We recognized each other immediately. I was overjoyed to find someone from my hometown in the big city of Syracuse, over two hundred miles from Underhill. He was happy to see me too.

Bill was a couple of years older than I was. We had been schoolmates in Underhill. His family was better off than we were. His mother had the post office in her house for many years. I remember when he got kicked out of school in his senior year by the principal, Mr. Sweat. He challenged Mr. Sweat to fight, but Mr. Sweat wouldn't. Bill's mother was on the school board. Mr. Sweat was not hired the following year. We sat and talked. He told me he had been an MP in the Army during the war. He had married a girl from the west side of Syracuse. They had one daughter, but were now separated. He was living alone in an apartment on the west side. Bill had a car.

Soon Bill and I were going out almost every night, drinking and girl seeking. So what money I made selling was quickly gone. Several times that summer I had to hock my typewriter for ten dollars to pay the rent and/or eat.

One night we were out drinking and there were two cute chicks and their guys in a booth near us. I looked at the girls with apparently too much admiration in my eyes. When I went into the rest room to empty my bladder, the two guys followed me in. They accused me of flirting with their girls. My immediate thought was of having my head dunked in the toilet. I did not want that. So I quickly denied their accusation. But I told them their ladies were very attractive and they should be complimented that I looked at them. Fortunately they accepted my fast-talking explanation.

Another time we saw two girls sitting on a park bench on the east side. We approached them and sat down near them. I struck up a conversation with the younger-looking of the two. She was probably sixteen or seventeen. Bill turned his attention to the older one. She told me they were waiting for a bus. She also informed me she had a boyfriend, perhaps to warn me to keep my distance.

"Are you going to marry him?" I asked her.

"No, we can never marry," she replied sadly.

"Why not?" I continued to probe. "Don't you love him?"

"Yes, I love him with all my heart and soul," she said. "But we can never marry because of his profession."

"What profession is that?" I asked.

"I can't tell you," she replied.

"Well, it's not too hard to figure out," I told her. "The only profession I know of that can't marry is the priesthood. Is he a priest?"

"Yes, he is," she admitted.

Bill and I had an unwritten, gentlemen's agreement that if one of us could make out with a girl he did not have to worry about the other one.

When her bus came I asked, "Can I see you home on your bus?" I hoped if a priest could screw her maybe I could too. "Then I can catch the late bus back."

"Okay," she agreed.

I think she lived in a Syracuse suburb called Mattydale. I can't remember for sure. Anyhow, by the time I got her to her house, talked a little and kissed her a few times at the door it was too late to catch a bus back to Syracuse.

"You can stay with me on the couch," she whispered as if she didn't want her parents, her priest and God to hear her.

"What about your parents?" I asked in a low voice.

"They will understand," she answered. "They would not want me to be unkind."

We entered the house very quietly and lay down on their living room sofa. It was dark. I held her close and kissed her silently. Her kisses were soft and responsive. They signaled, "okay".

I unbuttoned the top button of her blouse and reached in under her bra. Her breasts were soft and round. It was very exciting making love to her in danger of her parents catching us with our pants down. But I didn't pull my pants down. I unbuckled and unzipped enough to make contact. Then, after uncovering her love spot under her skirt, I entered her without removing her panties. I just pushed them aside enough so I could slip past their crotch. It was easy. A priest had already plowed the way. She was now wet with want. She moved cooperatively for my full penetration. The challenge of being caught created an almost immediate, silent, explosive ejaculation from me into her soft vaginal tunnel. We were sinners, fornicators. We knew it. We held onto each other in silent solace. I moved gently up and down in her, so as not to make the springs in the sofa squeak. She lay still and passive but that was okay. I did not need her to move. She felt good and I enjoyed it. I think she did too. The second time was the best. It took quite a while and gave her ample time for her own pleasure. We lay joined until I softened. Then we wiped ourselves with handkerchiefs, put our clothes back in place and lay close. We slept a little. As usual I became hard again in my sleep. I awoke and repeated my previous performance. This time

128

there was little fear of being caught. She was as willing the second time as the first. Slowly, silently we partook of the pleasures of passion, a repast of the devil.

The next morning, her parents were very understanding about my missing the last bus and spending the night on their sofa with their young daughter. They gave me breakfast and I left.

A day or two later I returned to see her. We went for a walk along a not-much-traveled road. I held her hand. We kissed. I tried to lead her into the bushes off the road. She would not go. She told me it was a sin what we had done before. We needed to pray for forgiveness.

"Isn't it a sin to have sex with a priest?" I asked.

"Yes, but I love him," she replied. "I can't help myself. I go to confession every day and pray for forgiveness."

I wondered if her lover was her confessor. I certainly did not want to commit myself to anyone who was committed to a priest. So I did not press the issue. I walked her home and left, never to return. It was one for the books. I had screwed a priest's concubine.

One night Bill and I were looking for girls again. We were drinking in some joint where there was also a dance floor. I got pretty drunk. There was another guy who had joined us. We spotted three ladies at a table. One of them had alluring brown eyes beckoning me to her bedroom. I asked her to dance. She told me her name was Claire. We danced until late at night. Then I rode the bus with her to her apartment on Westcott Street. Inside we lay on her davenport. We kissed. I played with her bare busts. They were soft and flabby but I didn't mind. I put my hand on her legs and crotch. But, try as I might, she would not let me pull her slacks down. Later on I was to learn why. She was expecting her son Lee, who was almost my age, to come home at any minute. I left early enough to catch the last bus home.

Apparently, I gave her my address and phone number because the next morning she called. It was a Sunday.

"Would you like to go to Green Lake Park?" she asked.

"Sure," I agreed.

"We'll pick you up," she said.

Lee, his fiancée, his mother Claire and another woman were

in the car that came to get me. There may have been another young lad to balance the sexes. I don't remember. The other woman's name was Josephine Kogut. She had been one of the women with Claire the night before. At that time I had not noticed her. I had focused my blurred vision only on Claire's eyes which I thought wanted me to come hither.

"You can call me Jo," she told me.

"You can call me Al," I told her.

Jo was a very attractive, dark-haired, blue-eyed woman with a slim, trim body. It turned out she was a nurse and had been a lieutenant commander in the Navy during WWII. She had been in the service for five years with overseas duty in the South Pacific. Her profession and military rank impressed me a great deal. I thought she was way out of my class.

Now that I was sober, I noticed Claire appeared to be about twice my age. To have a son as old as Lee she would have to be. She was pretty but not nearly as attractive in the daylight as she had seemed the night before on the dance floor. Jo looked younger and much more attractive.

While at Green Lake, about twenty miles east of Syracuse, I spent most of my time looking at Jo in her bathing suit. She was a good swimmer. I did not pay much attention to Claire. If there was another young lad in the group, I don't think Jo paid much attention to him either. She rubbed some stuff on my back and squeezed a pimple there. She told me I ate too many sweets. I liked her and got her phone number and address.

Jo and I saw each other a few times after that during the summer of 1947. Mostly weekend stuff, like going to the movies in the afternoon, lunch, etc. We would always meet downtown, never at her house, and she avoided letting me take her home. I'm not sure she ever told me why. But she lived in a poor section on the west side at 618 Otisco Street. Also I learned later she had a mentally ill sister. Maybe that was her reason. Or she might have been ashamed of me.

Our first big date was on the Labor Day weekend. We were to go to the 1947 Ice Follies.

Some time after we met, Bill had given up his apartment and moved in with me on Avery Avenue. The landlord increased the

130

rent to ten dollars a week, making my half only five dollars. So I saved a couple dollars. We slept in a double bed together. That would be frowned on by people who fear homosexuals today. But in those days nobody thought anything about it. Believe me, we were not queer.

A few nights before Labor Day, we were in a bar on the west side not far from Bill's old apartment. With us were Bill's wife, her father and somebody else. We were sitting in a booth. Bill, his wife and I were on one side. I was on the inside and his wife was between us. Her father and somebody else were on the other side. I was drinking boilermakers, southern comfort with a beer chaser. I'm not sure what the others were drinking or what they were talking about, not only because of the effects of the boilermakers, but also because my lustful eyes were focused on Bill's wife. She was quite pretty and her eyes sparkled as they responded to my gaze. I thought since they were separated, Bill no longer cared and maybe I could get a little from her.

"Your eyes are like stars," I said to her seductively.

Bill jumped to his feet, grabbed me by the hair and lifted me up from my seat.

"Let's go outside," he challenged me.

Others separated us and calm was restored. I apologized to Bill for my actions. We went into the rest room. We relieved ourselves and I combed my hair.

"Are you ready to go?" Bill asked me.

"Sure," I agreed. "I'm ready whenever you are."

I walked out the door ahead of him, thinking we were just leaving to go home. He rabbit-punched me in the back of the head. I was completely taken off guard. I turned and grabbed him around the waist, more to prevent him from hurting me than to hurt him. We fell to the cement sidewalk with me on top of him. He continued to try to punch me. He only succeeded in bruising his elbows on the cement. His wife's father and others again broke us up. It was a sobering experience.

As we rode back to our room in Bill's car we did not say much. Anger rose up within me. I was not afraid of Bill. If he wanted to fight again I thought I could kick the shit out of him. I felt a lump on the back of my head where he had punched me.

But it didn't hurt.

That night I lay awake thinking of my situation. I had wasted the summer. I had no money. I had a lousy job that did not pay much. I had become a drunken bum. I liked Jo but saw no future with her. If she really knew me she probably would not want me. I'd just been in a barroom fight. I felt low. I missed Vi. Except for my father, I missed my family. I missed the familiar scenes of my childhood. I guess I was homesick and afraid I might not make it in college.

Instead of taking Jo to the Ice Follies, I took the bus back to Underhill on the Saturday before Labor Day.

Chapter XXIV

While I was home on that Labor Day weekend I saw Vi. We went for a ride in Beverly's car. She had moved back home due to her pregnancy. She was now heavy with child. Apparently there was no animosity between her and her sister over her husband's taking Bozo with the connivance of her sister. Vi had made no effort to get her son back. Did she even condone the plan? I wondered...

She denied that she had cheated on me. But I was not convinced she was carrying my child. And even if she was, what could I do about it? I was in no position to support a child I could not legally claim as mine. She was still a married woman. I made no commitments to her. I touched her belly as if to feel if it were mine. We said our last goodby.

Vi and her family later were to move to a farm on the dirt road between Jericho and Jericho Center. A few years later Willard and Becky happened to pass their house, Willard told me they saw a young, skinny boy playing in the yard who looked like me. To this day I wonder...

When I returned to Syracuse, I moved from our room on Avery Avenue to a two-room apartment on Danforth Street on the north side. The rent was twelve dollars a week but there was a kitchen with a stove and refrigerator. So I could eat in and save money. I also got a job at Ross' Bakery making donuts for twenty dollars a week for twenty hours. Going out with Bill drinking and looking to get laid was behind me. I forgot about Vi.

I forgot about Bill. I heard that eventually he moved back to Underhill, became the road commissioner there, gained custody of his daughter, divorced his wife and remarried, bought the Benedict place next to his mother's house, was thrown from a horse and died from a broken neck.

I didn't forget Jo, but I put her out of my mind. I figured she would not want anything more to do with me after I stood her up.

At Syracuse University I registered for sixteen hours of courses. College credits are different than high school credits. A three-hour course in college meant that you attended three one-hour classes a week in that course. I signed up for three-hour courses in English, Latin, History, College Algebra, Citizenship and a one-hour course in Journalism.

Not long after classes started a dean called me in and gave me a check for fifty dollars from the Pepsi-Cola scholarship. He suggested I move into a college dorm or closer to campus so I could take part in more college activities. But I couldn't afford to. I now lived a bus and a transfer away – maybe a couple of miles as a crow flies.

In the first Latin class I attended, I learned it was too advanced for me. So the professor transferred me to Latin I. This was a repeat of what I had studied in high school so it was easy for me.

I went to the first football game because I thought I was expected to. I didn't understand the game and wondered why people got so excited about it. I didn't know anybody there so I felt lonely in a crowd, I did not attend any more games.

One day, I came home from school and found a note that had been slipped under my door. It was short, simple and to the point. Call Jo. Pleasant was my surprise. I called her. She did not know about the note. Apparently she and Claire had talked about me and wondered what happened to me. Then Claire had gone to the university to find my address and look me up. Whatever happened did not matter, as long as Jo was not angry that I had stood her up. We started seeing each other again. She was older than I was, but that didn't bother me too much. I liked her and hoped to make out with her. My intentions were somewhat less than marriage. She led me to believe she was only twenty-nine, young enough for what I wanted.

Eventually she let me take her home after evening dates. We would kiss good night in an entrance hallway of their two-flat house. She liked to kiss. She let me put my hand inside her bra and fondle her breasts. They were nice and pert. Not large enough to sag but ample to handle. Further advances she discouraged and avoided.

Claire bought a nice house in an affluent section on the east side. Jo and I visited her often. They were very close friends. One day we were sitting on Claire's davenport. There was no one else in the room. We kissed and hugged. She was wearing a pullover sweater. I touched her chest. Spontaneously, I raised the bottom of her sweater and lifted her bra above the nipple of her left breast. I knew what it felt like but I had not seen it in daylight. It was gorgeous. I kissed it. I covered it back up with her bra and pulled her sweater down. I didn't want anyone else to see.

"Let's get married," she blurted out unexpectedly.

I thought for a moment. "Okay," I finally agreed.

After that we spent a lot more time together getting to know each other better and making plans. Several times I had kiddingly told her I loved her in the heat of my lust and had noncommittally asked her to marry me. But now that she said it, it was serious business. We set the wedding date December 27, 1947. That was during the holiday break in classes at the university and would give us a week for a honeymoon. Now that I was committed to marry Jo and had fallen in love with her, I made a conscious vow to myself to wait until we were wed before taking her to bed.

Remember Jimmy Mansour, the young Catholic virgin who joined our outfit in Japan after the war? The one we tricked by putting a geisha girl in his bed? Well, we had maintained contact by letters. He started college at Le Moyne College in Syracuse the same time I did at the university. We met a few times during the fall of 1947 to talk over old times and renew our friendship.

Shortly after Jo and I had agreed to marry, Jimmy invited me to spend Thanksgiving weekend with him at his home in Binghamton, New York. Neither of us had much money so we planned to hitchhike the hundred or so miles. We got a ride out of Syracuse from a guy who said he was going towards Binghamton. We ended up going east almost to Albany instead of south to Binghamton. By the time we realized our error it was late at night. So we stopped at the police station of some small town and asked if we could spend the night. They offered us some wooden bunks in a cell. It was a hard night.

Jimmy had a nice family. His mother was short, sweet and maternal. His sister was short and pretty. His brother was also short and a nice guy like Jimmy. I don't remember anything about his father. They all treated me with great hospitality. One evening, Jimmy and his siblings took me to see a female cousin. I don't remember her name but she was a very friendly, warm person. She put on some records. We danced. Her conversation was lively. She fed us some home-baked goodies. Jimmy and his sister were lavish with their praise of her cooking and housekeeping talents. It was almost as if they were trying to fix her up with me, even though Jimmy knew I was unofficially engaged to Jo. The cousin applauded my dancing which wasn't that good. She was extremely attentive to me, almost to the point of being seductive. But she wished me well in my marriage to Jo.

I asked Willard if he would be my best man but he declined, due to his work schedule and the long distance between us. So I asked Jimmy if he would do the honors. He agreed to.

Before the wedding it was necessary to go through "instructions" from a Catholic priest. Right from the onset the differences between his Catholicism and my agnosticism were established. He was a nice person and did not dogmatically try to convert me. The mandated hours of instructions were spent in give-and-take philosophic discussion. The only thing I had to agree was not to interfere with Jo bringing up our children as Catholics. I agreed to that.

About two weeks before our wedding, Jo rented a two-room apartment on the south side, across the street from Syracuse General Hospital where she worked. It was not a very nice place. The bathroom had to be shared with the people in the adjoining apartment. The kitchen sink, stove and refrigerator were small, old and dingy. The small table and two chairs were dilapidated and rickety. Cupboard space was sparse. The locks on the doors were worn and insecure. It was not nearly as nice and spacious as the place I had on the north side. But the rent was reasonable and it was convenient for Jo since she could walk across the street to work. Jo bought a new maple double bed for the bedroom.

When Jo showed it to me the new bed was already made, inviting us to try it. We lay down on it to not only test it, but also to kiss, hug and be close. I felt the warmth of her body through her clothing. I wanted her. My organ pushed against my garments begging to go into action. I lifted her skirt and put my hand on no man's land between her legs. She did not resist. Then I remembered my silent vow to wait. I removed my hand from her privates and pulled her skirt back down. It was hard on me. We had talked about sex before. She told me she had lost her virginity in the service. I admitted to having been sexually active. Neither of us confessed completely.

I moved from my apartment to our apartment. For some stupid reason I thought all I had to do was leave and the landlord would automatically know I no longer wanted to rent the place. I was in for a rude awakening. When the rent was due the landlord showed up at Ross' Bakery and embarrassed the shit out of me. I ended up paying two weeks extra rent for not having given him notice. A cheap lesson in communications.

I had little money and was surviving from week to week on my $20 a week job and a monthly check from the GI bill. We shopped for rings. Jo made the down payment and we charged the balance. Jo had good credit. She had saved several thousand dollars while in the service. She bought me a new suit, a topcoat and fedora so I would look nice on our honeymoon. She paid all the wedding expenses. I made no bones about it. I was a poor struggling student with nothing to offer but a potential future. Jo was a functioning nurse already doing well in her career.

When we went for our marriage license I was in for my first surprise. Jo was thirty instead of twenty-nine as I had been led to believe. Although I can't honestly say she ever told me her age. That bothered me a little but not enough to shake my love for her. What's one year?

We were married as scheduled on December 27, 1947 in a Catholic church. After a sit-down dinner for family members at her parents' house, we boarded a bus for New York city. Jo had reserved a room at the Sheradon Hotel for our honeymoon stay.

Chapter XXV

It was a long bus ride from Syracuse to New York City. My joystick, swollen from hunger like the belly of a starving child, pulsed against the restraints of my jockey shorts and new suit. I put my new fedora over it so no one could see. I smiled at Jo. She smiled back knowingly.

At the hotel we rode the elevator to our room. I tipped the porter with Jo's money. It was late at night. I took Jo in my arms and kissed her. At last she was mine! But, despite my throbbing member, I was willing to wait a few more minutes.

"Would you like to go down to the dining room to get something to eat?" I asked my new bride.

"No," she replied. "Let's go to bed."

She showered first. It seemed to take a long time. She came out in a new, blue negligee. I showered quickly and came out in some clean underwear. I had no pajamas.

Once in bed I went right to work. Taking off my togs was easy. Taking off her gown was more difficult. I was all thumbs and she was of little help. But we were finally naked and ready for the grand entrance. This was much easier than I expected. She raised her knees and pushed up towards my eager probe. She was swollen with anticipation. How long we had waited for this one split second to come! I was surprised at how loose she was. It did not feel as if I was in a vaginal tunnel. More like a soft, pliant, warm, wet sponge. Many years later, in my studies of human sexual behavior, I learned a woman's genitals swell from great sexual expectations.

I ejaculated immediately and squeezed her close. Like a bullfrog who has finally landed atop his sex object, I held on for fear of losing her before I was done. Now I moved more gently and slowly to allow my sperm bank to build back up.

"I love you, honey," I whispered in her ear.

"I love you too," she whispered back.

I remained erect and it felt good. Her playground continued to be a swollen mass of looseness. It took me longer than usual to climax again. But I did. Since my best was three, I tried for a third. *At least on our wedding night*, I thought, *I should be in top form*. The flesh was willing but try as I might I could not pull the trigger for the third shot. As I pumped away a little more vigorously in the vain effort, strange suction sounds came from down there. They were unnerving. Probably her diaphragm reacting to my plunging. I stopped. We unconnected. We rested and slept a while. As per my wont, I became hard and horny again before dawn. I kissed her softly to see if she was awake. She was. We did it some more. She was still swollen, probably from lack of satisfaction. She did not tell me then but I found out later that she did not climax until several nights after we were wed.

On the second night I was eager for more married sex. But she said, "I've got my period. We'll have to wait."

Reluctantly, I agreed. Afterwards, she was to tell me that was when she first really loved me because I did not insist on having sex the first night of her period.

But on the third night my bone was so hard I had to beg her, "Let's just try it a little. I don't mind your period, I'll stop if it hurts."

"Okay," she condescended.

Sex during her period was much better for me. She was not swollen or loose. It was tighter and I felt the walls of her vaginal tunnel around my cock. She seemed to enjoy it more too. For the rest of her period and our honeymoon we did it every night. It was easier for her during her period because she didn't have to bother with her diaphragm. She was not fertile then. During our marriage I always looked forward to that time of the month because she was most willing to have sex then.

Back home from our honeymoon, I went back to work at the bakery. Jo returned to nursing in the hospital across the street.

The first morning for breakfast, Jo asked me, "Do you like cereal for breakfast?"

"Yes honey, I like cereal for breakfast," I said and started eating the cereal she put before me.

"Do you like bacon and eggs?" she asked.

"Yes honey, I like bacon and eggs," I said.

She fixed bacon and eggs while I finished my cereal.

"Do you like pancakes?" she asked as I started on the bacon and eggs.

"Yes honey, I like pancakes," I said. "But why don't you sit down and eat breakfast with me?"

She prepared pancakes.

"Do you like hash brown potatoes?" she asked as I became sated with the bacon and eggs.

"Yes," I said, "But honey, I can't eat so much at one time." I did eat the pancakes though, so she would not feel bad.

It was not a nice place to live. At night we could hear the cockroaches do close-order drill on the kitchen sink. As soon as they learned there was garbage in paper bags under the sink, large rats double-timed across our bedroom floor to get it. I got up one night to investigate. When I turned on the light I saw a rat under the sink so big I jumped back with fear. He ran back through our bedroom and under the door to the hallway.

Another night I had to use the bathroom we shared with our neighbors. As I opened the hallway door our male neighbor entered the hallway from his apartment. He was a short, middle-aged man. He was naked and had a hard-on sticking straight up about a foot long. It was twice as big as mine.

"Excuse me," I said and closed our door quickly. I didn't want Jo to see that.

The couple next door was not married. From the sound of their conversations they seemed to be, if not retarded, at least uneducated. We gathered that she was nearly blind. Once we heard them arguing about sex.

He hollered at her, "Why did you let that old bastard lick your cunt?" I guess he was referring to the landlord.

"I couldn't see to stop him," she whimpered.

From upstairs we heard the little old landlord yell at his fat wife. "You let him fuck you while I was downstairs fixing their sink. Why?"

"Because you can't get it up anymore," she yelled back at him.

It seems the male tenant had been paying his share of the rent by cleaning the stairs up to the landlady's quarters while the landlord had been fixing some plumbing for the female tenant downstairs. She invited him in for cookies.

This was not the kind of place I wanted to live with my new bride. We decided to look for a house. We found one we liked at 114 Miles Avenue. This was about a mile east of the Syracuse campus in a nice section, ideal for me. Jo's brother, John, loaned us $3,000 and Jo still had some savings left. Between the two it was enough for the down payment. We bought the house for $11,500. I had nothing to contribute but it was put in both our names.

But we could not move in until the first of March. Meanwhile we continued to live in the dump across the street from Syracuse General Hospital.

One night about two weeks after we were wed, when we were doing it, Jo pushed hard up against me and said, "I'm coming!" At last I had satisfied her. It made me very happy.

Bill and I had been talking about eating pussy once, as two veterans are apt to do in a jocular way, when he said in all seriousness, "Wait till you've been married a while. When you can't do it anymore you'll have to eat it."

Those words had stuck in my mind, as well as the feeling of Vi's lips around the head of my peter. I had to find out. So, as I would make love to my wife, I would kiss her body a little lower each time. Eventually, I went all the way down and kissed her vulva. As I stuck my tongue between the outer lips, lo and behold, I discovered a bit of sensitive flesh. I knew it was sensitive because of the way she moved and her juices started flowing. She told me it was her clitoris. My tongue tickled it. It was not distasteful for me. I think she liked it.

After that first breakthrough, we did a bit of oral sex now and then during the first few years of our marriage. But sixty-nine was not Jo's favorite number so it did not become a necessary part of our sex life. However the discovery of her clitoris was an important find. I learned to manipulate it with my fingers.

She would tell me, "Pinch it."

Willingly I obeyed her and she would lubricate and become ready for my penetration. From the first pinching Jo almost always would have an orgasm when we made love. Not necessarily at the same time I did, but sometime during the event.

In the first semester at college some things went well and some not so well. In Latin I got an "A" and in College Algebra a "B". All the other grades were "C"s. In Journalism that meant I would have to get an "A" in the second semester to pull my average up to a "B", a requirement to major in Journalism. Since I did not think I could do that I decided to change my plans. I did not like the course in Journalism, anyhow. There was too much emphasis on photography in it. I did not know anything about picture taking. I never had a camera.

History was another story. We had a great teacher, Professor Hodgekiss. He brought history alive in his classroom. But I did not take good notes in the beginning and sort of gave up taking them altogether. I figured it would be okay if I read the textbook. I kept putting that off too. In the end, I ran out of time and didn't do that either. I resigned myself to failing. On the final exam I guessed at the multiple-choice questions and gave up on the essay questions. I was sure I had failed. To my great surprise and joy I got a "C". A joke among students was that some professors threw all exam papers up a flight of stairs to grade them. The ones that stayed up on the upper stairs got an "A". The ones that fell to the bottom failed. Those in between got "B"s, "C"s or "D"s according to the level of stairs they landed on. I wondered if I had been lucky enough to be graded by that method.

At the end of the first semester, I quit my job at the bakery so I would have time to go out for the Freshmen baseball team. Even at the age of twenty-three I still had fantasies of playing pro ball. I didn't even make the first cut. Weak arm, poor hit, slow of foot.

Jo and I stayed at Clair's new house a couple of days before we moved into our new house, the difference between the end of our apartment rent and date of occupancy of our new residence. While there we engaged in our usual nightly lovemaking. She did not douche in between. We think that was when our first baby, Judy Joy, was conceived.

Chapter XXVI

114 Miles Avenue was a nice, two-story, three-bedroom house. It had green (my favorite color) wood shingles on the upper half and white clapboards on the bottom part. An open porch extended across the entire front. At the rear of a large back yard was a three-stall garage. Inside, an open stairway led from the large living room to the bedrooms and bath upstairs. Off one bedroom, was a closed-in sun porch. Downstairs was the large front room with a fireplace and built-in bookcases on each side, a kitchen with ample cupboard space, dining room and den.

A nice thing about it was that the three bedrooms were already rented to four roomers, two of them in the master bedroom, as were all three garage stalls. So we would have rental income to help pay the mortgage and other bills. We were in business. I felt on top of the world!

We used the dining room for our bedroom. We put our maple bed in one of the rooms upstairs and went shopping for new bedroom furniture for us. I think Jo would have chosen less expensive items, but I wanted only the best. With all the rent money, her income and my government check of ninety dollars, I thought we could afford it. We got a very nice, blond oak bed with matching chest of drawers and vanity dresser. While we were at it we also purchased a handsome, blond oak desk for me and my den. It was exciting for me to be setting up housekeeping on such a grand scale, even though it was mostly by virtue of Jo's good credit. I thought Jo was equally happy about it.

One day, not long after we had settled into our dream house, I decided to buy Jo a nice gift. So I went into Dey Brothers on Salina Street and bought some lovely silverware for her. It was not too much – less than $100. Of course, I did not have enough money to pay for it. Jo's credit was good so I charged it. When Jo came home from work and I gave it to her, she was madder than hell.

"How dare you buy something we can't afford and don't need?" she demanded. "I want you to take it right back. You don't even have a job to pay for it."

I was shocked at her ungracious reaction. "I'm not going to take it back," I retorted.

"I'll take it back myself then, if you're not man enough to," she continued angrily.

And take it back she did. All the while she was gone, taking buses to and from downtown, I sat with my head on the kitchen table, disconsolate and disillusioned about our relationship. In my book you didn't belittle the one you loved. Maybe I didn't have a job but I was studying hard to get an education which would lead to a good job in the future. Dark and defensive were my thoughts.

When Jo returned she was still mad. "I took it back and chewed them out for selling it to you," she raved at me. "I told them they had no right to let you charge it because you don't even have a job."

I did not bother to answer her. We did not have sex that night or for the next few days. Nor did we say much to each other. We stopped kissing goodby on parting or hello on returning. I started calling her Jo instead of honey, if I called her anything. We were mostly silent. In bed we did not touch.

Then one day she said, "I missed my period. I think I'm pregnant."

That good news plus my hardening male hormones softened my feelings for her. We made love again that night and things returned to an acceptable level of sociableness between us. But things were not exactly the same. The honeymoon was truly over. In my eyes she had sawed a few inches off the legs of her pedestal, I expect I never was her knight in shining armor. Probably a last resort as her biological clock was ticking.

Classes went fairly well at the University. I took Latin again because I had got an "A" in it the first semester and thought of majoring in it. But the second semester I got only a "C" in it. But I got "B"s in Physical Education (my baseball tryout), probably for effort, and a Philosophy course.

That summer I tried to get my old job back at the bakery. Mr. Ross had no openings but he sent me across town to his brother's dairy. I worked there a couple of weeks and was let go. But they referred me to a nephew who was a foreman at a foundry, I got a job there for even more money than Jo was making. She was getting about $10 a day as a nurse. I got nearly two dollars an hour at the foundry. I did a variety of tasks there; handling scrap metal and feeding a blast furnace, running a forklift, using a trip hammer to knock out a cement floor, painting, molding, and working in the carpenter shop. While I was a molder, making molds out of sand and pouring hot molten iron into them, I spilled a few drops of the hot liquid metal on my instep. Unfortunately, I was wearing combat boots instead of slip-on molder's boots. It took a few seconds to get my boot off. By then the hot metal had burned its way through to my flesh. That was the end of my molding. I wasn't very good at it anyhow. I took a couple days off with a sore foot. When I went back to work they assigned me to the carpenter shop. I liked that work.

Sometimes, we would get a chance to unload boxcars of coke or pig iron bars after work for twenty bucks a carload. It would take four or five hours of hard work. I volunteered to do that as often as I could. I was eager to earn all the money I could. I guess I needed to prove I was a hard-working husband and was also saving for the baby.

When school started again in the fall, I signed up for another Latin class, Greek, History, and two courses in Philosophy. I liked Philosophy. There is one bit of wisdom I have always remembered from the first philosophy class: behave in such a manner that, if everybody behaved in the same way, it would be a better world. I expect I have stretched that rule and done whatever I wanted to as long as it didn't hurt anyone. Anyhow, I thought it was better than the golden rule.

Our teacher also pointed out the paradox between the characteristics of the Christian God and the pain and suffering in the world. If God were omnipotent, omniscient, omnipresent and loving, how could he permit pain to exist? The argument that he gave man free will did not seem to hold water. If man has free will God is no longer all powerful. Placing blame for evil, on the devil would also be an admission of not having complete control. Saying that God acts in mysterious ways is a lame lapse of logic.

The philosophy teacher put into words what I already felt. He gave me good reason to continue to be a freethinking agnostic.

Jo's pregnancy proceeded on a normal path. She worked almost up to her due date. We needed all the money we could get.

Judy Joy was born January 10, 1949 while I paced the floor in the waiting room, as fathers were expected to do in those days. She was a nice, healthy baby. I was proud to be a new father. I did not pass out cigars though. We thought that was a stupid tradition. Some of my in-laws probably thought I was cheap.

Jo was a good mother. She taught me how to help her with Judy's formula, bath, diapers, burping, etc. We loved our little "bundle of joy". Even though she did not appear all that cute to me at birth, Judy became a beautiful baby and was a real joy to take care of.

Dr. Graeber was the teacher for my Latin II and Greek I classes. I did well in them and he seemed to like me. Maybe it was because we were both WWII veterans. And I called him Dr. Graeber. I think he liked that. He had just got his Ph.D. Anyhow, he was probably instrumental in steering me to choose to major in Latin, even though I had little idea what I would do with it. He gave me "A"s in both Latin and Greek. I was on my way to a major in Latin. So I continued my studies in the classical languages and also took German and Logic in the second semester of my sophomore year. I also signed up for Shakespeare but dropped it because I thought the teacher asked dumb questions. Dr. Graeber continued to give me "A"s in Latin and Greek and I got an "A" in German. Dr. Graeber became my scholastic advisor. He informed me that I needed another Latin course before I could start my major in it. So I would need to go to summer school. That summer I took Virgil, German, Roman Literature and Comparative Religions.

Even though I was an agnostic I did well in the religion class and enjoyed it. I got "A"s in it and in the Latin classes and "B" in German.

During that summer, I learned something that made the rest of my studies in Latin very easy. A fellow student gave me the address of a publishing company that published literal translations of Roman authors. When I got my translation of Virgil it was easy to read his works. The same was true of all the rest of the Roman writers I studied for the last two years of college. Of course, I never told Dr. Graeber or the other two Latin professors in the department about the translations.

The den in our house was right next to our bedroom. We made this into a room for Judy Joy. I moved my desk out into the front room. I used to get up early in the morning and study at my desk before breakfast. Occasionally, as I sat by myself studying I would have to fart. If I lifted a leg and one side of my ass I found it much easier to let it out. It became automatic. I would do it without thinking.

One day, I was doing some research in the library of the Hall of Languages where most of my classes were held. There were many other students there silently pursuing their studies. I was rapt in my reading. I forgot where I was. I had to fart. I automatically raised my leg and let her rip. It was a loud one. There was no mistake what it was or who did it. As it escaped it dawned on me where I was, I was too embarrassed to look up to see if anybody noticed.

Except for that slip of awareness, summer school was successful. I also found time to paint the house and put a new roof on it. Jo and I were getting along well with each other and our little Judy Joy.

In the fall of my junior year of college I learned of the ROTC program. Veterans could skip the first two years and become third year cadets. There were two definite advantages for me to take ROTC. It paid a small stipend of around twenty dollars a month and it was an easy way to get college credits. After taking it for two years I would be commissioned a Second Lieutenant in the Army Reserves. I registered for ROTC, never dreaming how it would change my life.

Chapter XXVII

Before Judy was born, the doctor told us we could have sex up until a couple days before delivery as long as we were careful. This meant changing positions with Jo being on her side so as not to put pressure on the baby inside her stomach. I could enter either from the front or the back. I preferred the back but Jo preferred the front. We did it her way. I was careful not to be too pushy.

The doctor told us to wait six weeks after Judy was born before having sex by normal penetration. He did not elaborate on alternatives. Sex was not the top priority then. Taking care of our baby came first. But I did get horny occasionally, and I must give Jo credit. She handled it quite well and even allowed for oral relief once in a while. Towards the end of the waiting period I talked her into letting me cheat a little. I put it in very gently to see if it was still sore. It wasn't and she felt good. The doctors had done a good job of stitching her back to her original size.

It was probably about this time that Jo made a somewhat fateful decision about our sex life. She decided once a week was enough. I didn't agree with her, I felt up to it every two or three days. But I did not argue with her. As I said before, Judy came first. However I did try to cheat a little and sometimes could sweet talk her into shortening the week. The return of her periods was welcome to me because I could usually get in a couple times during that week. She did not have to use her diaphragm then so it was less of a chore for her. So the once-a-week schedule may have been instigated by the bother of putting the diaphragm in. Whatever the reason, it had the effect of giving me a roving eye. Some of the young girls on campus started looking pretty good to me.

But during my third year of college I did not stray. I tended to my homework. School was now easy for me. With my "ponies" (literal Latin translations) reading Roman authors was a snap.

German and classical Greek were not difficult for me either. In ROTC it was fun ordering the underclassmen around in close-order drill. The class work was simply a repeat of what I had already learned in basic training six years ago. We were given a clothing allowance to buy pink and green officer uniforms. Once a week we wore them to class. I wore mine proudly.

I excelled as a cadet. Out of about fifty classmates I was in the top five. By the middle of the year I started seriously thinking of making a career in the Army. At about the same time I was beginning to question the value of my major in Latin. What good was it except to fulfill the requirement to have a certain number of hours in a major to graduate? Getting a commission in the Army and a military life as an officer became my short-term and career goals.

We learned that a few cadets in our class had a chance of being chosen Outstanding Cadets and being offered a commission in the Regular Army. Regular Army officers were considered the elite of the Army and were virtually guaranteed a career in the Army and regular promotions. Reserve Army officers on the other hand served at the discretion of the Army and were generally held in lower esteem.

A military career as a Regular Army officer became very attractive to me. What I had never dreamed possible while an enlisted man in WWII, now seemed within my reach. I got all "A" grades on the tests and "A" grade for each college semester of ROTC during my third college year.

There was only one obstacle. I had started wearing glasses after WWII and now my eyesight without glasses was not up to Regular Army standards. Twenty to forty visions were needed to pass the physical. I knew of no way I could change that. But perhaps I would still be able to have a career in the military as a Reserve officer. Anyhow, I continued to excel in ROTC classes. My hopes were high.

Between our junior and senior years we had to go to ROTC summer camp at Fort Meade, Maryland. Just before leaving for camp I got my hands on a book by Dr. Goddard entitled *Sight Without Glasses*. If I were a religious man I would have said it was a godsend. At the first opportunity, I opened it to read. The first sentence stated something like this: Take off your glasses and read this book. I did as it said but could not read the words even though the print was fairly large. The words were a blur. I stared at the page in sad resignation to my weakness. Miraculously, words began to form from the blur. Slowly I became able to read the book. In the book were directions on how to exercise and use your eyes. I followed those directions and did the exercises diligently during summer camp and my eyesight returned to about 20–30, more than adequate to pass the Regular Army Officer physical. I did not wear glasses for the next twenty years.

Unfortunately, I did not take summer camp training very seriously. It was so basic I thought it was a joke. I spent a lot of time laughing and kidding around with my buddies. During off-duty hours I would hold forth about eating hair pie down at the Y and other sexually risqué stuff. As a result I became thought of as a joker. The officers in charge of evaluating us apparently sensed my lack of seriousness.

Anyhow, I was not rated as an Outstanding Cadet in summer camp. When classes started in the fall of my senior year, the colonel in command of the ROTC program called me in and gave me the bad news.

After Judy was born Jo had gone back to work as soon as she was able. While I was at summer camp, we hired my sister Geraldine who was fifteen then, to come to Syracuse as a live-in baby-sitter for Judy, so Jo could continue to work. Financially we were doing okay, able to pay our bills and live fairly well. Admittedly this was due to Jo's earnings. But I was able to contribute enough for groceries from my government check. I thought I was doing my part. At that time Jo was able to feed a family of three on about twenty dollars a week. She bought a lot of hamburger at three pounds for a dollar. She was a thrifty housewife. The rent money from the roomers was adequate to pay the small utility bills and part of the house mortgage. Jo's income took care of the balance of the mortgage and her needs. I think she was able to save some also.

When I was a boy I had always wanted a dog. After WWII I had Tippy, who was now being cared for back home by my father. One thing I must give my mean old man credit for – he was very good to Tippy and took good care of her. When Judy was about one year old, I wanted her to have what I had wanted as a child, a dog to love. I thought it important to teach her to be kind to animals.

Jo did not share my feelings. Pets cost money to feed and you had to clean up animal hair after them. But I went to the SPCA over her objections and found a little, three-legged, black terrier. His sad eyes tugged at my heart. I brought him home for Judy. I called him Tripod. I loved him. Judy loved him. Being outvoted, Jo tolerated him.

As soon as I left for summer camp Jo took Tripod back to the SPCA.

When I returned I asked, "Where's Tripod?"

"I took him back to the SPCA," Jo explained.

Her cowardly deception angered me. But, for the sake of harmony in front of our daughter, I suppressed my ire. Besides, I was horny after being gone so long. For me it was impossible to have sex with someone I was angry at.

In June of 1950, Communist North Korea invaded South Korea. American occupation troops in Japan were sent across the Sea of Japan to fight for South Korea. At that time I hardly knew where Korea was. I was not worried that the United States military forces would have any trouble defeating the army of such a small country as North Korea.

By the start of my senior year of college my mind was made up to go into the Army when I graduated and get my commission. My dream was to become a paratrooper. I had heard paratroopers had to run five miles every morning before breakfast. I was afraid of not being able to do what I would have to do. So I started jogging. In those days one saw few, if any, joggers on city streets. I did not want to look weird so I went jogging after dark. At first it was hard. I could go only about a half mile. My muscles got sore. But gradually it became easier. Before I graduated in May 1951, I was able to jog five miles and was even bold enough to do it in daylight.

During the summer of 1950, the North Korean forces had driven the United Nations troops almost all the way out of Korea. Only a small pocket of resistance remained around Pusan. This was called the Pusan Perimeter.

I still did not think of North Korea as being much of a threat to us. However, Russia was another story. It was reported Russia was arming North Korea with planes, tanks and other weapons. Perhaps even military personnel as advisors. The cold war was on. I thought it wise to know your enemy. So I studied Russian in my last year of college.

General MacArthur, a war hero of WWI and WWII, was the Far East Commander. He had an excellent record of overseeing the occupation of Japan. In a brilliant move he masterminded an amphibious invasion at Inch'ŏn, on the west coast of Korea. In the fall of 1950, the United Nations forces moved up through North Korea to the Yalu River, the border of China. General MacArthur promised our troops they would be home for Christmas.

The Chinese entered the conflict in late fall, and poured over their border to drive the United Nations' forces back down through North Korea and across the 38th Parallel. General MacArthur wanted to send air raids beyond the Chinese border, perhaps even using the atomic bomb. Many have thought he wanted to start a third world war against the communist forces of the world and finish what General Patton had wanted to do at the end of WWII, defeat the Russians. Generals thrive on war. It is their occupation, their job, their career. They are promoted because of it, as are officers of lesser rank. History books parade the names of Great War generals. Their legends are made in battle. General MacArthur made public statements of his views, trying to influence our national policy as to how to conduct the conflict. President Truman, as commander-in-chief, fired him for insubordination.

General MacArthur returned to the United States. He was honored by a ticker tape parade in New York City. He spoke to the joint houses of Congress and made the sad, self-pitying statement, "Old soldiers never die. They just fade away." Truman silently seethed in the White house.

To me the conflict in Korea meant just one thing. I would be going into the Army after graduation whether I wanted to or not.

Chapter XXVIII

To the young people of today it may seem strange, but at the age of twenty-six I not only did not have a car, I did not know how to drive. Conrow had started to teach me to drive when we worked together for Burr Gleason on his farm in Jericho, Vermont. Conrow had an old Chevy coupe. I was about fourteen then, I put that car on a stonewall when I was trying to park it. After WWII, Ted Weatherbee let me drive his brother's car while he rode in the back seat with a couple of cute, young, high school girls. I ran that one into a bridge trying to go around a curve at the bottom of a hill.

Now, in my last year of college, I wanted a car. I decided to take driving lessons first. The lessons went well. When the instructor thought I was ready I took the test to get a license. The written test was easy. I failed the driving test. But I didn't give up. I took more lessons. Again I took the test. Again I failed. Then I did give up for a while.

A friend who was in ROTC with me told me about a 1940 Packard coupe. He said it was in good shape and a good buy for only $300. I bought it. This was during the last semester of my senior year.

During the first semester, I had completed the twenty credit hours in Latin needed for my major. I needed only five more credit hours to graduate. So I took only Russian and ROTC, six credit hours, in the last semester. That left me ample time to get a full-time job.

Jo's brother-in-law, Bill, who was married to her sister, Terry, worked at General Electric (GE) in Liverpool, just north of Syracuse. Bill helped me get a job there. I was hired as a material handler. Bill would drive across town to our house and then ride with me in my car to work. We both worked the three-to-eleven shift. After doing this for a while, I took the driving test again and passed it.

My first assignment at GE was to service several women on an assembly line. My duty was to handle their parts and satisfy their needs. This was a fun job for me. I was friendly and flirtatious with all the ladies. Most of them were older, married and not very attractive. But I treated all of them with gentle consideration. The majority of them seemed pleased when I flirted with them and some even flirted back.

Not long after I was there, a new girl was added to the line. I don't remember her name. She was short and fat. But she had a pretty face and nice, round breasts. She was younger than most of the other ladies on the line, about my age. She was also married. When I flirted with her and she responded in kind, the other ladies on the line became jealous. Someone from among them complained about us and I was transferred to another workstation.

My new assignment was in a sort of supply area where we handled incoming and outgoing parts. How she managed it I don't know, but within a few days the pretty, young, fat seductress was assigned to work in the same place I was. We were partitioned off from the rest of the factory so there was a certain amount of privacy. There were only a couple of other workers at that station. They were young, friendly guys who liked to joke around. As long as we kept the parts moving in and out, and kept our inventory organized, nobody bothered us.

After working together for a while it was obvious to our co-workers that my pretty little fat girl had the hots for me.

One evening while she and I were eating lunch in a small empty storage stall, our co-workers leaned a sheet of plywood over us and against the wall behind us. It gave us almost complete privacy. Most of the light was blocked. The privacy and dimness freed us from our inhibitions and created a seductive situation. No one could see what we did. We kissed, caressed and held each other close. We both knew what we wanted. But, of course, we could not do it there.

Sometime later we arranged to meet after work. Jo was now doing private nursing duty from midnight to eight in the morning. So it had to be on one of her nights off. Someone had to be home with Judy. We were in the front seat of my coupe. There was not much room to move. I tried mounting her from the top. That did not work. I think her belly was too big.

"Let me sit on you," she suggested.

So I moved over under her on the passenger's side. Her panties were already off. My pants were now at half-mast. She held me and slid slowly down around my shaft. I could feel the little lumps of fat in her love canal squeeze against my eager erection. It was good. She moved deftly up and down. As usual on the first time after much anticipation I came quickly. I thrust hard and deep up into her.

"Don't come in me!" she told me too late. "My husband will kill me. He always smells my panties when I get home."

All I could say was, "I'm sorry. I couldn't hold it."

Sometime later we decided to meet before work. We went for a ride in my Packard. We parked in a place where we would least likely be seen or disturbed, a cemetery. A narrow driveway wound its way in, around and out. I drove in to the area farthest from the entrance and exit. We kissed, caressed and warmed each other up. She took off her panties. I moved over under her on the passenger side as she had told me to do before and lowered my pants. I was ready for action. She knelt on the seat astraddle me. I waited for her to lower herself down upon me. But she didn't. She stayed high on her knees so that her genitals were near my face. Her curly, golden pubic hairs glistened in the sunlight coming through the window.

We didn't say much. It was a solemn site, sort of like a church. I tried to gently pull her down on me.

She said, "No, we shouldn't. My husband might find out."

"Did he before?" I asked.

"No, he wasn't home when I got home. I washed my panties out before he got home," she explained.

"Can't you do that again?" I asked as I thrust upward in a vain attempt to reach her playground.

"No, he might catch me," she argued. "We'd better go."

She kept her ballpark up near my face for many more moments as though reluctant to see the game end. Looking back from the vantage point of many years and much sexual education and experience, I realize now that she probably hoped I would lick her. But at the time I was too selfish to think of her needs, and besides she was in no position to reciprocate.

Finally I said, "Okay."

We put ourselves back together and I started to drive out of the home of the dead. As we went around the loop, I did not turn sharply enough. The right front wheel went off the driveway down a slippery slope. Perhaps a ghost from the past objected to our violating the sacred grounds. I tried to back up. The wheels spun. We were stuck. I was embarrassed for two reasons. Mostly for my poor driving but also a little bit for cheating on Jo. But not too much. She once told me, when I was trying to cheat on her once-a-week schedule, to get it somewhere else.

I went to a nearby house and phoned for a tow truck to pull us out. We were a little late for work that day.

By this time young men were being drafted and reserves were being called up for the conflict in Korea. Jo and I knew I would be going into the Army when I graduated.

"I'm going to change the house into my name in case you get killed in the war," Jo informed me.

"Why?" I asked. "If I get killed it will automatically be yours anyhow."

"But if we change it now it will save a lot of paper work. Besides we bought it with my money, not yours," she argued cuttingly.

"Okay," I agreed, "Have it your own way. See if I give a shit."

Now that I was earning pretty good money at GE, finances were another bone of contention between us. This added to the once-a-week sex schedule and other little irritating differences. She wanted more of my money. After she changed the house into her name only, I did not feel obligated to pay any household bills. Before I was earning money, I used to give her twenty dollars a week from my government check. That left me very little from the $125 check. My GI bill entitlement was now used up. Using some of it to finish high school had shortened its college duration. But I continued to give her twenty dollars a week for groceries. She wanted more but I refused.

I graduated cum laude from Syracuse University on June 4, 1951. ROTC cadets wore their green and pink officers' uniforms instead of caps and gowns. Our instructors, a colonel and a captain, pinned our gold second lieutenants' bars on our shoulders and handed us our commissions. It was a proud moment for me.

I was anxious to get started on my military career. I voluntarily signed up for three years of active duty rather than wait for them to call me. My dream was to go into the paratroopers, do well on all my assignments and eventually earn a chance to become Regular Army.

After I had signed up, Jo asked me, "Did you make out an allotment for me?"

"No, I didn't," I told her. "When I get paid I will send you money. The same as I have been giving you."

"But what if you get killed?" she whined. "What will I do?"

"If I get killed you'll get $10,000 insurance," I assured her. "I'm probably worth more to you dead than alive."

I was bitter about her materialism. She was upset over my insensitivity to her needs. We were both selfish. It was a power struggle. We did not communicate. But we maintained our cool in front of Judy. In fact, we never really argued. I refused to argue with her. That probably pissed her off. We were no longer in love. Our relationship was now based on physical needs, our baby's welfare, and a marriage contract.

Orders came for me to report for active duty at Fort Dix, New Jersey on June 28, 1951. As I was about to leave the house, one of our roomers came down the stairs and gave me an envelope.

"I was told to give you this," he said.

I was holding Judy in my arms. I kissed her goodby and put her down. I opened the envelope and saw what was inside. I did not bother to kiss Jo goodby. I walked out the door to my waiting Packard coupe and headed for Fort Dix. Inside the envelope was a summons to appear in court for non-support.

Chapter XXIX

My assignment at Fort Dix was to B Company, Forty-seventh Infantry Regiment. Their mission was to put recruits through basic training in preparation for the conflict in Korea. I asked for and was put in charge of the team of cadre who taught bayonet and unarmed combat. During WWII, I had always feared meeting a big German soldier in hand-to-hand fighting. Now I wanted to prepare myself as well as others for the ultimate test of a combat infantryman.

The officers' quarters were wooden barracks partitioned into two-men rooms. My roommate was an obese officer whose name escapes me. But I'll call him Fats. He was a friendly, jovial, large, short-peckered man who loved to sing in the shower (which, by the way, is where I learned of his shortcoming). Across the hall was a first lieutenant who had just returned from Korea. His name was Paul. He was a tall, well-built, dark-haired, handsome officer with a face expressive of his sad experiences in Korea. He had been with the Seventh Division, which took part in the march north to the Yalu River in the fall of 1950, and then the horrifying withdrawal when the Chinese entered the struggle. Paul, Fats and I became good friends.

The court summons? I ignored it. How the hell could you sue somebody for non-support before he had non-supported you? Her lack of logic seemed equal to her lack of love for me. *Piss on her*, I thought. When I got my first pay check I sent her eighty dollars as I had promised. I never heard anything more about her summons.

Not long after I got to Fort Dix, my 1940 Packard developed engine trouble. I traded it for a 1947, two-door, Packard sedan. Soon I discovered it needed some new tires.

I had settled in with my teaching team and everything was under control there. Our company did not have any recruits yet. My company commander was a WWII retread from western

New York. So, since there was nothing pressing for me to do one day, I asked him if it was okay if I went to town to get some tires.

He became enraged. "Chamberlin, I want to see you in my office," he ordered.

In his office he said, "Chamberlin, I think you're fucking off. You're never here at the company in case we need you. What do you have to say for yourself?"

I replied hesitantly, trying to choose my words carefully. "Well, I'm not much good at defending myself or making excuses. We don't have any recruits in the company so I've been spending my time with my teaching team and preparing lesson plans."

He cooled down a little. "I need to know where you are at all times. We never know when we will get a batch of men to train. Lieutenant Covington is always here. He's probably read all the magazines in the day room two or three times already. You should be here too. Or at least let me know where you are in case I need you."

"Okay, sir. I will from now on," I said. "I assure you, I have not been fucking off."

I waited for a more appropriate time to get new tires. I had learned another lesson in communications.

Our officers' quarters were the last barracks on a paved road which led into an unpaved road, which in turn led to a firing range about five miles from our billets. To stay in shape I continued my running on that stretch of road. I measured the miles with my Packard. Gradually I increased my distance from five to ten miles. *There*, I thought, *I have finally run the ten miles that corporal had bet I could not run when I was a raw ass recruit at Fort Bliss in 1944*. I now realized, though, I probably could not have done it then.

My friend Paul probably liked me because I had a car. We had a common lust for female flesh. Neither of us were inhibited by any puritanical moral codes. We started going pussy hunting on the weekends. He would always throw a blanket in the back seat just in case.

One night we met these two ladies in a bar. One was a very

attractive woman about our age, with a nice sexy body. The other one was a little older, a bit heavier and not as attractive. Paul liked the good-looking one. After a couple of beers I didn't mind the other one. Paul struck up a conversation with them. Soon we were in my Packard. We found a secluded place to park. Paul grabbed his blanket and led his lady into some nearby woods. The other one and I were now alone in the front seat of my love boat. For the lack of anything else to do we kissed. She offered me the full range of her tongue.

"Want to make love?" was all I could think of to say.

"Of course," she replied. "Why do you think I kissed you that way?"

It did not take us long to get into position with me on top and our heads towards the passenger side door. We bared ourselves only enough to make naked crotch contact. We had plenty of room. Packards were big, wide cars. She was good and I enjoyed her. When we were through we stayed together for a little while. But not too long. We didn't want to be caught when joined by Paul and his lover. So we uncoupled. As we moved apart, somehow my ass hit the horn on my car. It sounded loud and clear. It startled us. I thought Paul would have heard it and taken it as a signal we were ready to leave. We laughed and waited. Paul paid no attention to my horn. We talked a bit and then kissed and caressed some more. She had large breasts and I fondled them. My bone rehardened. So we resumed our prone positions and screwed some more. This time took longer but we still finished before Paul and his paramour returned.

When they returned, I dropped Paul and his ladylove off at the bar where her car was and took my sex partner home. Paul's woman had said she would take him back to Fort Dix. When we got to her house in some nearby urban area my woman invited me in to spend the night in her bed. I decided I'd better not. It was late and I had to teach a class the next morning. But I was willing to screw her again. So we got into the back seat. I did not want to toot my horn again. This time it took a long time. She seemed to enjoy every minute of it. It was a warm night in July. We were sweating profusely. After I came within her for the third time that night we rested and sweated together. I stayed hard inside her. Her love muscles squeezed against me and invited me to pleasure her more. I tried, thrusting vigorously in and out, up and down, and sweating even more. But I was drained. I could not come again. I finally stopped when we were ringing wet with sweat.

As we parted at her door she said, "You can come to see me any time you want to."

I said, "I will." I never saw her again.

Our company got a batch of recruits and I was put in charge of a platoon. When I was not teaching or practicing bayonet and unarmed combat or writing lesson plans, I spent all my duty hours with my platoon. My company commander never again had occasion to think I was fucking off. Fucking up was another thing. Once I planned to have a platoon from B Company make a bayonet assault from one training area over a stonewall into another area. The battalion commander heard about it and brought some VIPs in a bus to watch. Just as we were ready to charge into mock battle, we discovered the area we were going to charge into was being used for a map reading class. So I had to call off the assault. My company commander was there.

I meekly went up to him and asked, "Could you tell the colonel we had to change our plans?"

"Tell him yourself," he snapped back.

I did. I was thoroughly embarrassed. Another lesson in proper planning and communications.

Shortly after our liaison with the women we met in a bar. Paul's lover invited him to meet her in Jersey City, her home town. That was over fifty miles from Fort Dix. He asked me to drive him there. Fats wanted to go too. We met in some bar. She had a friend with her, named Lois. Lois was a tall, well-built, stately woman. Not beautiful, but good-looking. She did not say much. Her face was not happy, sort of between stern and sad. I liked her and ogled her most of the evening.

Unfortunately, Fats was there. He consumed some drinks quickly and was soon trying to consume the attention of Lois. I nursed a couple of beers and let Fats make his moves. Lois looked at me longingly as my eyes tried to undress and caress her.

The next day Paul told me, "Lois didn't like Fats. She likes you and wants to see you."

"I like her, too," I said, "I'd love to see her again."

But duty comes before pleasure in the Army. I was put on OD (Officer of the Day). ODs were to be on duty at all times for twenty-four hours. We were in charge of inspecting the guards, morning reveille and evening retreat. We wore armbands with "OD" in white letters on them. Most of that twenty-four hours there was nothing to do. During some idle time that evening Paul, Fats and I were talking in our quarters.

Paul said, "I wonder if any of those WACs over in that WAC outfit are good looking? I sure could use a piece of ass right now."

"They say all WACs fuck," Fats opined. "Why don't you call and find out?"

"No, that's not a good idea," Paul replied. "You might get stuck with a pig."

"Al, you're the OD. Why don't you go over and inspect them?" Fats suggested.

"I can't do that," I said. "I'm the OD for our battalion, not for their outfit."

"Yeah, but they won't know the difference," Paul said. "That's a good idea."

"Okay," I agreed. "But you guys have to come with me in case I get caught. Then we can all say it was a joke and share the blame."

So we got in my Packard and rode to the WAC quarters. Paul and Fats stayed in my car while I went in to inspect the WACs. A female corporal sat behind a desk when I walked into their orderly room. She was not the least bit attractive. She stood, saluted, and told me who she was.

"At ease!" I ordered her in a serious military manner. "I'm the Officer of the Day. I'm just checking to see that someone is on duty and that everything is okay."

"Would you like to inspect the living quarters?" she asked.

Just what I need to really find some good-looking ones, but also to get into some real trouble, I thought. "No, that's not necessary. Carry on."

I returned to my buddies and told them I had not seen any

good-looking WACs there. We laughed even though we did not accomplish our mission.

Soon Paul and I went back to Jersey City to see his woman and Lois. Lois and I hit it off well. We did not talk an awful lot. So we did not get to know much about each other. I no longer wore my wedding band. I had not worn it for some time. In fact, I did not even know where it was. That's how much it meant to me since I had fallen out of love with Jo. I did not tell Lois I was married. She did not ask. We would go out to eat and drink a little (although I never drank much then), then go for a ride and park somewhere. Paul always brought a blanket with him. Often, he would take his blanket and lover into some woods and Lois and I would stay in my car. Sometimes, Paul and his woman would cover themselves with his blanket in the back seat and Lois and I could hear their heavy breathing as they did their thing.

Lois was quite affectionate. She would snuggle close to me when I drove and I got a lot of left-handed driving practice. But she was not to be had. One evening, as we snuggled in my car while Paul and his lover were away on his blanket, we kissed passionately. I inserted my hand into her bra and cupped her right breast in my left hand. It was firmly soft, not flabby, sort of an unused, virginal condition. I fondled it with gentle eagerness. I wanted her. I reached down below and put my hand on her crotch with a confident, tender pressure.

"If you have any respect for me, you will move your hand," she told me.

"But I just want to love you," I argued as I moved my hand caressingly, not away.

"It is against my Catholic religion to have sex outside of marriage," she informed me. "So please remove your hand."

So I did as she bade me and removed my hand from my target. I had to settle for warm kisses and playing with her breasts, which she did not mind.

Towards the end of August, Jo wrote me that she was going to place the care of her house with her sister Millie and her husband, Al Deshaw, and come down to live with me. So I found a small apartment in Browns Mills, just outside Fort Dix.

Before she arrived I had one last date with Lois. I confessed to her I was married and that my wife was coming to live with me. She did not get angry with me. She was sad. I did not know for sure if I was sad or glad. At least I would be happy to see my little Judy Joy. And I would be back on a once-a-week schedule.

Chapter XXX

The first night in our apartment off base, of course, I wanted some. I guess Jo expected some too. She did not object. After all, it had been several weeks.

But little Judy objected. Not to her mommy and daddy making love, but because she was put in a crib to sleep by herself. She had become accustomed to sleeping with her mother while I had been gone. She cried loudly. I told her to stop. She continued even more loudly. Finally, in frustration, I rushed to her crib and gave her a good slap on her ass. Startled, perhaps scared, she stopped. Then Jo and I made love in serene silence.

I did not believe in corporal punishment. I had had enough of that from my mean old man. I guess that showed a sex drive can often win over reason. Slapping Judy on her rear end was against my better judgment and I have always regretted it.

Not long after Jo's arrival, I felt I was in good enough shape to pass the physical fitness test for the paratroopers. Out of 500 possible points one needed a minimum of 250. You were tested in five events: push-ups, sit-ups, squat jumps, pull-ups and running. I scored well over 250 points easily but was weak in the pull-ups and running. Even though I could run ten miles without stopping, I was not fast enough to score any points. In the running test you had to sprint 100 yards, turn around and sprint 100 yards back, turn around again and sprint another 100 yards in under one minute. I not only could not sprint very fast, I could not turn fast either.

I applied for Jump School at Fort Benning, Georgia, and was accepted. I was a happy trooper. Unfortunately, before I was to report for paratrooper training, orders came out for me to report to the Infantry School at Fort Benning, after which I would be sent to FECOM (Far East Command). Orders for FECOM took precedence over all other orders. There was a great need for lieutenants in Korea. They were being killed off fast.

Fats was also on the orders for FECOM. Before we left for Benning, he surprised us by marrying a schoolteacher from his home town. Being an officer, I suspect, made him much more attractive and outweighed his weight and other shortcomings.

Meanwhile, I carried on with the bayonet training and unarmed combat. I became quite adept at both. I was proud of myself. One day I taught a class in bayonet. I thought I did pretty well in demonstrating and teaching the long thrust, short thrust, vertical and horizontal butt strokes, etc. After the class, I approached the company commander of the men I was teaching.

"What did you think of my class?" I asked him.

"Oh, it was okay," he replied. "But that's not the best way to use a bayonet in combat."

"What do you mean?" I asked. "Is there a better way than the Army way?"

"Got five minutes?" he continued. "Grab a couple of rifles and I'll show you."

Holding a bare-bayoneted rifle at high port, he challenged me, "Come on, thrust at my throat."

He was a big, burly first lieutenant. I didn't want to make him mad by accidentally sticking him.

"I'd better put the scabbard on my bayonet just in case," I suggested.

"No, never mind the scabbard. Come on, give me your best shot," he ordered.

I lunged at him with a well executed long thrust. He deftly moved slightly to his right and parried my rifle down into the ground and aimed a horizontal butt stroke at my jaw. Fortunately he pulled it back before it connected, I tried a short thrust. The same thing happened. Everything I did he countered with simple movements and parrying with his piece held at high port. He was always on balance and in position to give me a butt stroke up side my head.

"Never stick an enemy with your bayonet," he explained. "If you do, you will be vulnerable while you are pulling it out. The next foe could get you. It is hard to pull a bayonet out of a man. Sometimes you have to shoot your rifle so the recoil will pull the blade out. Hold your weapon at high port and let the enemy make the first move. Then parry his piece and counter with a horizontal butt stroke. That may not kill him, but it will sure as hell rattle his brains. Then he might become a prisoner, which is more valuable than a dead man. This is called flat-blade bayonet. It was developed and taught to the Marines in WWII by Colonel Biddle. You can teach this to your men in one simple, short session. The Army method of bayonet training is good exercise. That's all I can say for it."

He convinced me completely. I went to the S3 (operations and training officer) and told him about flat-blade bayonet. He was a major. I told him I wanted to change the lesson plans I had so diligently written and teach flat-blade bayonet.

"I don't want to hear it," he said. "Forget you even mentioned it to me."

He was a short, little man sitting behind a large desk with his head in the sand. He did not tell me not to teach flat-blade bayonet.

I didn't change the lesson plans, but I made sure each bayonet class I taught thereafter was exposed to flat-blade bayonet. This usually caused a general stirring among the men. Words like, "Why didn't they teach us this before?" were often heard.

In unarmed combat, we taught the men how to disarm an enemy armed with a bayonet or knife, how to fight dirty, kick them in the balls, chop them in the throat, poke their eyes out – whatever it takes to kill or put them out of action. I enjoyed it and became quite good at it.

One day we put on a demonstration. As I was lecturing my class, one of my cadre, a corporal who was new to our team, came at me from behind with a bayonet. As he neared me I turned, parried his bayonet with my arm, grabbed it and twisted it out of his grasp. He fell to the ground. As planned I stuck the bayonet into the ground near his foot, symbolic of really sticking him. Unfortunately, the bayonet did not stick in the ground firmly. So I pulled it back to ram it into the ground more forcefully. As I did so, the corporal moved his foot and I plunged the bayonet through his foot and into the ground below it.

A gasp rose from the class. Somebody called an ambulance. I had a hell of a hard time pulling the bayonet out of his foot. To make things even worse, he was wearing very expensive jump boots, the kind paratroopers wear. When he was finally on his way to the hospital, I pulled myself together and carried on with my class.

As soon as I could I went to see my bayonet victim in the hospital. Luckily, the blade had not hit any bones. I paid him for a new pair of jump boots. He did not return to my teaching team.

Whether by design or accident, Jo became pregnant. We calculated it happened on our first night together in Browns Mills. I was not disappointed. We both agreed it would be nice for Judy to have a little baby brother or sister.

Before my tour of duty at Fort Dix was over, I pulled duty again as Officer of the Day. This time there was no foolishness with my buddies, Paul and Fats. Fats was now a married man and I had lost track of Paul since moving off post. Everything went fine until retreat. At the end of the day just before the evening meal, all the men of the battalion were gathered in company formations. In the center of the battalion quad I stood and took the reports from each company. Then music blared forth from a loudspeaker. At the end of the musical renditions our national anthem is played. At one point in the music the OD calls the battalion to parade rest. In this position the men stand with feet about a foot apart and their hands clasped behind their backs. When the "Star-Spangled Banner" is played the OD calls the men to attention and orders them to "present arms". At that command all salute the flag of our country. I have no ear for music. When I thought our national anthem was being played, I did as I was supposed to. I called the troops to attention and had them present arms. I saluted our flag and stood stiffly at attention, a proud officer in the United States Army. When the music stopped I dismissed the battalion, did a smart about-face and walked off the field.

However, the sergeants in charge of the men did not dismiss them. Just as I reached the outer perimeter of the formations, more music came out of the loudspeaker. The sergeants called their men back to attention and ordered them to present arms. This time the music was the real national anthem. As the troops stood rigidly saluting Old Glory, I hurried on to the cover of the orderly room in total disgrace.

Chapter XXXI

Towards the end of November, I took my pregnant wife and Judy back to Syracuse. Then I drove to Fort Benning, Georgia, and reported to the Infantry School on November 21, 1951.

We were housed in the typical wooden, two-story barracks with the latrine on the first floor. The living quarters were semi-partitioned into two-men stalls. A black second lieutenant shared a stall with me. He was a tall, friendly, well-spoken, bright young man. We hit it off well from the start. I forget his name but I'll call him "Buddy" because we were buddies.

Most of our classes were held in a large lecture hall. We were taught everything an infantry officer has to know, all the way from how to wipe your ass with a single sheet of toilet paper for supply economy to more erudite things such as map reading. There was not much emphasis on bayonet, unarmed combat or physical training – the areas in which I was most interested. During the lectures we were given large amounts of typed material. We were supposed to study these in the evening or on the weekends during our free time. Most of it was a rehash of what we had already learned in ROTC and previous training. So I did not pay much attention to it.

The classes were made up mostly of second and first lieutenants. The former had not yet been to Korea; the latter had. They had been rushed into combat during earlier stages of the conflict. Now they were hardened warriors from whom we could learn much.

Fats was in our class, but he did not stay in the barracks. He had brought his new bride with him and rented a place off post. He became very friendly with a good-looking, well-built, rugged, combat veteran, a first lieutenant. They were together most of the time. Some of us wondered why. They were so different. Soon we found out. It was not because Fats' loud, melodious singing was so attractive. It was his wife who was winsome. It seems that

Fats invited his combat hero to his apartment. Fats got drunk on screwdrivers (vodka and orange juice), passed out on the couch and his buddy came to know his wife in the Biblical sense. This went on for the four months we were at Benning. So it eventually leaked out. Maybe Fats preferred screwdrivers over screwing.

While at Benning I continued to stay in shape. I jogged a little on a nearby parade ground. In the mornings, I got up early and did pull-ups on some water pipes in the latrine, before anybody else was up to see how few I could do.

But all was not study and work for me. In fact, I seldom read any of the long, boring handouts we were supposed to. They were too dry and repetitious. During the weekdays I would usually go to bed early so I could get up early to exercise. All of this early-to-bed, early-to-rise and exercise kept me healthy and horny.

Not long after we were there, three of us took off one weekend in my Packard for Atlanta, Georgia, many miles north of Benning. Our mission was to get laid. None of us were heavy drinkers, so we did not go bar hopping. We parked my Packard and asked a cab driver where we might find some. He took us to a Hilton hotel. We asked the doorman what was available and for how much. He said there were some black ladies up on the top floor for twenty bucks apiece. We were all white. We decided the price was too high and we didn't really want to change our luck.

So back on the street we went. As we were walking along we met three young ladies. At a distance of perhaps ten feet on a well-lit sidewalk, my eyes and the eyes of one of the female trio locked on to each other. They joined in a mutually lustful, magnetic embrace. As we passed, our eyes slowly turned to maintain contact. As though forcefully pulled we turned with them. After we passed by a few feet we returned to each other, drawn by a common desire. I took her hand. For a moment we ignored the other four people in our groups.

"I like you," I said. "Can I walk with you? Maybe we could go someplace and have a cup of coffee and talk?"

"I like you too," she replied. "Why don't we all go to my trailer and we can make some fresh coffee."

So the six of us walked to her trailer. It was not a large trailer. There was a living room, kitchen and bedroom. In the living room was a couch and a stuffed chair. In the bedroom was a double bed. One of the girls was the sister of the one I was with. The other was just a friend. As soon as we entered I saw the bedroom through the open door. Being the oldest of us men, I felt obligated to assume leadership.

"We get the bedroom," I announced decisively.

My lady followed me eagerly into her love nest. We closed and locked the door. The other couples were left to the living room and kitchen to make coffee or whatever. We forgot about coffee for the moment. We were both hungry for each other. Other things could wait. Soon we were naked under the covers.

There was no great amount of foreplay needed. I was immediately hard. She was already wet. Anticipation had prepared us. She assumed the missionary position and I penetrated her with little ado. We kissed as we came together and tried to swallow each other's tongues.

She was short, slightly plump, with dark wavy hair and a pretty face. Her breasts were firm and pert. They felt warm and nice under my chest. We stayed joined and soaked up each other's juices. Soon we were ready for more movement. This time we took our time, moving slowly up and down in happy harmony. We fit well. She was not tight, but not loose either. She had good vaginal squeezing control. We were good for each other. We had found what we wanted. We lay together for a while in serene sexual satisfaction.

Before I left her bedroom I got her name, address and phone number. I promised I would return.

My poor buddies did not score. They did not have the privacy we did. But they did not hold it against me. In fact, they expressed amazement at my seductive power. As a matter of fact, I was a little amazed myself. All I can say is that our eyes spoke the truth to each other. They stripped away all moral taboos.

As promised, I returned the next weekend. She was not home. Her sister was. She told me, my lover had a policeman boyfriend. She said they might be home at any time. I did not really want to tangle with a southern, redneck cop. But to be polite, I tarried a while to chat with the sister on the couch. I could tell the cop I had come to see her. She was a pretty, sandy-haired girl with a nice body. I could not help but notice a lot of peach fuzz on her face.

As I was about to leave, I touched her arm and stood close to her. Too close I guess. For somehow we started kissing. Perhaps platonically at first, but more passionately as the danger of being caught increased with the passage of time. She gave me ample access to her tongue. Soon her back was to the wall and my body was pressed against her. She was a little taller than her sister and by bending my knees slightly I was able to make genital contact. It was hard for me, she was so warm and soft. She must have wanted me for she started pushing against me in a circular movement, the same as that Japanese geisha had used in the hills near Nagasaki in 1946. I could not stop myself in time. My seeds spilled inside my pants. Somewhat embarrassed, I left with soiled shorts.

Not wanting to get mixed up with a lawman, I did not return to see my Atlanta lover or her swivel-hipped sister.

Things went fine for me at the infantry school. I had no trouble passing the tests at the end of each segment of instruction. One thing I discovered about myself that I did not know before was that I had excellent night vision. To determine this they turned the classroom into total darkness by shutting out all light with shades, etc. Then they directed our eyes to one side of the room and gradually turned on a small light. As soon as one saw it, he was to speak up. I was tops in my class. They said it was because of the amount of purple in our eyes, whatever that means. Good night vision was important in combat because during WWII it was learned it was more practical to fight at night than in the daytime. Casualties were less. Now most of the fighting in Korea was done at night.

But I did not pass all the tests on the first try. We had extensive instructions in map reading. I learned the material well, including how to use a compass. On the final test we had to find our way through some thick woods, following azimuths and map coordinates and ending up at a particular stake along a road leading back into camp. There we would be picked up by trucks and brought back to camp. If we took too long, missed our stake or got lost, we were ordered to wait alongside the road until we were picked up. That way we would be accounted for.

I plotted my course on the map using the coordinates given me for my test. Every place on a map had two coordinates, a vertical north and south one and a horizontal east and west one. Unfortunately, even though I knew better, I used the horizontal when I should have used the vertical and vice versa, when I plotted my path through the woods. By the time I realized my mistake, it was too late. I did not come out where I was supposed to and I missed the regular truck ride back to camp. So I had to wait as ordered.

It was late in the afternoon. Evening mess was at five o'clock. I was getting hungry. As it neared mealtime I became concerned I would be too late to get any chow. So I moved to the edge of the road and hitched a ride into camp. I decided to eat first and then report in. I did not want to miss supper.

As I was about done eating someone from the orderly room found out I had returned without reporting in. I was ordered to report to our commanding officer immediately.

Chapter XXXII

"Where the hell have you been?" the commanding officer bellowed at me. "I've had people looking all over hell for you."

"Sorry sir," I answered meekly. "I got lost."

"Why did you disobey orders to wait to be picked up?" he continued.

"I thought maybe I'd been forgotten," I lied.

"Why didn't you let us know you were back as soon as you got here?"

" I should have sir, but I was hungry," I said truthfully.

"You're damned right you should have. You know I could court martial you for disobeying orders – insubordination. But I'm not going to, because that might keep you from going to Korea. They need cannon fodder like you over there. So I'm going to make damn sure you go. Now get the hell out of here. I don't want to ever see your face again," he said ending the discussion.

"Thank you, sir," I said sincerely.

I certainly was not trying to get out of going to Korea, but I was glad he thought so. It saved my ass.

That Saturday afternoon I was unable to continue my normal pursuit of sex. Instead, I spent the time repeating the map reading test. This time I made sure I read my coordinates right and passed.

But it was only a temporary slowdown. The next weekend one of my classmates came up with a brilliant idea to get dates – call up a local nursing school dormitory and ask if any of the students wanted to go out. He buddied up to me because I had a car. He called and arranged for us to pick up two student nurses. We took them out for a movie and a ride.

My buddy was younger than I was, so he got the younger, prettier girl. My date was a tall, slim, flat-chested, dark-haired girl. There was no chemistry between us. She was not very bright and had little sense of humor. She was neither sexually attracted nor attractive to me. Being with her was a waste of time.

The younger girl did not hit it off well with my buddy either. He was sort of flaky. He seemed more interested in having a teenage type, platonic relationship rather than getting down to the practical business of setting the groundwork to get laid. I sensed that his date was more interested in me than him.

Anyhow, I arranged to see her. I took her for a long ride up towards Atlanta. We talked, had something to eat and got acquainted. She told me she liked brandy. So I got her a pint. On the long drive home, at my encouragement, she consumed quite a bit of brandy. As I hoped, she became rather drunk and went to sleep at my side, I pulled off the road into a secluded spot and tried to pull her slacks down without disturbing her, so I could sneak in before she awoke. I knew I would have it made once I was in. She awoke briefly and took my hand that was tugging at her pants.

"Kiss me," she said.

Kiss her I did, thinking she was giving me a green light. I tried to push my tongue into her mouth but her lips resisted my effort.

I gave her another drink. We drove a little farther down the road. She returned to dreamland. I found another private place to park. This time I touched her breasts. They were well molded and spongy, as they were supposed to be. She didn't seem to mind. Again I attempted to slide her trousers down slow and easy. Again she intercepted my hand.

"Kiss me," she demanded again.

I did as she told me. Only this time I moved my body more on top of her so she would more fully understand what I wanted. But if she did, it was not what she wanted.

She pushed me away and repeated, "Kiss me."

I kissed her some more and took her home – mission thwarted.

There was a drugstore in Columbus, Georgia, where some of us went sometimes because it had a snack bar where we could get something to eat or drink. There was a cute little waitress who exchanged smiles with me on occasion. She was short and slim with well-rounded breasts. I liked her.

I asked her if she would like to go for a ride one evening. She was happy to go with me. She did not waste time in letting me know she liked me. It did not take me long to know she was an easy make.

We soon found an out-of-the-way parking place. I took her young, little body in my arms and kissed her. She welcomed my tongue. I started to reach into her bra to massage her breasts.

"Wait a minute," she said.

She reached in herself and unloaded two wads of toilet paper from her bra. She was totally bustless. But that did not matter to me. For what I wanted tits were unnecessary.

She took off her panties and spread her legs willingly. I lowered my pants and entered her eagerly, thinking she would be young and tight, maybe even a virgin. To my great surprise, she was anything but tight. She may have been young, but she was no virgin. She felt like she had been screwed many times by dicks much larger and longer than mine. But we worked at it and finally I came. Strain as I might against her little body, however, I could not touch the bottom of her cavernous receptacle. We did not stay together long. There was no flesh-on-flesh feeling. It felt more like a vast void.

But she did not complain. Nor did I. She seemed happy a second lieutenant would want to do it to her. After we sat a while and kissed some more I grew hard again. This time, remembering that I had liked doing it doggy fashion with my wife, I turned her around and put it in from the rear. This was not much better than the other way. It took me a long time but finally I got my rocks off again.

As soon as she had taken off her panties I had noticed a bad odor from her privates, sort of like rotten fish. Now that we were through screwing, the smell seemed even stronger. I decided to take her home as fast as possible and find a drugstore to get a pro kit. I did not want to get any venereal disease.

She directed me to her house in some place outside of Columbus. I had no idea where it was.

At the door she clung to me and begged, "Come on in. You can sleep with me. My father won't care."

From inside a voice hollered, "What the hell's all the noise.

Get your ass in the house and go to bed."

I kissed her hurriedly and said, "Good night."

On the road again I looked for two things: a drugstore and road signs so I could orient myself and find my way back to Benning. This was a road map test. After driving around the back roads a while I finally found a drugstore, bought a pro kit and applied it as I had learned so well to do in Japan after WWII. Then I found my way back to camp.

I felt sorry for that young, flat-chested waitress, but not sorry enough to ever go back into the place where she worked.

One weekend a buddy of mine named Ralph and I decided to go over to Auburn, Alabama, to look for female flesh. Ralph probably liked me because I had a car and he didn't, the same as Paul had at Fort Dix. But I welcomed his company. Two men can find willing women easier than one. Ladies seldom travel alone. Often they are in pairs. Ralph and I had a common, healthy lust for sex.

We found a large dance hall in Auburn and went in. Soon I spotted a gorgeous lady sitting on the sidelines. She had dark, wavy hair, beautiful blue eyes, a rosy complexion that appeared unmade-up and the most luscious bosom I've ever seen on a woman. She was very neatly dressed with a tight, form-fitting sweater on top which showed off the rich roundness of her torso in all its splendor.

I forgot about Ralph for the moment. I asked her to dance. She was like a dream in my arms. We danced together as long as the hall was open.

Fortunately, she had a friend with her with whom Ralph hooked up. Ralph's partner was also a well-built, comely woman. We all left together. Ralph's lady had an apartment. I took them there. My girl's name was Ruby. She lived with her parents. So we went parking.

I took her in my arms and kissed her, long, tenderly and sweetly. She was totally responsive. Chemistry flowed warmly between us. My left hand cupped her right breast. It was so perfect. I pulled up her sweater and unhooked her bra to expose her beautiful busts. I had to kiss them. My lips encircled her left nipple as my left hand squeezed her right bust. They dilated with desire. My maleness hardened with wild anticipation. My left hand caressed her body as it moved down to her thigh. She pulled it back up to her breast. I continued sucking and massaging. Suddenly a spasm shook her body and she pressed hard up against me. Again I reached for my target area. Again she pulled my hand away.

"No, I can't," she explained.

"Why not?" I asked as my sperm suddenly shot forth into my shorts.

Embarrassed, I got out of my car, went to the back of it and wiped myself with my handkerchief as best I could.

"I'm sorry," she said when I returned.

"So am I," I replied.

I took her home, picked up Ralph and returned to Benning.

Ralph scored that night and wanted a repeat performance the next weekend.

This time as we parked, Ruby and I talked a bit.

"I can't have intercourse because I'm deformed down there," she told me.

"What do you mean?" I asked.

"I have no pelvic bone and cannot control my bladder. So I have to wear rubber pants all the time," She explained. "I was married once and my husband left me because sex with me did not satisfy him. I would like to but I don't think I could please you either."

"Why don't we try and see what happens?" I suggested.

"Okay, but I have to keep my rubber pants on," she agreed. "Love me first like you did last week."

So we kissed and I fondled and sucked her breasts to prepare for the invasion. After the sweet sucking session her body shook with an orgasmic spasm.

"I love you," she whispered in my ear.

Then we both reached down, after I had dropped my pants, to push and pull the rubber pants aside for my grand entrance. They were so tight it was almost impossible. I think some famous general once said it takes a little longer to accomplish the impossible. It took some maneuvering to finally get in sidewise from an angle. It was a tight squeeze, too tight for comfort. But I accomplished my mission like a true soldier.

We continued seeing each other on nearly every weekend. Eventually I convinced her to trust me enough to take her rubber pants off. I would always make her get her cookies by kissing and sucking on her breasts. This was almost as good as the actual screwing for me. Probably better for her. When she would take her pants off there was a foul odor of urine underneath, but after I entered her it did not bother me. She had no control of her love muscle. It felt like dipping my dink into a soft, wet mass of loose meat. But I had no trouble reaching a climax. The foreplay with her busts had me ready. She was always very neat and we were careful not to stain or stink up the interior of my Packard.

Ralph, his lover, Ruby and I often went on Sunday picnics. Ruby would fix fabulous picnic lunches with southern fried chicken. Ruby invited me into her home to meet her parents and partake of a home-cooked meal with them.

I told Ruby I was married and probably encouraged her to fall in love with me by telling her my wife and I did not get along too well.

Inevitably, our Infantry School training days drew towards an end. My black buddy and I would laugh and joke about a two-week cleansing period before we graduated and returned to our wives for thirty days before being sent overseas. But I kept seeing Ruby until near graduation, I knew there was no future for us. But I hated leaving the warmth of her bosom.

Meanwhile, I had kept practicing my pull-ups in the latrine in the mornings and exercising in preparation for the final physical fitness test. On the day of the test the first exercise was pull-ups. I did eighteen, the most in the company, and scored 98 out of 100 possible points. Then on push-ups, sit-ups and squat jumps my score was 100 in each. So going into the run I had 398 points. But in the run I did not earn even one point. The tester took pity on me and gave me one point. So I ended up with a 399 total out of a possible 500. One ex-football player from West Point beat me, but I don't think anyone else did. When the final graduation scores were posted, I ranked in the top third of the class despite having not taken much of the instructions very seriously.

After I said goodby to Ruby, I promised her I would write to her when I got to Korea. It was a sad parting. I think she truly loved me. And I loved at least a part of her. But I also loved my little Judy, my wife and our unborn child.

When I got home in the first part of April. Jo's belly was full and round with child. Judy was adorable. I was glad to be home. Jo was certainly a good mother.

Chapter XXXIII

The first night home was not bad. We worked around her belly to the satisfaction of both of us. But the next day Jo started harping again about money.

"When are you going to take out an allotment for me?" she asked.

"I'm not," I informed her.

"But what if you get killed in Korea?" she continued. "Then what will I do?"

"Don't worry," I said, "If I get killed you'll get all the pay I have coming and $10,000 insurance."

Since our earlier disagreements over money, I felt compelled to control my earnings the way I wanted to, not the way she wanted. She did not seem to have the slightest clue of how to get me to do her bidding. Our relationship had become a series of confrontations with brief time-outs for sex. Love for our little Judy and unborn child tied us together.

I did not stay around long to argue with her. I drove to Vermont to see my family and friends there.

Kermit had remarried and built a small house on a small piece of swampy land in Jericho. He was now barbering in Essex Junction. He and his new wife Betty now had a couple of boys.

Willard was now living in Claremont, New Hampshire, in an apartment with Becky and their two boys. He had a good job as a machinist for Jones and Lamson in Springfield, Vermont. I spent some time with them. Willard and I tossed a baseball back and forth some and told tales about playing ball. He had a lot more to brag about than I did.

Gerald had married his sweetheart Lorraine and was now doing a hitch in the Air Force. They also had a family started.

Geraldine was now seventeen and had dropped out of school. She and our mother were at odds about her dating a boy who our mother thought was low class. While our mother was in the hospital for something or other, our old man had allowed Geraldine's boyfriend Ernie to come into the house and have his (or her) way with her. They were to marry later.

My mother was still working in Burlington and supporting our dead-beat father who was now in Mary Fletcher Hospital in Burlington. He was recovering from rectal surgery to remove a large cyst. He now shit through a colostomy in his side.

Perhaps as a last-ditch effort to gain approval from him, or maybe just to show him I had succeeded in spite of his constant sarcastic put-downs when I was too small to whip his ass, I visited him in the hospital. It was a disappointment. All he did was complain about his condition. He described his operation in detail and seemed only concerned with himself. Never a word from his lips about my going to Korea or care that I return. I listened awhile and then left with no change of heart towards him.

While in Vermont I was as horny as ever. Thinking I might get another piece or two from her for old times' sake, I called Vi. She wanted nothing to do with me even though I told her I was now an officer in the Army. It did not impress her. Maybe she'd been screwed by officers before.

After I returned to my wife in Syracuse, she started nagging me about getting an extension on my leave to be with her when our baby was born. She was due at any time. I refused. I did not think having a baby was that big a deal, at least not as important as the war in Korea. I did not want anybody to think I was a coward hiding behind my wife's petticoat. Being a coward was my biggest fear. Besides, they were already talking of peace. I wanted to get there and be part of the action. That's the way military officers get ahead in their careers.

In hindsight, I now realize I was very insensitive to my wife's needs. I more concerned with my own career. Of course, I rationalized that I was doing things for the benefit of my family and our country.

Anyhow, in early May I boarded a plane for Seattle, Washington. From there they flew me and other officers to Japan.

The Japanese are very industrious people. They had cleaned up most of the destruction of WWII and rebuilt their homes and businesses. But their culture remained pretty much untarnished by the presence of United States occupation forces. Honey carts still made their rounds collecting human shit which Americans normally waste by flushing down toilets into non-productive skeptic tanks or sewers. Little Japanese men still scampered from house to house, shop to shop, with honey buckets on each end of a yoke over their shoulders, gathering the human excreta and dumping it into the honey carts. They usually wore white masks over their mouths and noses, but I doubt that the mask filtered out all the shitty stink. This human waste was used as fertilizer to grow rice and other nice vegetables.

Geisha houses were still easy to find. I did not delay long in finding one. As soon as I was settled in our temporary billets and had organized my gear, I set forth to find some Japanese pussy. It still cost only two dollars, a pack of cigarettes, a cake of soap or a candy bar. So my wife could not accuse me of wasting a lot of money.

We were in Japan about a week before being sent on to Korea. During that time I visited geisha houses a couple of times, wrote letters home, exercised, kept my gear in order and waited.

Some of the officers, perhaps the lucky ones, were assigned to the First Cavalry Division in Hokkaidō, the northern island of Japan. My friend Fats was sent there. I did not want such an assignment. I wanted to go to an outfit in the thick of the fight in Korea. I got my wish. Several of us were assigned to the Forty-fifth Division in Korea.

We traveled by train across Japan to the port of Sasebo. From there we crossed the Sea of Japan on an LST (Landing Ship Tank) to Pusan, Korea. It was one of those flat-bottomed ships on which I had become deathly seasick during amphibious training in WWII. If I remember correctly, we crossed Japan during the day and the Sea of Japan at night. I tried to sleep part of the way. The sea was calm so I did not get seasick.

A few miles out to sea from Pusan, before we could see land, we got our first whiff of Pusan. It stank like stale shit. As we got closer and began to see the land of the morning calm, the stink strengthened. It reeked of urine, feces, sweat and all other foul odors combined. It permeated the air and the sea. I wondered how fish could live in it or how people could stand it. But then I remembered how bad our father used to smell from never bathing. So I guess it was easier for me to tolerate than for others. Farm boys were used to the smell of manure piles and fresh cow shit. In my teens, I had helped my brother Conrow clean out gutters full of cow shit and piss and spread manure many times on the fields of Burr Gleason's farm in Jericho, Vermont.

As we came closer to Korea and the land rose higher out of the sea, the men stirred and stood at the rail. Bill Brownly and George Goodboy joined me. We had been at Fort Dix and Fort Benning together. We were friends but not awfully close. They had never joined me in my search for sex. I didn't know much about them. I guess they respected me because I was a combat infantryman and a little older than they were.

"What a terrible odor," remarked Bill. "The Koreans must be very primitive and uncivilized."

"What a fucking place to have to fight for," George complained.

"It does smell like shit," I agreed. "But we'll probably get used to it."

"I hope I don't get assigned to a rifle platoon," Bill said. "I think I could handle a mortar Platoon. They're not on the front lines."

"I don't want to be a rifle platoon leader either," George agreed. "I'm not sure I'd know what to do. How about you, Al? You've been in combat before. How was it?"

"Well, I was in a machine-gun platoon, so it wasn't like being in a rifle platoon," I explained. "Most of the time we didn't know where the hell we were or what was going on. We got shelled some and I was pretty scared. But I plan on a military career so combat experience will help me get ahead, if I don't get killed."

"Not me," Bill said. "I'm not going to stay in the Army. I've got better things to do."

"Me neither," agreed George. "I would not have signed up for ROTC if I had known we were going to be in a fucking war."

After we landed, had some chow and stowed our gear in our billet, we took a stroll through Pusan.

A young, barefoot, dirty-faced little boy approached us.

"Hey, GI, want pretty flower girl?" he asked. "Only ten

dollars. Come on. I take you to her. You have good fuck."

He took Bill's hand. Bill withdrew his hand and cringed away.

"Go away," he told the little pimp. "We don't want any Korean girls. Leave us alone."

"Maybe you like *sucha hachi*," the little fellow continued his sex sales pitch. "Me number one *sucha hachi* boy. Come on. I show you. Only five dollars."

"No, no," George backed Bill up. "We don't want any of that stuff. We're just looking for souvenirs. Don't bother us."

"You like cherry girl?" the boy persisted. "I let you fuck my little sister. She number one cherry girl. I know. I fuck her myself."

Bill waved him away with his hand. "Go on, get. We don't want any whores."

"Wait," I said. "Let's talk to him. I wouldn't mind getting laid."

"Are you out of your mind?" asked George in amazement. "We don't want to get VD from a dirty prostitute or a knife in the back from a communist guerrilla."

Bill agreed with him. "I've never been promiscuous in my life. I'm not about to lower myself now by having sex with a Korean whore."

"Oh, come on," I said, "I'm horny. I'd like to try some Korean pussy. We'll be okay if we stick together. And I've got some pro kits with me, just in case."

"You go ahead if you want to," George said to me. "We'll wait for you up the street."

"I won't be long," I told them.

I took the little boy's dirty hand and let him lead me down a narrow alley towards my mission.

"Wait," I ordered him, "How much?"

"Twenty dollars," he upped the price. "Number one cherry girl. You fuck all day."

"No, no," I told him. "Two dollars. Only one time."

"Okay, GI, you give me two dollars," he agreed.

"No, no," I said. "I pay mama-san."

"Okay," he said. "Let's go."

He led me to a house. My right hand tightened its grip on the stock of my M2 carbine slung over my shoulder, as a sense of the alley closing behind me crept through my mind. What if it was an ambush? Many a man's hormones have brought him into harm's way, somebody probably once said.

I relaxed a little as I entered the house and saw GI boots lined up just inside the door. I took my boots off and put them at the end of the line. A young businessman led me down a narrow staircase. At the bottom he held out his hand and pointed to a door. I gave him two bucks and entered the sliding door made of paper on a flimsy wood frame.

Inside was the smallest fucking room I was ever in, about four by six feet. Awaiting me on a narrow quilted pad, which took about half the room, was a young Korean workingwoman. She was plain, but not unattractive. Not as well made up as most Japanese geisha girls. Her equipment was placed neatly near her small pillow – a box of tissue and a jar of lubricant.

"Hi, GI," she greeted me, as she slipped out of her scanty white shift. "Come on, let's go."

She lay on her back with her legs spread and her knees drawn up so her feet were flat on the straw floor next to her buttocks, an easily penetrable position. I stripped for action and made my invasion. She did not wiggle up and down as a prostitute normally does, pretending it is pleasurable for her. Instead, she lazily flapped her knees back and forth horizontally to create a minimal squeezing effect. I suspect she was tired and this was an easy way to save energy. But she was not too bad. Not the worst, but far from the best. It was a release for my pent-up sexual drive and a livelihood for her.

After applying a pro kit, I dressed and rejoined my companions. I slept well that night.

Chapter XXXIV

The next day we moved up through the replacement pipeline by train. Like the train cars in Japan, the Korean train cars were equipped with holes in the floor in the rear of the cars. These were for passengers to relieve themselves. The train moved slowly and stopped occasionally. When it stopped some of us would disembark to take a leak. Little Korean kids and old people would look at us and grin.

We saw peasants working in their rice paddies in the hot sun. They protected their heads from the heat of the sun with cone-shaped straw hats with wide brims to shade their faces. We saw a few old men with the traditional black stovepipe hats like Lincoln used to wear. Wrinkle-faced little old men carried huge loads on A-frames strapped on their backs. These were three-pronged crotches cut from trees of the right size and shape to fit the back. Between the upward pointed prongs were balanced loads often much heavier than the little old men carrying them. Big logs, firewood, building materials, bundles of produce or personal belongings were some of the things carried on the A-frames. I did not see any women laboring under A-frames. They carried their burdens in baskets balanced on their heads. The little old men bent forward under their loads; the women stood straight. Few, if any, young men were to be seen. I guess they were all off to war. Whenever the train stopped in a station, we were greeted by hungry, dirty-faced, ragged, barefoot, chattering children begging for handouts.

After a brief stop at Division Headquarters, Brownly, Goodboy and I were transported to the 179th Infantry Regiment. Brownly and I went on to the Third Battalion. I think Good boy was assigned to the Second Battalion. I never saw him again.

The battalion commander, Lieutenant Colonel Spottswood, interviewed Brownly and me separately. Brownly was sent to M Company where he became the leader of the Mortar Platoon. Just what he wanted.

Colonel Spottswood impressed me as being a very nice man. He was of average size with silver, thinning hair. His pale blue eyes looked me over carefully as he spoke to me. I was wearing my Combat Infantry Badge. I had noticed that other soldiers were wearing theirs as we had come forward from the rear. Colonel Spottswood was also wearing his. On his was the stainless steel star signifying a second award. That told me he had been in WWII.

"I see you've been in combat before, Lieutenant," Colonel Spottswood said. "Is this your second tour in Korea?"

"No, sir," I replied. "I was in WWII."

"Good," he said. "We need officers with combat experience. What outfit were you in?"

"The Ninety-seventh Infantry Division in Germany, sir," I told him.

"What was your MOS?" he asked.

"I was a machine gunner, sir," I said.

"We don't have an opening for a machine-gun platoon leader," he informed me. "So I'm assigning you to L Company. Lieutenant Pierce is the company commander. He's a West Pointer – a fine officer."

I was delivered by jeep, ever closer to the front lines, to L Company. The company was occupying a reserve, blocking position. First Lieutenant James Pierce greeted me with no great excitement. Immediately, I noticed he was not wearing a Combat Infantry Badge. I felt a little embarrassed that I was. He did not say anything about it.

Pierce was not a tall man, nor was he heavy-set. But he did not seem small. His shoulders were broad and his jaw square. His fatigue pants fit tightly around heavy thighs. He appeared strong and rugged. He wore his silver first lieutenant's bar. A white bar was also painted on his steel helmet. A Colt .45 hung from his cartridge belt at his hip. The short stub of a cigar occupied his mouth.

Lieutenant Pierce introduced me to First Sergeant James Baker and then took me to Sergeant Burfoot's mess tent, where the other company officers were having coffee. First Lieutenant

Mike Moroney was his executive officer. First Lieutenant Jules Buckhuyt had the first platoon and First Lieutenant Jim Rau had the weapons platoon. The second and third platoons did not have officers to lead them, not an uncommon thing in war.

"Which platoon do you want me to have?" I asked.

"I don't know yet," Pierce said. "I have to think about it."

Being out of range of enemy artillery the men of L Company were living in pup tents. They all had rubber air mattresses to sleep on. *Somewhat different than WWII*, I thought, when we slept on the hard, cold ground in Germany. The officers lived in a squad-sized, tepee-shaped tent. They had cots to put their air mattresses on. The supply sergeant furnished me with one.

At my first opportunity for privacy, I took off my CIB and put it with some personal stuff, I certainly would not want to wear it when we got up on the front lines in combat. And I did not want my fellow officers and men to think badly of me. None of them were wearing theirs. I guess only rear echelon troops wore them to prove they had been in combat.

Sometime ago, my brother Willard had sent me a gift of twin, double-edged daggers with leather scabbards, a supplement to my other weapons of war. Now, while I was alone, I pulled them out of my duffel bag. I wondered where best to carry them, on my cartridge belt or in my boots? My cartridge belt was already loaded with a carbine bayonet, a canteen, an ammunition pouch and a first-aid kit. There was not much more room on it. So I stuck them in my boots and stood up to see how they would feel. Not too bad. But I decided not to display them yet. I put them in my knapsack which I expected I would be wearing on the front lines. Then when the time came I could quickly stick them in my boots and be ready for action.

The next morning nobody told me what to do. So after breakfast, I found an improvised pull-up bar at the back of our tent. I stripped to the waist and did some pull-ups. When strength was needed to fight I did not want to be found lacking. Lieutenant Pierce found me there.

"Want to go and relieve Jules on a detail?" he asked me.

"Sure," I agreed, as I put my T-shirt and fatigue jacket back on.

"They're working on a secondary line of resistance," he said. "The men know what to do. All you'll have to do is keep them busy."

Because of my inferior rank I got into the back seat of the jeep we were to ride in. Pierce rode up front. When we came to the bottom of a high hill we stopped.

"Wait for me," Pierce ordered the driver.

Pierce led the way up a steep trail. He did not look back. I followed him. I thought I was in good shape. Keeping up with him would be no sweat. Pierce did not stop. Soon my thighs became weak from oxygen debt. My lungs gasped for air and my heart pounded. Sweat poured from my body. The distance between us increased but Pierce did not look back or stop for a rest. Was he testing me? Paths forked off from the trail we were on. There were sharp turns. I lost sight of Pierce. I did not know where or how close the enemy was. Could I get lost? I had no map or compass. I did not even have my daggers with me and only one fifteen-round clip of carbine ammunition.

Suddenly I had to urinate. I stopped and took a leak at the side of the trail. I rested and took a drink from my canteen. *If this is the way Pierce is, piss on him*, I thought. Anger mixed with my apprehension and my fears faded. When I was rested I continued to climb, hoping I was on the right track. I rounded a bend and saw Pierce up ahead waiting for me. When I neared him, he turned without a word and led me to the top of the hill.

The men were building bunkers with overhead cover out of logs and sandbags. These were being connected by trenches dug in the sandy soil. Some of the men were digging and filling sandbags, some were cutting logs from trees in the surrounding woods and others were constructing the fortifications. Nobody seemed to be working very hard.

Lieutenants Pierce and Buckhuyt left and I stayed with the work detail. I walked around for a while to figure out what was going on. The front lines or secondary lines I had been on in Germany were never like this. This was all new to me. It reminded me a little of what I had read about trench warfare in WWI in high school history classes. I asked questions but gave no orders. I was not sure what orders to give.

One group of men were sitting idly confronting a large, dead stump. They seemed to be contemplating and speculating on the difficulty of removing it. Apparently, it was blocking the field of fire of a machine-gun emplacement.

"Lieutenant," spoke up a short, young black soldier. "We need some dynamite. You can get us some dynamite, can't you, Lieutenant?"

"I don't know if I can get any dynamite or not," I replied. Nobody had told me what I could or could not get. "Have you tried chopping it out? That would probably be quicker than getting dynamite."

"Oh, we can't chop it out. It's too hard to chop with an axe. I've been chopping on it all morning." The black man continued to be the spokesman for the group.

"Let me see your axe," I said.

He handed me the axe he'd been leaning on. I took it and felt the blade's edge with my thumb. It was not very dull. It did not appear to have been used much. I spit on the palms of my hands and rubbed them together like I used to in the woods of Underhill, Vermont. That gives you just the right amount of friction. I faced the stump and placed a couple of light chops on it to get the feel of the axe and zero in on the target.

I stopped. The man smiled as if to say, "I told you so."

The black soldier voiced their thoughts, "See, sir, it's too hard. You can't do it."

I did not answer him. I took off my cartridge belt and laid it near where I had put my carbine. Then I took a few more swipes at the stump. We were all wearing steel helmets. We were within range of Chinese artillery and an occasional round landing in the area was a reminder of that. So it was ordered that the men wear steel helmets at all times in this area.

But I have never swung an axe while wearing a steel helmet. It was not comfortable. I took it off and my fatigue jacket as well and set them neatly next to my other gear. Now I was ready to cut the stump.

The men sat back and watched as I wielded the axe with an expertise born of many years' experience cutting wood as a youth, and the determination of a lieutenant who had to prove himself.

The stump was not nearly as hard as I had been led to believe. In fact, it was quite rotten. I chopped it out of the way in short order.

I looked at the men and explained, "I used to be a lumberjack."

For the rest of the day I chopped logs, dug trenches, filled sandbags and helped build bunkers. It was on-the-job training. I learned a great deal from the men, I think the men worked harder because I worked along with them. It was not necessary for me to tell them what to do. They knew as much, if not more, about what we were doing than I did. I felt no need to assert the power of my authority. When the day was done I was as dirty, sweaty, tired and smelly as the other men. I knew how they felt.

The next day Pierce assigned me to the second platoon.

Chapter XXXV

As I had promised, I wrote to Ruby as soon as I had an address for her to write to. I knew there could be no future for us, but I will never forget her beautiful, bare breasts.

Of course, I also wrote my wife and hoped she would send me a telegram as soon as our baby was born. I assumed that was the traditional thing to do.

I got letters off to my mother and my brother Willard as soon as I had time. They wrote to me regularly. Other siblings and friends wrote less frequently.

Rocky was born on May 24, 1952. I got a letter with an eight cent, regular postage stamp on it from Jo on June 12, telling me of his birth and that everything was fine. I was elated at the good news, but a little pissed off that she had not sent a telegram or even bothered to use an airmail stamp. I made sure none of my fellow officers noticed that I had found out about my new baby in such a way. It was embarrassing to me that she was so stingy. Of course that was just a reflection of our cool relationship. I had not tried to be with her for the birth, so why should she be concerned about letting me know as soon as she could? Notwithstanding that, I might have been killed by the time her letter arrived. But if that were the case, would it have mattered to her?

After he learned I had a son, Lieutenant Pierce told me he also had a son. His son was James Pierce III. I called my son Rocky, even though his mother had named him Ronald Mark.

"I have a four-month-old son who is going to be a football player," Pierce told me. "I have not seen him yet. I can't wait to go back to the States to see him."

"My son is going to be a baseball player," I bragged, thinking of what I had wanted to be.

For the few days L Company was in the rest area, where I joined it, things were quite peaceful and relaxed. Very few demands were placed on the men. There was no formal reveille or retreat. Platoon leaders and platoon sergeants saw to it that the men kept their areas reasonably neat and policed up. There were showers within marching distance to the rear. I recall taking the second platoon back there at least once. Generally, steel helmets were used to wash up in and shave. I remember only one formation where the officers inspected the men. It was sort of an introduction to my men for me.

While inspecting my platoon I acted as sharply and militarily as I could, I slapped the rifles out of the men' hands crisply. I looked at the open chambers and squinted down the barrels knowingly, as if it mattered. The men' fatigues were wrinkled and sometimes ill fitting, their boots unshined. I understood that and made no negative comments about it. The men themselves were clean and well shaved. When I came to Bob Browne, the second squad leader, and the biggest man in the platoon, I had to look up to him. He was several inches taller than me. His scowling eyes silently challenged me to find anything wrong with him or his piece. I felt compelled to say something.

"The bore of your rifle could stand a little more cleaning," I said.

"Our rifles are so damned pitted you can't get them clean," he answered defiantly, as if speaking for all his men.

My platoon sergeant was Jimmy Sides. He was a tall, well-built, neat soldier. During the stay behind the lines I found him to be sharp, bright and well organized.

The assistant platoon sergeant was Art Amos. He was a short, small, well-spoken man who appeared to be efficient.

Sergeant Jim Crimmins was the leader of the first squad. He was a fairly tall, slim soldier. Sergeant Bill McAfee had the third squad. He was also quite tall and well built. Corporal Cecil Jackson was in charge of the machine-gun squad.

By the time I learned of Rocky's birth I had already received mail from Mom, Willard and Ruby. All the more reason to think Jo had taken her own sweet time to let me know. But there was not much time to worry about it. Soon we were moved up on the main line of resistance. This line was made up of trenches extending across the higher ridges of the entire Korean peninsula, with gaps in the lower valleys. To hold the high ground is important for fighting forces. Low lands were no man's lands where it was dangerous to move or be seen for fear of being shelled by artillery and mortars. At points along the trench were bunkers with overhead cover where the men lived. They rested mostly during the day. They were alert at night. By now Chinese attacks were pretty much limited to night assaults. At this time the front was pretty stabilized across the mountainous middle of Korea, about where the "Police Action" had started two years before.

Directly across the valley from our position I could see a Chinese outpost called "Eerie". Eerie was the southern end of hills extending northwards. A little beyond Eerie a ridge cut across the main ridge to form a tee. So it was called "T-Bone". A long trench leading northward towards the Chinese main line was visible from our position.

No one had told me much about the status of the "Police Action" of the United Nations forces, which were made up mostly of United States troops. What I knew had come from reading the papers and listening to the news on the radio. I knew that peace talks were taking place in Panmunjon. But they seemed to be all political and were not amounting to much. It seemed to be generally understood that the conflict was stalemated as far as taking territory was concerned, except for fighting over small outposts between the main lines.

At the time I was not aware that the Forty-fifth Division was in the final phase of operation "Counter". From historical accounts I was later to learn there were about a dozen Chinese outposts strung out along the front of the 179th, 180th and 279th Infantry Regiments which made up the Forty-fifth Division. General Ruffner had decided to take these from the Chinese. I suppose his rationale was to take away their forward observation posts. Then they would not be able to shell our positions as accurately, thus cutting down on casualties. I think he perhaps failed to factor into his plan the number of casualties it required to take those hills. But then, he could well have been less concerned about casualties than he was about getting another star.

As soon as we were situated on the MLR (Main Line of Resistance), I stuck my twin daggers in my boots. I no longer was concerned about how they appeared to others. If I needed them they would be there. They fit neatly in my combat boots. My boots were a little fancier than the split-leather ones the men wore. At Fort Benning, I had had zippers sewn on the inside of them to save lacing them every day. Leather thongs, through slits in the sheaths, and tied around my legs helped hold them in place. I also tied down my bayonet scabbard with a leather thong around my thigh. This would keep it from flopping up if I had to pull it out quickly. At the time I did not know of General Ruffner's dislike of leather thongs. They were a no-no in his command. Nobody had told me.

On the morning of June 13, Lieutenant Moroney called me on the field phone. "Chamberlin, Battalion wants us to occupy Uncle and dig machine gun positions there to fire on Eerie. It's your platoon's turn, so send a squad out there."

I knew where Uncle was. It was a small knoll out in front of the MLR in no man's land, a little to the right of my platoon's position.

This is it, I thought. My first mission as a leader in combat. Could I handle it? Would I be scared like a boxer entering the ring for the first time, or a speaker before a speech? Would I mess up? Like Roosevelt had said at the beginning of WWII, my biggest fear was fear itself. I was terrified of being afraid, of being a coward.

My reaction on the phone surprised me. My voice was calm and steady. I think I asked the right questions. "What's the situation, Mike? Are there any Chinks out there?"

"I don't think so," Mike answered.

"Should I go with the squad or stay here?" I asked.

"You'd better stay there, where most of your men are. If you have any questions, ask Sergeant Sides. He knows what to do. The main thing is to get those gun positions dug out there," Mike said in an impatient, somewhat excited voice.

"Yes sir," I answered.

I was a little disturbed that Mike had not given me many details and had implied that Sides knew more about what to do than I did. If I needed advice from a sergeant, I would ask for it. I did not need to be told to. A bit of anger rose inside me. But not much.

In my CP (Command Post) bunker were Sergeant Sides, Sergeant Amos and private first class Harry Cottrell, my radioman. We made up our platoon headquarters.

"Sergeant Sides, whose turn is it to go out?" I asked. I had already learned that platoons and squads took turns on dangerous details.

"Sergeant Browne's," answered Sides. He seemed to be suddenly nervous. "What do we have to do?"

"We have to send a squad out to Uncle," I told him. "Harry, call Browne and have him report here."

Before Harry could call, the phone rang again. It was Moroney.

"Chamberlin, have the men pick up picks and shovels at the Company CP. Have them ready to go in fifteen minutes. The artillery is going to lay a smoke screen to cover them when they move out," he told me.

"Yes sir," I answered. "Call Browne," I told Harry. "Tell him not to come here. We'll go there. Tell him he has to move out in fifteen minutes. Jimmy, you come with us. Harry, bring a roll of commo wire and a phone. Amos, you stay here while we're gone."

Standing tall, I led Sides and Cottrell to Browne's squad area. It was finally happening. I was giving orders in a combat situation and my men were following me. As if to punctuate the reality of the scenario, a couple of mortar rounds landed close enough so that I heard the whirring sound from their fins. I had heard in WWII that the ones you hear won't hurt you. A comforting thought. We paid them little mind.

Sergeant Browne had his men ready. As instructed, they collected digging tools from the Company CP and proceeded down the slope towards a dip in the terrain between us and Uncle. A smoke screen spread across the valley hiding Browne's men from the Chinese.

From the MLR I watched their progress through field glasses. One of the men carried the field phone hooked to the roll of commo wire.

Lieutenant Pierce came to watch with me. They were as much

his men as mine. He had known them longer, knew them better and was more attached to them.

"Good job, Chamberlin," he said as he patted me on the shoulder. "Good timing."

"Thanks," I replied. "Maybe I should've gone with them."

"No," he reassured me. "You did the right thing."

Mortar rounds landed not far from Browne's men.

"Those fucking Chinks aren't so dumb," I remarked. "They know we're moving men out to Uncle."

"Yeah," agreed Pierce. "But they can't see them. That's better than being wide open."

More mortars hit the knoll a few yards to the left of Uncle in a saturation pattern. Browne's squad moved swiftly onto Uncle. Mortar rounds followed them, as though drawn by human scent. They found cover in bunkers and foxholes already there and stayed low. The shelling stopped and Cottrell and I went back to our CP to stay in touch by phone.

Later Browne called. "We're getting the hell shelled out of us out here. Coplin has already been hit. He's bleeding badly. He needs medical attention. We need a stretcher for him. We can't do anything out here. As soon as we start digging they throw shit at us. They can look right down our throats from the high ground on both sides of us."

"Okay Bob, I'll see if I can get some more smoke out there and send some help with a stretcher," I told him.

"I might as well send Charles back too," Bob continued. He cracked up and I can't do anything with him."

I had Harry call the Company CP for the needed help for Bob and his men. I was to learn later, that the rescue squad was led by none other than Bob's brother Bill who I had not met yet. They hurried Eddy Coplin on back to the Battalion Aid Station with a badly wounded arm.

I tried to talk to Charles Hale, a casualty of a different sort. It was no use. He had lost all contact with reality. All he wanted was to go home to his mother. Probably that's what happened to him. I wondered how many men crack up under fire for that reason. I remembered how General Patton had slapped that young lad suffering from battle fatigue in Italy, during WWII. I did not think that was the answer. Later Bob told me he had slapped Charles. It had done no good. I wondered if I would ever crack up.

Towards evening a mortar round cut the commo wire between Browne's squad and my CP. Moroney had ordered me to have my men stay on Uncle all night and get those machine-gun emplacements dug at all costs. We had to have communications.

"Want me to find the break?" Cottrell asked me.

"Can you?" I asked.

"I'll try," he offered.

I saw Cottrell in a new light. It is not common in the Army to volunteer for anything, much less a dangerous job.

"I'll get some smoke out there to cover you," I said.

I watched from the MLR as Cottrell moved down the trail towards Uncle. He lifted the wire hand over hand searching for the break. Smoke landed out in front of him but there was not enough of it and the wind blew it away. But Cottrell continued on his mission. He was all alone. He could be seen by the enemy. A mortar round landed near him. He ducked a little but kept going. It was my first look at real courage on the battlefield. I was proud of him. I felt a need to protect him, a need akin to the need of a father to protect his son. To hell with what Moroney and Pierce had advised me to do. I moved swiftly down the slope to be near him.

Chapter XXXVI

It did not take me long to get within a few yards of Cottrell. I stopped before I got too close to him so as not to make a bigger target. Probably the enemy had seen me come down the forward slope into no man's land. They lobbed a few mortar rounds in our direction. They landed mostly between us and the MLR. I dropped to my knees to lower my silhouette. Cottrell found the break and spliced the wires. We were now closer to Uncle than to the MLR. It seemed safer to run for Uncle than to return to the MLR. I hollered to Cottrell to make a dash for Uncle. When I saw that he had made it, I jumped up and sprinted to the top of Uncle and eased myself into a bunker occupied by Browne and most of his squad. Mortars and direct-fire weapons pounded the position. But the bunker we were in had overhead cover of logs and sandbags. So we were relatively safe except from a direct hit. The Chinese seemed to know exactly where we were and what we were up to.

"Here, Lieutenant," said Browne. "Take my place and let me sit next to the entrance. I've got an armored vest on and you haven't."

"No, that's all right," I replied. "Stay where you are."

"But you might get hit by shrapnel," Browne argued.

Before I could continue the discussion, an attention-commanding voice came from outside. "I think I see the bastards."

I looked out and saw Private first class, Jack Neathery lying on his belly on the crest of the hill, peering through field glasses towards Eerie. His right arm was bare. I later learned he had torn off the sleeve of his fatigue jacket to use as a tourniquet for Coplin's wounded arm. His blond, rumpled hair stood out vividly as he laid his steel helmet aside to prevent it from deflecting the magnetic needle of his compass as he took an azimuth reading. His sky-blue eyes sparkled with excitement as he shouted an azimuth and calculated range to an enemy weapon. I watched, listened and learned as Browne relayed the firing data to the artillery observer at the Company CP. Within seconds an artillery round was on the way. It fell short and to the right.

"Up 200, left 100," ordered Neathery.

Another round landed. This one was too far and still to the right.

"Down 100, left 50," Neathery was bracketing in the enemy position.

I was fascinated. I had learned this stuff in training, but seeing it in action was a hell of a lot different than reading it in a manual. I stuck my head out to watch the friendly fire move in on the enemy. An unfriendly round exploded a few feet in front of our bunker. I flinched. Neathery did not bat an eye.

"Up 50, right 25. Okay, let 'em have it," Neathery ordered.

In a few seconds several rounds of artillery exploded in a cluster on the side of Eerie.

Neathery stayed outside the bunker and continued to scan the hills to the north for puffs of smoke, evidence of enemy weapons.

"Jack is the best fucking combat man I ever saw," Browne told me. "He ought to get a medal for what he's done today."

"Put him in for one," I said. "I'll recommend him for whatever you say when we get back."

"Vincent is another one," Browne continued. "He saved Eddie's life. Tony gave him first aid when shells were landing all around them. He would have bled to death if it hadn't been for Tony."

"Put them both in," I said. "Sounds like they deserve it."

Tony Vincent was the medic assigned to my platoon, I barely knew him before our trip to Uncle. Nor had I known much about Neathery.

At dusk, hostile mortar rounds started pounding Uncle. Neathery had not been able to spot the enemy mortar positions. They could fire at us from behind the hills out of our sight. No way could the men dig during such a barrage.

"Those bastards know we're here," Browne said. "They'll hit us with a patrol tonight."

"Think we can hold them off?" I asked him. I thought he

would know better than I would. He had been in Korea much longer than I had. I did not think rank mattered much in a situation like this. I was not too proud to ask for advice from battle-hardened veterans of lesser rank than mine.

"I don't know," Browne replied. "Two casualties already. I've got six men left. At the rate they're shelling us, we won't last long."

Browne's count did not include Cottrell and me but I did not say anything about that. Pride is a poor protector.

"What do you think we should do?" I asked.

"I think we ought to get the hell out of here before it's too late," Browne stated with a voice of experience. "They're on top of you before you know it."

"Get the CP for me, Harry," I ordered.

Moroney answered.

"We're getting the hell shelled out of us, Mike," I told him. "Browne thinks we ought to pull out before they hit us with a patrol."

"I know you're getting hit," Moroney replied. "But Battalion says we've got to get some gun positions dug out there. You can't pull out."

"Well, we can't dig while they're throwing shit at us, or listening for a patrol," I informed him loud and clear.

"You want to talk to Battalion?" Moroney offered.

"I don't give a shit who I talk to," I said. "I'll talk to the fucking general if you want me to. I don't want my men getting killed out here for nothing."

"Okay, I'll get Battalion for you," Moroney answered.

Major Moore, the battalion operations officer (S3), answered. I told him basically what I had told Moroney. This was more than Moore could manage. He put Colonel Spottswood on the phone.

"What's the problem, Chamberlin?" Spottswood asked.

"We're getting a lot of hostile fire and think we'll be hit by a patrol soon," I told him. "We want permission to get the hell out of here."

"Chamberlin, I can't tell you why, but it's critical that we get those positions dug out there," he informed me.

"Well, dead men can't dig," I shot back. "What the hell are we, a suicide squad? I did not think American forces used those tactics."

A short silence sounded over the wire.

Spottswood broke it, "Chamberlin, can you pull back to the knoll behind you until the shelling lets up, and then go back and dig those positions?"

"We can try, sir," I said. "That's better than getting killed here now."

"That took guts, talking to the battalion commander like that," Browne commended me.

"Not really," I replied. I knew it did not compare to the courage of Neathery and Vincent.

"Who knows how to get back to the left knoll?" I asked. It was pitch dark and I did not trust my sense of direction.

"I do," volunteered Neathery. "I was out here with the First Cavalry."

"Okay, you lead," I ordered. "Bob, have your men follow Jack. I'll bring up the rear." I wanted to be sure they all made it.

We wormed our way slowly and silently westward, towards the knoll to our left. The footing was treacherous. A slight drizzle had turned the sandy soil into a slippery goo. But we made it. We found cover in a bunker large enough to hold us all. I could not see how big it was, nor what was inside. Were there rats, spiders, or even snakes? Maybe dead bodies? I had heard there were no snakes in Korea, that the natives ate them all in their *kimchi*. But I don't know if that is true. Getting under cover and hiding from the enemy was more important than the fear of the unknown. We communicated by touch and low whispers. No one dared to strike a match or light a cigarette.

Cottrell had carefully carried the phone along with us. Moroney called. He said there had been a change of plans. We did not have to go back to Uncle.

In the damp darkness of our hiding place I leaned back against a sandbagged wall. I felt a hand on my thigh. I spread my legs gently so as not to hurt anyone. Someone squeezed in between my legs and leaned back against my chest. He smelled of sweat but he was warm. His body heat felt good. There was no place to put my arms except around him.

"What's your name?" I whispered.

"Bowman, Mason Bowman," he answered in a soft southern drawl.

"Try to get some rest, Mason," I advised him.

I thought Bowman was the short soldier from Louisiana who carried a BAR (Browning Automatic Rifle), which was almost as long as he was tall. The men called him Frenchy.

As we rested and gained comfort and warmth from our closeness, the bond between me and my men grew. It seemed only natural that I would hold one of them in my arms.

Chapter XXXVII

I did not know it then, but learned later that we had been ordered to prepare machine gun, mortar and recoilless rifle positions on Uncle to support the taking of Eerie. Eerie was the last Chinese outpost that General Ruffner wanted taken in his operation, "Counter".

We were called back to the MLR before dawn of June 14. I discovered I had lost one of my daggers. The zippers on my boots had given out. They were now useless. Fortunately the supply sergeant had a pair that fit me. They were split leather with the two-buckled top parts – the kind you could not shine. I also learned that my remaining dagger fit nicely in a carbine bayonet scabbard. So I got another scabbard from supply and added it to my cartridge belt on my left hip opposite the bayonet scabbard on my right hip. I tied this one down with a leather thong to my left thigh. If nothing else, I looked gung ho.

After morning chow, all hell broke loose out on Eerie. Mortars, 87-mm recoilless rifles and machine guns commenced fire on Eerie. Heavier mortars and artillery from further back opened fire also on Eerie and the trenches behind it. Low-flying, fast jets swooped in and pounded the hill with rockets and bombs. A lone spotter plane hovered high above the hill to direct the deadly fire. Slower flying, propeller-driven planes of WWII vintage stirred up trails of dust across Eerie with their 0.50-caliber machine guns and 20-mm cannons. In the afternoon the flyboys made it even hotter by blanketing Eerie and the trenches leading to it with napalm. I watched and wondered how anyone could survive such a bombardment.

Big brass – majors, colonels and generals – with their aides tagging along obediently, wandered around the MLR. Most of them had binoculars and expensive-looking cameras. They seemed to be looking for the best spot to take pictures of the fireworks out front. *Probably they'll take these shots home to show their friends and families and brag about the action they were in*, I thought.

A half-track with quad-fifties lumbered up to a position close to me. The gunner fired a few bursts at Eerie. I spotted a bunch of Chinese, moving down the long trench towards Eerie, from the higher ridge to the north. I saw a phone on the back of the half-track. I used it to give a firing order to the gunner. His fire raised a cloud of dust in an elliptical pattern where the Chinese had been. I didn't see them anymore. I wondered if we got them. If we did, it was probably the first time I had ever been directly involved in killing enemy soldiers. In WWII we were always on the move. When we did set up to fire our machine gun it was usually indirect fire. We could not see what we were firing at. It is doubtful if I ever killed anybody in WWII. I had no particular feeling about whether I had helped kill some Chinese or not.

At 1600 hours, a company of American soldiers moved out across no man's land towards Eerie. Despite the heavy bombardment and napalm burning, the enemy welcomed them with withering fire and rose from their foxholes to meet them in hand-to-hand struggle for the hill.

Lieutenant Moroney called on the phone. "Al, get your men ready to move out. E Company is having a lot of trouble out there. We may have to reinforce them."

"Okay Mike. What should we take with us?" I asked.

"One K ration per man and all the ammo they can carry," he told me. "I'm sending some K rations over to your CP now. Stay on the phone for further orders."

Questions entered my mind. Which way would we go? Straight out across the valley floor in front of them, or back around the hill to the left? What would the men do with the rest of their stuff? Should I call a meeting?

"Jim," I addressed Sergeant Sides, "we may have to move out."

"Move out!" Sides cried in instant panic. "How can we move out? The men are not ready. Where are we going?"

Sides' panic had a strange effect on me, a combination of anger and calm.

"Don't get your piss hot, Jim," I said slowly. "Harry, get the squad leaders on the phone for a conference call."

The squad leaders reported: "Crimmins, First Squad; Browne, Second Squad; McAfee, Third Squad: Jackson, Weapons Squad."

"Men," I said, "we may have to move out. Have your men pack their gear and stand by. K rations are on the way. Send one man from each squad to my CP to get them. One K ration per man and all the ammo they can carry. Have the men pack the rest of their stuff separately. Be sure they have a full canteen of water and salt tablets. It's hotter than hell out there. Stay by the phone for further orders."

I told Sides to man the phone. I went outside to watch the battle for Eerie.

Men rushed up the slope a few yards and then hit the dirt. Others leapfrogged over them. A few turned and ran back. I wondered if they were bugging out. I hated those words. Everybody used them, almost as if it was okay. I thought only cowards bugged out. Being a coward was my greatest fear. Through my field glasses I saw a man's helmet and part of his head lift off from his body. The body sagged to the ground and rolled down the slope a few feet. Then it stopped and stayed still. The dirt near the top end of the body darkened from its blood. The helmet with its load of flesh and bone rolled a little further and bloodied another spot of soil. *Poor bastard*, I thought.

Moroney called again. "Al, have your men get their extra stuff ready to turn in, to supply. Just stay ready, in case we have to move up."

"Okay, Mike," I answered.

I passed the word on to my men and told them to get as much rest as they could.

Corporal Garrett, our mail clerk, brought us mail. There was a letter from Ruby. It was a sweet message and she signed it with all her love. After reading it, I put it in my breast pocket. I did not think of the possibility of its getting back to my wife in case I was killed. I closed my eyes and visualized her beautiful breasts.

I glanced at my right palm. The lifeline still extended down towards my wrist. The words of "Old Lady" Cushion darted through my head. She had told me not to worry. I was not going to be killed in WWII. I hoped her prediction was good for this conflict also. The lifeline looked long enough to reassure me.

The next morning we moved out – not forward, but back behind a hill on our left. There we had a hot breakfast and turned in our extra gear to supply. Then we waited. Rumors flew. We heard E and F Companies had taken Eerie and the cross of T-Bone and had sustained heavy losses. We had another hot meal at midday. Then trucks took us along a dusty road to an assembly point behind a hill that screened us from Eerie.

Lieutenant Pierce met with his officers. Lieutenant Rau was no longer with us. His time in Korea was up. He was now on his way home. Pierce introduced his replacement, Lieutenant George Price, a tall, well-built black man.

"We have to relieve E Company on Eerie," he told us. "We'll move out in this order: First Platoon, Weapons Platoon, Second Platoon and Third Platoon. Jules, your platoon will occupy the trench around the top of the hill and be responsible for a perimeter defense from ten o'clock to two o'clock." Pierce drew a circle on the dusty ground with a stick to symbolize the face of a clock. "The Weapons Platoon will be attached to you and set up in your area. My CP will be with the First Platoon. Al, move your platoon to the right side of Eerie. Your part of the perimeter defense will be from two o'clock to six o'clock. George, your platoon will be responsible for the left side of Eerie from six o'clock to ten o'clock. We move out at 1400 hours. I'll be with the First Platoon. Mike, you'd better stay with the Weapons Platoon. I'll see you on Eerie."

I returned to my platoon and assigned the order in which we would move out: First Squad, machine guns, Second Squad and Third Squad. I told them I would be behind the First Squad.

As Lieutenant Buckhuyt's platoon and the Weapons Platoon moved out across the valley towards Eerie, my men waited behind the hill. I positioned myself where I could keep my eyes on them and watch for the signal to move up. This was our last safe spot. Around the bend in the road ahead, the hill would no longer shield us from the enemy's sight. It would not protect us from hostile fire. Some of my men were seasoned combat veterans; some were raw replacements. They were all scared, except maybe Jack Neathery and Melnie Dawes. Dawes was an Indian boy from Kansas. Indians didn't seem to show fear. Maybe they were taught to be brave. I did not know. I had heard everybody was scared in combat. I knew I was. But I was afraid to show it. I did not want my men to think it was okay to be a coward or bug out.

From up ahead a jeep came around the curve. A Catholic chaplain dismounted and asked my men if they would like him to say mass for them. Most of my men were grateful for this. They might die soon. Perhaps this was sort of the last rites, a sure ticket to heaven. I did not know. The short, chubby chaplain performed an elaborate ritual.

Unfortunately, the spot selected for the ceremony was on the narrow road. No vehicle could pass while the chaplain continued to try to save souls. I could not have cared less about that except that a convoy of several jeeps came around the bend. They were coming from the battle area and were loaded with stretchers bearing wounded men.

They stopped, blocked by the religious ritual. The rear ones were still unprotected by the hill. I looked at the chaplain and my men kneeling in prayer. They were still healthy and whole. *They will surely give way for the wounded and dying*, I thought. But they did not move. The chaplain continued his Latin mumbo-jumbo and moved his hands in the sign of the cross. For a few minutes, which seemed like an eternity he kept up his religious foolishness. Mortar rounds landed near the rear jeeps as if to punctuate his pronouncements. Perhaps the priest thought he was saving the wounded men from hell too, if they were to die. I was not sure what to do – tell him to get the hell out of the way and let the jeeps pass, or keep quiet. He was a captain and I was only a second lieutenant.

Suddenly I had to urinate. I decided to let nature take its course. I moved a little off the road, turned my back for the sake of modesty and relieved myself. I wondered if the chaplain would consider it sacrilegious that I pissed while my men prayed. *Tough shit*, I thought, *if he did*. I had no fucking concern for how he felt.

The signal to move up was passed back. The priest finished his crosses and rode away in his jeep. I moved back towards my men. They rose from their knees.

"Okay men, let's go," I ordered softly. "Stay spread out and keep moving."

Following Dawes, the point man, we rounded the bend and moved out in the direction of danger.

Chapter XXXVIII

As soon as we were in their sight, the Chinese lofted some mortar rounds at us. They buzzed as they landed close. I'd heard that those you hear won't hurt you. But they scared the shit out of us. We hit the ground. *This is a hell of a place to die*, I thought. I rose to one knee to survey things. We couldn't survive here, I figured. Eerie was not that far away. If we move fast we might make it, I calculated.

"Come on," I hollered over the din of the exploding rounds. "Let's go. On your fucking feet. Move."

Dawes, Neathery and Browne responded to my command. The rest remained prone. Browne prodded his squad to their feet. Neathery shouted encouragement. Dawes moved silently forward. I moved back among my men and nudged them with my boots and rifle butt. I made sure everybody was up and moving towards Eerie.

"Stay low and move out fast," I ordered.

All of my men had on heavy armored vests. They were also carrying burdens of ammo and weapons. I had not felt comfortable wearing the heavy vest, so had chosen not to weigh myself down with one. I could move faster without it.

I was scared like everybody else when the first rounds hit near us. But something happened to me when I saw my men hugging the ground, immobilized by fear. Suddenly my mind seemed to function more clearly. I was cognizant of everything around me. I felt stronger and quicker. Fear produced adrenaline. Adrenaline gives one the power to fight or flee. In this case, we were fleeing to the cover and protection of Eerie, for when we got there we would be out of sight of the enemy gunners.

The safety of my men became paramount to me. Up and down the line I moved and urged them forward. They responded to my orders and followed Dawes swiftly towards Eerie. Luckily, we all made it. We moved up the rear slope and around to the right side. Shell holes reminded us of the battles for this small piece of land. Did they also warn of the battles to come?

"Dig in as soon as you get into position," I told my men.

I chose a spot at the back of the Second Squad and towards the top of the hill for my CP. I told Cottrell to string wire to each squad so we would have phone communications. Then I went to the First Squad and made sure they had made contact with the First Platoon at ten o'clock. From there I moved down the line through the Second and Third Squads. I wanted to see if all my men were okay, that they were where they were supposed to be and to make contact with the Third Platoon at six o'clock. All of my men were in position, but I could not locate the Third Platoon.

As I rounded the curve of the south side of Eerie, I saw a still body lying face down on the ground. Long, black hair covered his bare head. There were no visible signs of wounds. I touched him. He was stiff and cold. A closer look revealed he was Chinese. Probably an officer because of his long hair. I looked around the battlefield, both for members of the Third Platoon and anyone else. I was alone with the dead foe. It was an eerie feeling. Suddenly I felt lonely and insecure. I needed to get back to my men and get dug in before dark. It was not my fault if the Third Platoon was not where it was supposed to be.

I hurried back to my CP. I called Moroney and told him my men were in position, but I had not been able to link up with the Third Platoon. He told me not to worry about it. They probably had not got out there yet.

I was a little disturbed with myself about my reaction to the dead Chink. Why hadn't I searched him for papers, maps and stuff? But I did not dwell on it.

I went over to check on Sergeants Sides and Amos. They were well dug in and had plenty of ammo, including a whole crate of grenades. I noted that Sides seemed to be functioning okay now. Since his moment of panic the day before, he had been quiet and followed orders. However, he had not done much leading, as you would expect a platoon sergeant to do. Browne and Neathery had appeared to be the most conspicuous leaders so far.

Cottrell had connected us to each squad and the Company CP

while I had been gone. Now we started digging a two-man foxhole for ourselves. It was easy digging in the sandy soil with our entrenching tools. By dark we had a hole deep enough so that our heads were below ground level if we sat or squatted. I figured that was deep enough. I wanted to be able to get out of it if I had to and I didn't want it to be so deep we could be buried in it. So we rested.

"Harry," I addressed my foxhole buddy. "You did a good job getting the phones hooked up. You're a good man."

"Thank you, sir," he replied.

"Let's have a bite to eat," I suggested.

So we ate our K ration, assuming food would be brought out the next day if we had to stay out there that long.

Darkness and silence settled over Eerie. Harry and I huddled in our foxhole, glad that we were not alone. We kept our eyes peeled for any sign of movement and our ears open for the sounds of an approaching enemy. The darkness was both a shield and a danger.

Suddenly all hell broke loose. Hostile hardware poured down upon us. Mortars, artillery, machine guns, recoilless rifles – everything opened fire on Eerie and T-Bone just north of us. I felt the earth shake. Dirt, debris and shrapnel filled the air around us. Some of it inevitably landed in our foxhole and on us. Harry and I huddled together as close to the bottom of our foxhole as we could get. I expect many of my men prayed to their God not to be hit. I hoped they would also protect their weapons and ammo and be ready to defend their positions when the enemy assaulted us. I did not pray to any God. I did not become a foxhole Christian. How could I believe in a God who was supposed to be omnipotent, omniscient and merciful and let men be so brutal to one another? But I did hope after each close strike that this would be the last one. Maybe you could call that praying. However, I was just hoping the Chinese would stop shelling us, not that God would stop them or protect me.

There was no doubt in my mind that the Chinese intended to take back the real estate they had lost. I wished they would hurry up and come. For I figured that when the assault began, the artillery barrage would let up or move to our rear. I felt an assault from foot soldiers was less dangerous than the artillery barrage. What good was my carbine, dagger, bayonet and grenades against flying shrapnel? Against an enemy infantryman, I could use my weapons and stand a fighting chance.

After an extremely close strike I felt for Cottrell, "You all right?" I asked.

"I'm okay," he whispered.

Suddenly he started to climb out of our foxhole.

I grabbed him and demanded, "Where do you think you're going?"

"I have to urinate," he explained.

"Well, stay in our foxhole while they are shelling us," I ordered. "Piss in the foxhole if you have to."

"I can't do that," he replied. "That's not right."

"You don't have to be modest around me," I told him. Fumbling in the dark I found an empty ration can and gave it to him. "Here. Piss in this and dump it outside. Then give it back to me. I have to piss too."

Pissing in the same can in the closeness of our foxhole did not make me think less of Cottrell. We had been warned in ROTC classes not to fraternize with enlisted men for it would breed contempt. I hoped this was not the case with Cottrell and me. How could I help but fraternize with him in our little hole? I certainly did not want to be in a foxhole alone. I was glad he was with me.

The shelling slowed a little. I stood up in our foxhole. I wanted to be able to see what was happening if or when the Chinks came back to claim Eerie. I heard a lot of small-arms fire from the top of the hill and sounds of small explosions, probably from grenades. *They're coming*, I thought.

I think Jack Neathery saw them first. He was the first to alert us.

"They're coming this way," he hollered. "Yell at the yellow bastards, men. Holler '*dunee*' at them. That means 'fuck you' in Chinese. It scares the shit out of 'em!"

I saw Bob Browne rise to his full height in his foxhole. His thunderous voice challenged the enemy and encouraged his men to action. "You dirty, little yellow bastards, come on up and tangle assholes with some real men. I'll cut your damned hearts out with my bayonet. *Dunee, dunee!*"

I joined in with my men. "Give 'em hell men. Kill the fucking little bastards. Show 'em how we can fight. *Dunee, dunee!*"

Somehow the hollering and cursing was inspiring and contagious. All of my men joined in except Sergeants Sides and Amos. It seemed to lessen our fear and increase our courage.

Suddenly, I saw some men from the top of the hill run down the slope through my platoon area. A couple of my men joined them. Was my worst fear coming true? Were they bugging out?

A loud, excited voice came from the First Platoon area. "They're breaking through up here! Al, bring your men up here!"

It sounded like Moroney. I didn't give a shit who it was. I didn't want my men making targets of themselves by running around in the open. Besides, they were busy fighting off the Chinks coming up our side of Eerie. So I ignored the order from above.

"Stay in your foxholes, men," I shouted. "Fight from your positions. You have the advantage. You can see the enemy but he can't see you?"

By now friendly artillery had flares in the air over the approaching foes. They lit the battlefield underneath them as they parachuted slowly to earth. Outside our perimeter of defense the enemy lost their protective cover of darkness.

Private first class Calvin Knox and Sergeant Bill West, Bob Browne's assistant squad leader, were the men who had seemingly bugged out with the men from the top of the hill. But they were not bugging out. I watched from my CP as they intercepted the crazed men.

Knox was new in our outfit and had already gained the reputation of being a loudmouth. He was not well liked. Now he put his loud mouth into action. "What the fuck do you think you're doing?" he shouted. "You stupid bastards, you're running right into their artillery. Get your fucking asses back up the hill and defend your fucking positions."

The men turned and did as Knox told them.

Apparently, some Chinks had broken through the First platoon area on top of the hill. A phone call from my First Squad reported that Melnie Dawes and Sergeant Crimmins had been wounded by grenades thrown into their foxholes by Chinks, who had penetrated the trench around the top of Eerie. They had been evacuated to a first aid station somewhere near the Company CP. By now the Chinks had been driven out of the First Platoon area. But they were now coming up the east slope of Eerie towards my platoon.

"We need grenades," Sergeant Webster said. He was now squad leader by virtue of Crimmins becoming a battle casualty. "We're all out of grenades and most of our weapons don't work. The Chinks are moving up on us."

"Tell him grenades are on their way," I told Cottrell. "Amos, take some grenades to the First Squad," I hollered to Sergeant Amos, whose foxhole was within shouting distance.

I watched Amos leave his foxhole with a crate of grenades. But the damned fool went in the wrong direction. He headed around the curve of the hill and towards the top of the hill, so as not to expose himself to small-arms fire from the enemy approaching from below our positions. I had expected him to go straight towards the First Squad. *Stupid bastard, he'll never get there in time*, I thought. His circuitous route was much longer and more difficult than a straight one.

Adrenaline was flowing through my veins. I was mad as hell. I loaded my pockets and hands with grenades from our foxhole and ran across the open area in a beeline for the First Squad. Now that the artillery was not shelling us, the small-arms fire from the assaulting troops seemed like nothing. I paid it no mind.

I got there just in time. The few men left in the First Squad awaited the foe with fixed bayonets. I handed my grenades to them gently.

"Up here," hollered Amos from the trench above, "I've got more grenades up here."

Amos had finally reached the top of the hill at the back of the First Squad. But I could tell that he had no intentions of exposing himself by bringing them to the men who needed them.

I moved a little closer to Amos and stood tall to make a good target. Flares lighted up the battlefield as brightly as a night game at Yankee Stadium.

"Toss 'em down to me one at a time," I ordered. "I'll catch them."

Like a second baseman in the middle of a double play, I caught the grenades from Amos and passed them on to the men in the foxholes without an error. I must give Amos credit for making accurate tosses to me. The First Squad held their ground, as did the rest of my platoon. I was proud of them.

The battle dwindled. I went over to a foxhole in the First Platoon area. A young lad was there alone. A BAR lay on the rim of the hole. I fired it at a back flash, from an enemy recoilless rifle. The hot barrel burned my hand. The lad explained to me how to hold it. We worked as a team for a few minutes. He loaded clips and I fired at retreating Chinks.

"Are you scared?" I asked the young soldier.

"I was," he replied. "But I'm not now with you here."

"You're doing a good job," I told him. "You'll be okay. We've got 'em licked now."

I put my arm around his shoulder in a paternal gesture of approval. At the age of twenty-seven, I felt like a father to these brave youngsters. I had another young man from my platoon move into the foxhole with him.

I walked the line of my platoon. Corporal Jackson was trying to get a machine gun to fire. I tried to help by adjusting the head space, the distance between the rear of the barrel and the face of the bolt at the time of firing. I knew how to do it by tightening the barrel all the way and then loosening it a couple of clicks. But we could not get the gun to work. I left Jackson and his assistant gunner, Private first class Walter Johnson, to continue to work on it. I patted them on their backs for their courage.

The Second and Third Squads were weary, but they were okay. I praised all my men for their determined defense. My men were quiet now. I told them to take care of their weapons and ammo and rest as much as possible.

I returned to my CP. Miraculously, the phone lines between my CP and all my squads and the Company CP were still intact.

On the phone I heard Lieutenant Buckhuyt say with a weak voice, "I've been hit bad. I need help." I learned later that his leg had been blown off and he bled to death.

Lieutenant Moroney called and told me Lieutenant Pierce had gone to help Buckhuyt and was now missing.

Tired and hungry, but proud and happy that we had held our position, I slumped down in the bottom of our foxhole with Cottrell and tried to rest.

Chapter XXXIX

As dawn descended upon Eerie, Moroney told me by phone, Lieutenant Buckhuyt had died, Lieutenant Pierce was still missing and Lieutenant Price had been wounded and evacuated. He also said I Company had been overrun. Their company commander had called friendly artillery in on their positions. It was not now known who held the cross of T-Bone. I also learned Melnie Dawes had been killed by a direct hit from a mortar round, as he lay on a stretcher at the Company Aid Station. And that Sergeant Crimmins had been evacuated.

"How are you and your men doing?" Moroney asked.

"Not too bad, I guess," I replied. "The First Squad lost a few men. We don't have much ammo left and most of our weapons don't work. My men are tired and hungry. We don't have much water, but other than that we're okay."

"You and I are the only officers left," he said. "Have your men ready for whatever happens. Maybe we'll be relieved today."

"I hope so," I replied.

We rested for a short while. As I half dozed, I thought of the night and how my men had done. Neathery had been great in inspiring the men to action. Browne had been a fierce fighter. Knox had surprised everyone with his battle savvy. Amos had been a coward. Sides had shown neither leadership nor courage. I would miss Dawes. He had been a brave man. But courage could not always win in combat.

Soon Moroney was on the phone again. "Al, we've got to go out and retake I Company's positions. You're the only platoon leader I have left. Get your men ready to go. Leave the machine guns here. Assemble your men behind my CP as soon as you can."

"Okay, Mike." What else could I say?

I wondered if the Second Platoon would have to go alone.

I called my squads. Browne's squad seemed the most ready to

go. I told them where to assemble, what we had to do and that the Second Squad would lead the assault.

When we were gathered, more orders came from Moroney. "When you get into the trenches just keep going as far as you can. Move out as quick as possible."

Sergeant Browne loomed above me. "How come my squad gets all the shit?" he demanded. "It's not our turn to lead."

I looked up into his mean-looking face, a face that would make weak men shiver with fright, and even cause a bold man to step back a little. He scowled down at me. Before last night's action, his ugly mood would have scared me. But not today. I knew what I had to do, something I could not ask any of my men to do unless I were willing to do it myself.

"Bob," I spoke to him softly so only he could hear. "Your squad will be in the lead because you're in the best shape. But you will be behind me."

"Sorry, sir," Bob replied quietly.

I think he knew that lieutenants did not usually act as point men in assaults. He lowered his eyes and returned to his men.

"Sides, take a position between the Second Squad and the Weapons Squad. The Third Squad will follow the Weapons Squad and the First Squad will bring up the rear. Let's move out," I ordered.

"Lieutenant," Sides cried in instant panic. "I can't go out there! My rifle is jammed."

"Fix your fucking bayonet and take your position," I snapped. "Be ready to take over if anything happens to me. Amos, you bring up the rear."

I knew that Sides was not capable of commanding a platoon in combat, but I also knew Browne, Neathery or some other brave soldier would take over if necessary. Leadership in combat did not depend upon rank. I had learned that the night before.

I moved close to Browne again and asked in a low voice, "How do you think we should do this, Bob?"

"I think we ought to move out in a skirmish line, sir. That way we would be less vulnerable to machine-gun fire."

Good thinking, I thought. I remembered that machine-gun fire hits the ground in an elliptical pattern. So Bob was right. A machine gun could rip hell out of a column of men, whereas a skirmish line would pose a wider target.

"Okay, Bob," I agreed. "When we get to the bottom of the hill we'll form a skirmish line to the left." I did not have to tell the rest of my men. I would use a hand signal when the time came. For now I gave the signal to move out in single file.

"Follow me, Bob," I said, as I moved down the forward slope of Eerie, towards the valley floor in front of the cross of T-Bone.

As decided, when I got to the bottom of the hill I signaled my men to form a skirmish line. I saw the rest of L Company following my platoon. I felt better that they were with us. Lieutenant Moroney signaled us to hold up. Then he sent the whole company into a long skirmish line.

When all the men were in position we moved across the valley floor and up the western slope of the cross of the T-Bone. My end of the skirmish line moved faster than the others. I reached the top of the slope first, followed closely by Bob, Jack and the rest of my platoon. The trench was on my right. I leaped into it with my bayonet-tipped carbine held at high port.

No foe was in sight. The remains of the shot-up I Company were scattered along the trench. A few were whole. Many were wounded. Most of them were dead.

I did not hesitate long. I could have turned south towards friendly forces. But Moroney had said to go as far as we could, so I turned north towards the enemy. My men followed me bravely. We passed several cave-like holes leading off from the main trench. Weak voices from within them could be heard. I could not tell if they were Chinese or American. If they were Chinks I wondered if they could cut us off. I stopped.

"Maybe we'd better not go any farther," I told Browne and Neathery, when they came up to me.

"You're right," agreed Neathery. "There's Chinks in those holes. I could tell when I heard 'em talking."

"We may have to blast the bastards out with grenades," Browne said.

I thought about trying to get them to come out of their holes. But how could we do that without exposing ourselves in front of their holes? That could be dangerous. We could not see them but they could see us. They might have some ammo left. And if we took prisoners, what in hell would we do with them? Somebody would have to guard them. My men had enough to do already. They needed rest, not to have to watch prisoners. We had no food, water or medical supplies.

"Okay, men, blast 'em out," I ordered.

But even after my order, Browne and Neathery tried to coax them out. But none came out. We could hear them crying and moaning in pain and peril. They screamed with greater pain when Browne and Neathery tossed grenades in amongst them. Browne and Neathery laughed with pleasure at the muffled explosions.

My men huddled and waited in the trenches. If any of them had any water, it was soon gone. It was hotter than hell. We heard we were going to be relieved. I hoped it would be soon.

I saw a wounded Chink in a shell hole about fifty yards west of the trench. He tried to raise himself up. He appeared to be in pain. I watched him for a few minutes. I thought, *why should he suffer?* I took careful aim with my carbine and shot him. He moved no more.

I looked at the trench south of us. Many men lay dead along the bottom. Outside the trench the bloody stump of a leg stuck out of the dirt like a post. It appeared too large to be Chinese.

There were no signs of any officers from I Company. A black corporal seemed to be in charge.

Wounded men were piled together. I wondered why. Was it for warmth? I had heard that when men lose a lot of blood they go into shock and feel cold even in hot weather. One man's head was a ball of bloody bandages. A large young lad had a hole in his thigh as big as a grapefruit. The hot sun beat down on it. Flies were crawling over it. The man with the head wound cried out in pain whenever a member of the pile moved. The medics were out of medicine and painkillers. They had no plasma or bandages left. They were helpless. One medic wept; another slept. What else could they do?

The lad with the hole in his leg called to me, "Hey, Mac, can you give me a hand?"

"Sure, son. What can I do for you?" I asked.

I moved closer to him. He said, "I have to urinate. Can you

help me up?"

I tried to help him to his feet. The man with the head wound screamed in pain. It was no use. I couldn't help one man without hurting the other. After many futile attempts, I gave up.

"Sorry," I said. "I can't help you without hurting your buddy. Why don't you let it go where you are?"

"I can't do that," he replied.

"Well, damn it, there's nothing I can do," I said helplessly.

I moved away from my failure. Then I saw a great example of determination and courage. The lad, whom I could not help, slowly disentangled himself from the pile of wounded warriors, painfully rose to his feet, moved a few feet away and urinated in the most modest manner possible.

The day passed slowly. Men from other units made many trips to carry back the wounded and the dead. I heard later that Lieutenant Pierce's best friend, a lieutenant from Headquarters Company, searched the battlefield for many hours looking for Pierce's body in vain. Forty-seven years later, I learned that Pierce's remains were found in August 1952, out in front of Eerie.

A story spread among the troops, after that battle for Eerie, that the assistant division commander, General "Bulldog" Smith, visited the front lines in his helicopter. His whirlybird alit near where Pierce's friend was lining up some dead bodies. He asked the lieutenant to show him some of the fighting men. He said he wanted to talk to them.

The lieutenant took him to the dead soldiers and turned back the blankets from their silent faces. "There are some fighting men, sir. Talk to them," he said.

It was said that the speechless general beat a hasty retreat to his helicopter and flew away.

While we waited for relief on the cross of T-Bone, we witnessed propeller-driven Navy attack planes fly low over Eerie and drop their 500-pound bombs on the position. A few L Company men were left there. There was a question as to whether the nylon markings had been put out to let the Marine pilots know Eerie was now in friendly hands. Fortunately, their bombs were not effective. There were no casualties from the misguided missiles. But they did not boost the morale of the already battle-weary ground troops.

Finally, towards dusk, we were relieved. My platoon was the last to leave and I brought up the rear of my platoon. I wanted to be sure all my men had made it. Sporadic hostile shelling hastened our departure. As I left, a litter team was carrying a large lad on a stretcher. They needed a fourth man, so I helped. Our load was the young soldier who had had to urinate. His head was towards my end of the stretcher.

"Glad you made it, son," I said to him gently.

He turned his head towards me. "So am I," he said. When he saw who I was, he continued, "Thanks for trying to help me."

"That's okay, son," I assured him.

"Sorry I called you 'Mac', sir," he apologized.

Did it dawn on him that I was an officer? I don't know. I did not tell him. I was wearing no insignia.

When we were again behind the hill and safe from hostile fire, I became very weary. I sat down beside the road and rested near the spot where I had pissed while the men had prayed the day before.

Chapter XL

What was left of L Company returned to the rest area where I had joined them. We rested and recuperated from the battle on Eerie. We cleaned up our weapons, equipment and bodies. New weapons and gear were supplied to us as needed. One nice thing about combat was that you did not have to pay for things lost or broken.

I was proud of my men and talked openly about how well they had done under fire. And I encouraged my men to talk about the battle. I put Browne, Neathery and Vincent in for Bronze Stars for their actions on Uncle. From what I had seen of the action on Eerie and from what I was learning from my men, I planned to make more recommendations for medals for some of my men for the action on Eerie.

But before I had time to do that, Moroney sent me to attend a battalion staff meeting. This was a first for me. At the meeting were all the battalion staff officers and representatives from each company, usually the company commander. Also, of course, Colonel Spottswood, the Battalion CO (Commanding Officer) was there. All the staff officers and most of the company officers were dressed in clean, neatly pressed fatigues and well-shined combat boots. They wore their polished brass and insignia of rank.

My fatigues were clean too. I had changed my dirty ones the day before at the field shower, where I had taken my men, for unpressed, ill-fitting ones – the same as my men did. I wore no brass. I had lost it. I had an olive drab, GI towel around my neck because I sweat a lot. It was handy to wipe the salty moisture out of my eyes. My twin bayonet scabbards, one of which was for holding my double-edged dagger, were held down with leather thongs tied around my skinny thighs. I did not yet know that General Ruffner frowned on leather thongs. Not that it would have mattered to me. My carbine's barrel and firing mechanism were encased in the dust flap I had ripped out of a fatigue jacket to keep them free of dust and sand. I found out later this was also against Ruffner's rules. But combat men do not always go by the book on the front lines.

When it was my turn to report about Company L, I was nervous and did not know exactly what was expected of me. I don't remember what I said, but I guess it was okay.

When I was finished, Major Moore complimented me for putting three of my men in for medals. He said medals were a boost to morale and officers should be alert for acts of gallantry. He expected there would be more recommendations for awards after the action on Eerie and T-Bone. He suggested, that any soldier who stood his ground and used his weapon or grenades to fight off the enemy, deserved at least a Bronze Star. It was common knowledge that many men hid from the foe and did not fire their weapons for fear of revealing their positions. Only two of my men fell in that category: Sides and Amos.

When I returned to the company, I called a meeting of my squad leaders. Using Major Moore's criterion, it was decided to put everyone in the Second Platoon in for a medal for the action on Eerie, except Sides and Amos. I decided to recommend Dawes, Browne and Neathery for Silver Stars, the rest for Bronze Stars.

A few days later I asked the company clerk, "How are you coming with the recommendations for medals?"

"I have the ones for Uncle done," he said. "I'm working on the ones for the officers now – Pierce's, Moroney's and yours, sir."

Looking back, I should have told him to work on my men' awards before mine, but I didn't. I was so surprised and pleased that I was being put in for an award that I lost track of my priorities, an error for which no amount of rationalization will ever erase my sense of guilt. So I did not press the issue as I should have.

Moroney asked me to hold classes for the men. This was new to me – teaching combat men about combat. I thought they should be allowed to rest up, write letters and maybe drink a little beer. But I did not argue with him.

"What do you want me to teach them?" I asked.

"Anything you want to," he replied. "Whatever you think they need."

I was surprised at his trust in me. His attitude towards me seemed to have changed since the battle on Eerie.

So I held some classes, and taught them what I knew best and what I thought would help them most in future fights. I showed them flat-blade bayonet, how to use knives and how to protect themselves when unarmed. I told them what I had learned from Neathery – to holler and swear at the enemy. Then in a soft, low voice, I spoke to them about fear, courage and caring for their buddies. I marveled at how the whole company listened to me so attentively, as if I were some sort of authority.

*

Letters had to be written to the relatives of those who died on Eerie. Moroney asked me to write to Lieutenant Buckhuyt's parents. He told me he would write to Lieutenant Pierce's wife. I did not know Lieutenant Buckhuyt well, but I wrote as nice a letter as I could to his mother and father. I also wrote to the parents of Melnie Dawes. I tried to emphasize his courage and camouflage the pain and suffering. That was easy with Dawes. It was harder with Buckhuyt.

I also wrote home to my mother and brother Willard, and to my wife Jo. Our mail was not censored like it was in WWII. So I told them about the battle on Eerie. My mother wrote back telling me to stop "showing off". Willard's lovely wife Becky told me to be careful. They wanted me to come home. For some reason her message touched my heart deeply.

Two new second lieutenants, Eugene Porter and Allen Fanjoy, were assigned to our company. Porter got the Weapons Platoon and Fanjoy the Third Platoon. Lieutenant Price was expected back and would take over the First Platoon when he returned.

I treated the new officers the same as I had been treated when I joined the company a month ago. I was friendly in a condescending way, but did not encourage real closeness. I now knew that true friendship depended upon how you acted when

228

your guts were exposed. They had to prove themselves under fire.

Soon we were sent back to the MLR, this time facing Baldy. The company had been there before I joined them and it moved into familiar positions with no difficulty.

One of the first tasks assigned to me was to send an overlay of our position back to battalion. I was not good at drawing maps, even though we had been trained in this at Fort Benning. I learned that Sergeant Amos was very adept at drawing, so he came to my rescue. I must give him credit. He did a good job for me.

Another assignment, was to take my Second Platoon out into the valley between the MLR and Pork Chop on the right and Baldy on the left, at night. This was another first for me. Fear of the unknown stirred in my guts. This seemed as terrifying as the move to Eerie.

A young lieutenant from S2 (Intelligence) came up to the MLR to brief Moroney and me on our mission. My nervousness and fear were revealed by my many questions, probably dumb ones.

Our task was to set up three listening posts in no man's land between the MLR and the two outposts, Baldy and Pork Chop. One was to be placed between the MLR and Baldy to watch for enemy movement from around Baldy. Another was to be positioned near a gap, between some ridges on the right towards Eerie, to listen for enemy activity from that direction. The third was to be set up farther out near a gap, between a ridge on the right and the foothills of Pork Chop. Apparently, attacks were anticipated on Baldy or Pork Chop.

We set out after dusk in single file. I had the men maintain an interval of two or three yards between them. I told them to move as silently as possible. Browne's squad was to peel off and establish the first listening post towards Baldy. Webster's squad was to set up near the gap looking towards Eerie. McAfee's squad was responsible for the listening post out near Pork Chop.

The moon was bright that night. Patches of clouds moved across the sky and hid the moon sporadically, creating alternating moments of good visibility and darkness. I'm not sure which was worse, not being able to see or being visible. Anyhow, for me at least, the fear of possible danger seemed to lessen with each step we took towards our goal.

It was hard to move silently. Every little sound stood out in the stillness. Cloth rubbing against cloth, metal touching metal, a blade of dry grass or twig cracking, tiny night creatures scurrying in the grass, all disturbed the quiet.

As planned, the Second Squad moved a little to the left and took their position. Cottrell, my trusty radioman, and I stayed with them for a few minutes to be sure they were set. The other two squads moved on out ahead of us.

When we were ready, Cottrell and I followed to check on the other two listening posts. We walked over to the right where the First Squad was supposed to be. There was nobody. We moved farther out in the valley to where the Third Squad was supposed to be. There was nobody there either.

"Where the hell are they?" I mumbled to Cottrell.

"Maybe they went farther," he suggested.

So I led Cottrell on through the gap at the base of Pork Chop. With each step I became angrier, more worried and closer to the enemy.

"Maybe we missed them on the way out," Cottrell offered.

"Okay, let's go back," I agreed.

They must be somewhere, I thought. They couldn't have been ambushed. We had heard no shots. The artillery was silent. No land mines had exploded.

We passed the Third Squad's spot again. There was still no one there. We went on towards the First Squad's area.

Suddenly from the black, sheer side of a hill came a low whisper. "Lieutenant, over here."

Cottrell and I moved quickly into a large, dark cave from whence the whisper came. Inside were all the men of both listening posts.

"What in hell are you doing here?" I demanded.

"We got lost," replied McAfee lamely.

"Are you all here?" I asked. It was too dark to see.

"Yes, sir," Webster spoke up.

In the cave they were safe from any encounter with the enemy. But they could not have spotted any movements of enemy troops towards Baldy or Pork Chop. However, it was more important to me that they were safe than it was to be angry at them. Besides, now was not the time or place to chew anybody out. What good would it have done? Who was really responsible, I or they? Looking back, I had to admit I was. I should've led each squad to its designated spot.

It was now creeping towards dawn. Too late for the enemy to attack. Soon we all returned to the MLR. I told Moroney that our mission had been accomplished.

Chapter XLI

Pork Chop was occupied by a platoon from K Company on the night of June 24 and 25. A fierce firefight took place that night. Chinese forces overran the outpost on Pork Chop. Communications were lost. On the morning of June 25, it was not known who held Pork Chop, friend or foe.

L Company was given the dangerous mission of sending out a reconnaissance and rescue patrol to see who was on the hill and to bring back the wounded and dead. The First Platoon, under the leadership of Lieutenant Price and Sergeant Bill Browne was given this task.

We had just finished a hot meal at the base of the rear slope of the MLR. Bob Browne, Jack Neathery and I watched as the First Platoon moved out across the valley floor in broad daylight.

Bob and Jack had had something to drink that morning. Drinking on the MLR was taboo, but many men did it if they could get anything to drink. I never did, but I realized it was a way for some men to tolerate the hardship and horror of war in the trenches. So I overlooked their indulgence.

We watched Bob's brother, Bill, and his platoon as they moved up the rear slope of Pork Chop. We saw some mortar rounds burst among them. They hit the dirt. We could not tell if any of them were hit. Bob became very upset. I would have been too, if my brother had been out there. The beer, or whatever he had to drink, did not improve his judgment. Maybe it boosted his courage.

"I'm going out there to help Bill," he cried. "He needs me."

"You can't go out there alone," Jack told him. At this point Jack seemed to have more sense than Bob. Maybe he'd had less to drink. Also it wasn't his brother out there.

"Yes I can," bellowed Bob. "And you can't stop me. You're only a damned private first class. You can't tell me what to do."

"Then I'm going with you," Jack said. "You damned fools will get yourselves killed if I don't take care of you."

I think he meant both Bob and Bill. They had all been in the First Cavalry together before transferring to the Forty-fifth. They had bonded long before I knew them. I understood their concern for each other, but we were soldiers. We could not choose and pick our missions. We were obligated to do as we were ordered.

I spoke to them in a low, slow voice, "Bob, Jack, you're not going anywhere. There's nothing you can do."

They stayed there with me. We continued to watch the progress of the men on Pork Chop.

The patrol completed its mission. A few of K Company's men still held the outpost. The patrol brought back the dead and wounded. Lieutenant Price was again among the wounded. He had to be evacuated. Platoon Sergeant Bill Browne, who had been only a squad leader when I joined the company, became the acting platoon leader.

After the noon meal on June 27, my platoon received three new replacements: Carl Fields, John Partin and Jack Tally.

Fields spoke up to me. "Lieutenant, you have to put me and Partin in the same squad. We take care of each other."

Partin reinforced his demand. "I don't think Kentucky – we call him Kentucky – could take care of himself without me to look after him. He's not too bright. Only his mother loves him and I promised her I would look after him." Partin smiled knowingly as he spoke.

Instead of getting angry at being put down, Kentucky agreed with Partin. "With a face like mine, you're lucky if your mother loves you."

Nearby listeners laughed at Kentucky's sense of humor. But I don't think Kentucky was trying to be funny. He was very homely. He had big ears and a small, twisted nose that looked like it might have been broken in fights. Floppy lips covered yellowish-brown, crooked teeth. He was small of stature.

"Why do you let Partin make fun of you, Kentucky?" Browne asked.

"I'm on duty today," Kentucky explained. "It's his day off. I have to do all the work and take his shit all day while he fucks off."

"What do you mean?" Browne asked. "Nobody fucks off all day."

"Maybe I'd better tell you about these two," Tally announced. "All three of us are from Kentucky and took basic training together. Partin and Kentucky have an unwritten agreement. One day one is on duty and has to do the work for both of them and take care of the other one. The next day they switch. The one that's off duty fucks off if he can get away with it. They both drink like hell, but the one on duty never gets drunk. They'd be a lot better off if you can keep them together, sir."

I didn't want new men to think they could drink on the front lines. So I warned them. "You can't drink up here on the MLR."

"They'll drink if they can get their hands on any liquor," Tally said simply.

Before I could press my point, a messenger told me to report to Moroney. So I assigned the replacements quickly. Partin and Kentucky went to Browne's Second Squad and Tally to McAfee's Third Squad.

Moroney told us we had to relieve F Company on Baldy. He decided to place my Second Platoon on the left of Baldy, the Third Platoon in the middle and the First Platoon on the right. We would be moving onto Baldy from the right, so my platoon had the farthest to go. The order of march would be Second, Third and First Platoons. Units of the Weapons Platoon were attached to each rifle platoon. Moroney chose to be with the lead platoon, so he asked me to bring up the rear and join my platoon as soon as they were all out there.

Moroney's orders were simple: go over the top of Baldy and take up positions on the forward slope facing the enemy. If we could not get to the forward slope, we were to dig trenches through the crest of the hill to the forward slope. Whatever happened, we were to be in defensive positions before dark. From there we could see the enemy coming and lessen the element of surprise. For some reason, I seemed to have the same feeling that I had had when we went out to Eerie less than two weeks before. The Chinks would be coming that night.

I didn't like being separated from my men. But orders were orders. I could not expect my men to carry out my orders if I didn't carry out Moroney's orders. I told my men what Moroney expected us to do. I told Sergeant Sides to position the First Squad on the left of our platoon area, the Second Squad in the middle and the Third Squad on the right.

Soon after the company moved out, Browne called me on the radio. "What should I do about White? He refuses to go. He just sat down and started bawling. I slapped him a couple of times and kicked his ass but he still won't go."

We couldn't let one coward hold up the whole company. I made a quick decision, "Leave him there. We can't fuck around with him now."

I did not know much about White. I remembered him as a big, well-built, black man. He had not been on Eerie with us. He had joined the company since then.

When I got to where White was, he was still sitting by the side of the trail. His head was between his knees and his arms covered his face in shame. He was still sobbing and shaking with fear. I did not have time to worry about him. If he was such a coward, we would be better off without him.

When I rejoined my platoon on the left side of Baldy, they were not on the forward slope. Bullets were snapping overhead. Mortar rounds landed on the hill intermittently. Just enough to keep our heads down.

Browne came to me. "That damned Sides has got the men all screwed up," he told me. "He's so damned jumpy, he's got everybody scared shitless. I can't do anything with my men."

"Are any of the men on the forward slope?" I asked.

"Only Jackson with a machine gun," Browne replied. "We could not stay there. Too much incoming sniper fire."

"Is Jackson okay?" I asked.

"I don't know. Things are all screwed up. F Company bugged out before we got here. Nobody knows what the hell they're supposed to do. I think I'm going to crack up too. Just like White." Browne was really wound up.

Somehow Browne's nervous ratings seemed to have a calming effect on me. Maybe the realization that my men needed me helped me to rise to the occasion.

"You're not going to crack up, Bob," I reassured him. "You're a damned good squad leader. Don't worry about Jim. He's close to rotation. That's probably why he's so nervous."

"He's got the First Squad where you wanted the Third Squad," Browne continued to complain.

"Where's the Third Squad?" I asked.

"I don't know," Browne said. "You wanted them on the right, I think they're on the left."

"Where's Harry?" I asked about my radioman.

"The last I saw him, he was with McAfee's squad," Bob said.

"I wanted him over here in the middle where I plan to have my CP," I said.

"I know," Bob agreed. "But he was with McAfee when we started and things were so confused, he just stayed with him. Sides had everybody so confused, nobody knew what to do."

"What the hell difference does it make?" drawled one of Browne's new men who was sitting on the ground nearby smoking a cigarette. "We're all here, ain't we?"

I recognized Kentucky. He continued, "Lieutenant, you want me to go over the top of the hill and take care of Jackson?"

Partin was prone on the ground near us. He spoke up. "You can't leave. You have to dig me a foxhole, you lazy bastard."

"I ain't going to dig no fucking foxhole here," Kentucky argued. "The lieutenant said to dig in on the other side of the hill. I ain't going to dig no hole for nothing."

The conversation between Kentucky and Partin, seemingly serious to them, was humorous enough to me to lighten the gravity of the situation.

"How you guys doing?" I asked.

"I need a drink," Kentucky said. "My canteen's empty. Got anything to drink, sir?"

Figuring he meant water, I offered him my canteen. He took a sniff of the contents and handed it back to me with a wry face.

"Shit, lieutenant, I thought you had some booze," he said. "I thought all officers had booze on 'em to keep up their courage."

"We don't drink on the front lines," Browne said sharply to Kentucky. "The lieutenant doesn't need liquor for courage."

"Neither do I," Kentucky shot back, undaunted by his squad leader's rebuke. "But I sure need a drink when I'm dry."

A mortar round landed close. Browne hit the dirt. I crouched on one knee. Kentucky remained sitting calmly.

As had become a custom in tight spots, I had to go. So I stood up, turned my back, moved a few feet away and took a leak. Kentucky moved down beside me and did the same. I took no offense at this unusual gesture. I rather admired his balls.

Browne looked furious. But before he could jump on Kentucky for his audacity, I put my arm around Kentucky's shoulders and said, "Looks like you got some good men here. They don't seem to be afraid at all."

"What's to be scared of?" Kentucky asked. "Running a still back home is more scary than this."

"What do you want me to do?" Browne asked.

"Make contact with the Third Squad on your left," I ordered. "The squads might as well stay where they are. Dig in enough to protect yourselves and move to the forward slope as soon as it gets dark. My CP will be behind your squad. I'll go over and tell the First Squad."

"I'll go over and contact the Third Squad," volunteered Kentucky. "I want to see if Tally's okay."

"Can I go with him?" Partin asked. "He's so stupid he'd get lost. Besides, I have to start looking after him in a few minutes."

"Let 'em both go, if you can spare them," I told Browne. To Partin, who appeared to be the smarter of the two, I said, "Bring Cottrell, my radioman, back with you."

I went to the First Squad and told Webster what to do. Then I crawled to the crest of the hill and looked for Jackson.

"Where are you, Cecil?" I hollered. "Are you okay?"

Jackson stuck his head out of a hole, "Over here, sir, I'm okay."

I saw where he was. He was only a few yards down the forward slope and in a large foxhole. A tripod left by F Company was perched on a shelf-like ledge of the hole.

"You got the machine gun?" I asked.

"Yes, sir," he replied, "It's here in the hole with me."

"Good," I reassured him. "Keep it clean. We'll be with you as soon as we can."

"I hope so, sir," he said.

I viewed the terrain between us on Baldy and the Chinks to the north on higher ground. A valley of about 300 yards width separated us. A low ridge reached out towards them from us. It seemed like the most likely approach. It was a logical place to station a listening post. It was directly in front of the Second Squad's central position. From there they could hear movement coming along the ridge and on either side of it. I saw that a machine gun in Jackson's position could cover the top and right side of the ridge and the valley out front. I hoped the machine gun with the Third Squad could cover the left side of the ridge. I planned to check on them as soon as I could.

I returned to my temporary CP, which was nothing more than a spot of dirt on the rear slope of Baldy at the back of the Second Squad. I told Browne where to place the listening post. Jack Neathery volunteered to man it.

I was weary so I decided to rest a bit. I should have gone over to check on the Third Squad, but decided to wait there until Kentucky and Partin got back with Cottrell.

There had been mail call just before we had moved out to Baldy. A letter had come from Ruby. I had not had time to read it yet. Nothing from my wife. Ruby's letter was in my fatigue jacket pocket. I opened it now to read it before dusk.

Chapter XLII

Ruby's letter emitted the sweet scent of her body. I could visualize her beautiful busts as I read it. It contrasted sharply with the dirty smell of the battlefield. She wrote the usual sweet stuff. I put her letter in my pocket again and buttoned down the flap. Again the thought crossed my mind. If I got killed, would Ruby's letter along with my other personal belongings be sent to my wife? Probably not, but I didn't give a shit one-way or the other. I'd be dead. Maybe it would remind her of her rude send off – serving me with non-support papers when I left for active duty a year ago.

At dusk, my men moved over the top of Baldy to its forward slope. Jack Neathery and Virgil Johnson, another recent black replacement, went out to be a listening post a few yards in front of Browne's squad.

I set out to check my men. First I went to where Jackson was. I wanted to be sure he and his machine gun were okay. Jackson was not alone when I got there. Several members of the First Squad had joined him and so had Sergeant Sides.

Sergeant Jackson had done a good job of keeping his machine-gun clean and ready to defend our positions.

Some clever American soldier had figured out how to make a 30-round clip out of two 15-round clips and tape four of them together, staggered top to bottom. After the battle on Eerie, I had replaced the regular 15-round clip in my carbine with one of these concoctions. So I now had 120 rounds at my fingertips. I could fire thirty rounds, release the clip, turn it over, reinsert it into my carbine and fire thirty more rounds, continuing this until all 120 rounds had been fired in less than one minute, if my piece was on full automatic.

As I approached Jackson's position, I held my carbine (equipped with this 120-round, awkward looking, multiple clip) loosely at the balance in my right hand. The leather thongs tied around my slim thighs made them appear even skinnier. I knew I looked different. I also knew my men could easily recognize my figure in the dim light of night. To me this was as it should be. I had no fear they would ever mistake me for the enemy.

As I lowered myself into the already crowded foxhole, I inquired, "Everybody okay?"

"Yes, sir," answered Jackson.

"How's the machine gun?" I asked. "Ready to go?"

"I think so, sir," Jackson said, "I kept it covered until almost dark."

"How much ammo you got?" I asked.

"F Company left us a thousand rounds and we brought another thousand," Jackson replied.

In the dim light I took visual inventory of the 0.30-caliber, air-cooled machine gun in place on its tripod. The legs of the tripod were held firmly in place by sandbags. A wooden ammo crate was sitting next to it on the left. Four 250 round belts of ammo were joined together and lay neatly folded in the crate. One end of the belt had been fed into the left side of the machine-gun receiver. It was loaded and ready to fire at the rate of 400 rounds per minute. The other thousand rounds were near by in the foxhole.

This was the first I had seen of Sergeant Sides since I got out to Baldy. As platoon sergeant, he should have been the one reporting to me when I got there, instead of Sergeant Browne. But this was no time to make an issue of his lack of leadership under fire. I had already learned that in combat, leadership did not always come from those in leadership positions. It often came from soldiers not in positions of authority. After Eerie, I knew what to expect from Sides.

Sergeant Webster and a couple of other lads from the First Squad were also in the foxhole with Jackson and his assistant gunner.

Suddenly, some muffled whispers could be heard out in front of us. An enemy grenade exploded near the edge of our foxhole. The men in the foxhole instinctively cowered as close to the bottom of the hole as they could.

"Somebody give me a fucking grenade," I snapped.

A grenade was put in my outstretched hand. I stood erect,

pulled the pin and tossed it where I thought the voices had come from. Then I stepped behind the machine gun, loosened both horizontal and vertical clamps and fired a burst at where I thought the enemy was.

"I hope I got the bastards," I muttered to nobody in particular.

I relaid the machine gun on its primary target and clamped it tight.

Enemy artillery opened up on our positions, as if the burst of fire from our machine gun had been their signal. If they did not know it already, the tracers revealed our exact location to them. Artillery and mortar fire rained down upon us. Most of it landed on the rear slope. Perhaps they thought we were still there. But enough of it landed among my men on the forward slope to scare the shit out of us. We were not the only ones hit. The whole of Baldy was showered with a deadly barrage, which was so heavy it could mean only one thing. The Chinks were coming to reclaim this damned piece of real estate.

Some phosphorous grenades landed out in front of our position and lit up a small area. Somebody from Browne's squad area had probably thrown them.

"Tell Headquarters we need some flares," I shouted above the din of battle sounds.

Webster, who was on the phone, relayed my orders to our company CP. Soon the company's 60-mm mortars had flares in the air, lighting no man's land in front of us, as they parachuted slowly to the ground. Before they burned out, larger and longer-burning flares from 81-mm and 4.2 mortars and supporting artillery units lit up the battlefield even brighter. Ere the night was over, B–26 planes of WWII vintage took to the air and circled ever the battle area, dropping their sparklers that burst forth in multiple stars of light and spent a long, lovely time floating to earth. The Chinks had very few moments of darkness the entire night to cover their approach to Baldy.

Despite the heavy hostile barrage, I had remained alert with my head high enough to watch for enemy foot soldiers who I knew would be coming. I was afraid of being taken by surprise and being shot in our foxhole or even bayoneted if I were not on guard. I knew that Neathery would also be looking out for their assault, if he was still alive (which I could no longer be sure of).

Soon the strike zone of the barrage moved a little to our rear. Then I saw some Chinks jogging along the crest of the ridge towards Neathery's listening post and Browne's squad.

"Get on the gun, Jackson," I ordered. "Here they come. Tell Browne to get the listening post back."

Jackson did as I ordered. The machine gun was already aimed at the ridge line where the Chinks were coming. He fired a burst of four or five rounds, ducked down into the foxhole and rotated the gun two clicks to the right with his upstretched hands. He peeked again and fired another short burst following a pre-arranged firing plan, just like they taught us in basic training.

But this was not basic training. Those were real enemy soldiers coming at us. They were too close and coming too fast for that kind of fire to be effective against them.

The adrenaline was again flowing through my veins. Quickly I realized what I had to do. "Give me the gun," I told Jackson. "You watch the ammunition and keep it feeding, Cecil."

In infantry training, they never allowed us to fire a free-swinging machine gun. They told us it scattered the strike of the bullets too much to be effective. Don't believe everything you see in the movies, they told us. We were taught to pull the trigger with the left index finger, turn the horizontal dial with our right hand and the vertical dial with our left hand. We were to fire in short bursts to keep the barrel from overheating and to conserve ammunition.

Fortunately, when I was in an anti aircraft artillery unit during WWII, I had learned to fire free-swinging 0.50-caliber machine guns at targets towed by airplanes. We aimed them by watching the flight of tracers.

I took the gun from Jackson's hands and loosened both the horizontal and vertical clamps. Like I had fired the 0.50-caliber machine guns at Fort Bliss, Texas, I pulled the trigger with my right middle finger and helped guide my fire with my left hand on top of the receiver. I fired a stream of tracers into the front-running Chinks, who were getting close to Browne's squad. I fired a long burst of thirty or forty rounds, swinging the gun in a slow arc. It jumped a little at first, but a little more pressure with my left hand on the receiver and a bit more lift with my right hand steadied the weapon.

From front to rear, the Chinks silhouetted on the skyline of the ridge fell like dominoes. Bullets tore up the ground at their feet. It almost looked like they were diving into the fire.

"Look at the little bastards drop!" I yelled excitedly. "Good job, Cecil. You got this baby firing beautifully."

What fear I had had was now gone. I was high on adrenaline. Killing the enemy to save my men and my own ass gave me a thrill beyond words.

"Come on you little yellow bastards," I yelled. "Step right up and get a bullet in your balls. *Dunee! Dunee!*"

From across the valley a recoilless rifle with its telltale back flash fired at the source of the tracers from my machine gun. How could the bastard miss from such short range and with such a visible target? By most standards he did not miss. The shell plowed into the dirt about two feet below the barrel of my machine gun. Like a line drive home run ball off the bat of Ted Williams that hit a few inches below the top of the green monster in left field at Fenway Park, this missile of death with my name on it fell short of its mark.

It blew dirt all over my machine gun and into my face. Instead of frightening me, it thoroughly pissed me off. As I wiped dirt from my eyes and spit it from my mouth, my anger mounted.

"You dirty, fucking son of a bitch," I muttered. "Did anybody see his back flash? Keep your eyes open, men, and see if you can spot that bastard."

As the shell struck, a lone, dark figure ran towards our foxhole from Browne's squad on our left. He was hollering, "Chamberlin! Chamberlin!"

Perhaps the sound of my voice cursing at the Chinks directed him towards our position. From about twenty feet away, he dove headlong for our hole and slid in on his belly like Ricky Henderson stealing second base.

I recognized Virgil Johnson, the black man who was on the listening post with Jack Neathery.

"You all right?" I asked.

"I'm hit," Johnson answered. "I'm bleeding. My pants are all blood."

What he thought to be blood turned out to be urine.

"Is Neathery okay?" I asked him.

It's not that I did not care about Johnson, but I was more worried about Neathery. I had not bonded with Johnson as I had with Neathery by our mutual courage in combat.

"I don't know," Johnson said. "I think they killed him."

I wasted no more time on Johnson. There were more Chinks running towards Browne's squad. I yanked the bolt back twice to check the feeding mechanism. It worked. I poured more hot lead at the advancing foe. They were now near Browne's squad. My fire was close to my own men. But I could tell the Chinks from my men. They wore soft cloth caps. I could see my tracers mow them down. I didn't see anybody with a steel helmet on in my line of fire. So I was not too concerned about hitting my own men.

Suddenly, most of the flares burned out at the same time and the battlefield was again shrouded with a mantle of dark danger.

Chapter XLIII

"Get some more fucking flares up," I ordered.

I felt insecure in the darkness, but kept my eyes peeled and ears open for any further approach of the enemy.

Almost simultaneously, more flares relit the battlefield and another round from our recoilless rifle nemesis hit a few feet to the left front of our position. Surrounding the burst of its explosion were members of a bazooka squad in the brilliant glare of the new flares. They were headed for our position. The long tube resting on the gunner's shoulder was aimed directly at us, probably about to be fired. The whole squad of three or four foes seemed to disintegrate in the blast from their own recoilless rifle. But just to make sure, I sent a burst of machine-gun fire where they had been.

"Look at the stupid bastards," I yelled with glee. "Shooting their own men."

Soon I saw more Chinks running along the ridge line.

"Come on, men, help me pick 'em off," I said, as I started mowing them down again. "It's like shooting ducks on a pond."

My example seemed to encourage the others in the foxhole. They began to stand up next to me in the hole and fire at the approaching Chinks with their M1 rifles. Another round from the hostile recoilless rifle landed near by.

"I saw him," shouted Webster. "Over there." He pointed to my right.

"So did I," I replied. "I'll get the mother fucker."

I swung the gun to the right and sprayed the area where I had seen his back flash.

"I think you got him," said Sides, who had finally drummed up enough courage to join us in watching for the enemy and firing upon them.

I don't know if I got him or not, but no more shells from that gun came our way for the rest of the night.

But the Chinks kept coming along the ridge line towards Browne's squad in human waves.

"You guys pick off the singles and I'll take care of the bunches," I suggested. "That way we'll save ammunition."

Sides, Webster and others fired their rifles at the continuous stream of oncoming Chinks. I continued to mow them down with long bursts of machine-gun fire. I was firing much more rapidly than the manual called for. It is a wonder the barrel didn't burn out. But it didn't and there was a replacement in case it did. So I was not operating completely recklessly.

Fear in the foxhole seemed to have disappeared, except from Johnson, who remained cowering at the bottom of the hole at our feet. The courage of some of us seemed to have spread to most of us. Was it as contagious as fear?

Suddenly Sides' rifle jammed. The sand stirred by the shelling had got into its receiver and prevented the bolt from operating, as it should.

"My rifle is jammed," he said nervously. "I can't fire anymore."

"Piss on it," I suggested in all seriousness. Though I had never heard of urine being recommended to clean one's piece, I instinctively knew it would work.

"I can't do that here," replied Sides, as if modesty mattered. He seemed shocked at my solution.

"Here, give it to me," I said. "I'll piss on it for you."

I needed to go, so pissing on his rifle served two purposes. It relieved me and made his piece function perfectly. Sides was able to continue to pick off some of the assaulting Chinks.

I wondered how McAfee and his squad were doing over on the left flank. I worried about Neathery and Browne. I could see that other elements of the First Squad and the Second Squad were firing at the enemy. I hoped the Third Squad was doing the same. I remembered that I had heard most soldiers were too scared to fire their weapons in a firefight for fear of giving away their positions. I was glad and proud that most of my men had courage enough to fire at the Chinks. I wished the firefight would let up and the Chinks would stop coming so it would be safe enough for me to leave the foxhole and check on my other men. But the battle continued and the Chinks kept coming. I felt more useful on the machine gun than I would running around out in the open. So I stayed on the gun until it was nearly dawn. The Chinks made at least three major assaults against my platoon that night. As the last one petered out towards daybreak, so did the last of the 2,000 rounds of machine-gun ammo in our foxhole. But I still had my carbine with its 120-round clip intact. There were also a few grenades left.

With my carbine and a few grenades in my pockets, I set out to check my men. I went to Browne's squad first. When I got to where Browne was, I asked him, "Are your men all right, Bob?"

"We're not all right, but we're all alive, except maybe Johnson," he replied. "I don't know where he is. He bugged out when the artillery started coming in. A few of my men got hit. I think my eardrums are busted."

"Johnson is okay," I said. "He came to our foxhole. How's Jack?"

"He's okay," Browne said. "He did one hell of a job all night. He's the best damned fighter I ever saw."

"Good," I answered, with relief that Jack was alive.

I saw two Chinks in a shell crater a few yards down the slope from where we were. One of them moved. I was still on a killer's high.

"Cover me, Bob," I told Browne. "I'm going to bayonet the bastards."

I moved quickly towards the prone Chinks. Most likely they were wounded. One of them might even have been dead. He was not moving. *But I'll stick 'em anyhow*, I thought. If they were dead it would not hurt them. If they were not dead they might as well be. I had felt the thrill of mowing down the foe with machine-gun fire. Now I wanted the feel of my bayonet plunging into enemy flesh. I hated them.

As I neared my goal, one of the Chinks rose to one elbow. I could have shot him, but I wanted to stick him. I didn't see what he had in his hand.

Browne hollered at me. "Watch out, lieutenant. He's got a grenade."

Browne threw one of his own grenades into the hole with the

Chinks. The Chink heaved his grenade towards me. It went about two feet and rolled back into the hole with the Chinks.

I saw the two grenades and hit the dirt. I was close enough for the double blast to almost lift my body from the ground. But I was not hurt. I rose and looked at the mutilated Chinks. Blood was oozing from the various openings in their heads. It didn't make sense to stab them now. I walked slowly back up to Browne.

"What in hell did you do that for?" I asked him. "I wanted to bayonet the bastards."

"That was stupid," he answered. "One of 'em had a grenade."

"Yeah, but shit, I would have got him," I said cockily.

But we were not angry with each other. The bond of battlefield courage tied us too closely to allow any ire to come between us. We had probably both saved each other's lives that night.

Neathery came to us. "There's a lot of fucking Chinks in the holes out in front of our positions," he said. "I heard them talking. We ought to try to get 'em out of there before daylight."

So Neathery, Browne and I went down the forward slope into no man's land. There we discovered several cave-like holes dug into the side of the hill. From inside we could hear some enemy soldiers jabbering. There was also some moaning – a sign of wounded men.

We tried to coax them out. The only words I could think of were Japanese. "*Itawah, boysan*," I said. It meant, "Come here, boy." I don't know if the Chinks knew what it meant. They did not come out. Neathery tried other words. Nothing worked. We didn't have enough grenades between us to blast out all the holes. It was nearing daylight, so we retreated to the safety of our perimeter defense.

I learned bits and pieces of what had happened to Browne and his squad that morning. What I didn't find out then was told to me later when we were resting in reserve.

Johnson had taken off from the listening post when the barrage started. He fled through Browne's squad area in search of cover while hollering for me. The new men, Kentucky and Partin, were bravely waiting in their foxhole for the enemy. When

Johnson passed near their foxhole in scared flight and yelling my name, Kentucky yelled at him, "He's over there, you yellow, black nigger." Later Kentucky was to admit he thought of shooting the "coward", but his rifle was temporarily jammed.

Neathery had stayed at his post. He saw the first few Chinks trotting towards him. He decided to slow them down a little so his comrades could get ready for them. By now flares were up and he could see the Chinks clearly. He shot the leading Chink. His rifle jammed. He jumped out of his foxhole to meet the foe on their level. He smashed a Chink on the side of the head with a butt stroke. His rifle was knocked from his hands and he was knocked to the ground. He grabbed his entrenching tool, a short-handled shovel, and rose to his feet, swinging the shovel. It slashed a Chink's throat. He smashed another one under his ear. Then those who were rushing at him started falling. He noticed the stream of tracers coming from his right. Later he learned they were coming from my machine gun. He was grateful for my timely fire, which may have saved his life. I later learned of his heroic hand-to-hand fighting, which may have saved many lives.

Neathery then withdrew to the squad perimeter. He took up a position in a foxhole just in front of Browne's. A round landed close enough to nearly bury him and his equipment. He took off his steel helmet and started digging himself out.

Browne noticed his plight and rushed to his aid. He, too, took off his steel helmet and started to dig Neathery out.

I don't know if this is true or not, but this is what they told me they said to each other.

"Are you hit?" asked Browne.

"Of course I'm hit, you stupid bastard," answered Neathery. "Can't you see the dirt all over me?"

As some Chinks who got past my machine-gun fire moved closer to them, Neathery said to Browne with deadpan seriousness, "Turn around and smile, Bob. There's a photographer from Stars and Stripes who wants to take your picture."

According to Neathery, Browne did glance back, but quickly turned back and retorted, "Shut up, you damned asshole, and dig."

Just as they got Neathery out there seemed to be a surge of Chinks coming towards them. I think this was when the shell from the recoilless rifle hit so close to my machine gun that we were out of action for a moment.

Browne shot a Chink with his rifle. The bolt jammed. He tried to pull it back by hand, but could not. He put the butt on the ground and tried to kick it back with his foot. But it was too late. The Chinks were upon them. So he held his rifle by the barrel and clubbed the head of the front foe. Neathery's rifle was also clogged with dirt so he joined Browne in clubbing Chinks into dreamland.

As my machine gun opened up on the Chinks again, Browne and Neathery were able to withdraw into a tighter defensive circle with their squad.

Not long after Browne and Neathery had narrowly escaped being killed or captured by the Chinks, a round exploded close to Browne's head. It knocked him unconscious. (Many years later, a doctor explained to him that such an explosive force slams one's brain against the back of the skull with such force as to cause great trauma.) When he came to, he could neither see nor hear. He thought he was dead. Being a Christian, he wondered if he was in heaven, hell or purgatory. It hurt too much to be heaven. It was not hot enough to be hell. Must be purgatory, he concluded. Gradually his mind cleared. He hollered, but could not hear his voice. Sergeant Bill West, his assistant squad leader, came to his aid. A medic came too. There was no blood or outward signs of injury, so the medic went to help others.

Browne forgot that Neathery was already back safe from the listening post. "I've got to go get Jack," he screamed.

He started to leave the foxhole in the midst of hostile fire. West grabbed him and pulled him back. "You can't go out there now," he yelled. "It's too dangerous. Jack is okay."

Browne did not know who West was. He could not see or hear him. He thought he was invincible, but he was actually weak from the concussion. Perhaps that is why West, who was much smaller than Browne, was able to get him down and sit on him until his senses returned.

After telling me some of these things as we rested after the all-night battle, Browne told me, "I have a splitting headache, sir. Would it be all right if I go back to the aid station?"

Word had come from the Third Squads. No one had been killed. They had fought bravely. Cottrell was wounded and had to be evacuated.

Fatigue suddenly hit me as daylight spread over Baldy. I felt limp and wanted to rest.

"Sure, Bob," I said. "You can go back. We'll be okay. They'll probably relieve us soon anyway."

I stretched out on the rear slope of Baldy, where I had originally intended to have my CP, and closed my eyes. *I would check on the Third Squad after I rested a bit*, I thought.

Chapter XLIV

I never did get over to the Third Squad area to check on them. But I was to learn later what they went through from first hand accounts.

Partin and Kentucky had made contact with them before dark, as I had asked them to do. First they found their buddy, Tally, and made sure he was okay. Then they located Cottrell and told him I wanted him and his radio over at my CP. The radio had been hit and no longer worked. But Cottrell was going to report to me anyhow. However, Kentucky and Partin had trouble explaining where my CP was. Maybe because I didn't really have one. So McAfee told Cottrell to stay with his squad. He needed all the help he could get.

Just behind where Cottrell was on the rear slope before dark, a 60-mm mortar squad dug a crew-size foxhole for themselves and their mortar. They dug it very deep, too deep as it turned out. Many years later, when I was writing *Circle of Courage*, another book about the Korean War, Cottrell told me on the phone what happened to them and how it had affected him. He remembered the name of only one of the four men in that foxhole. But he could recall vividly how they died. A round landed dead center in their hole. Blood spurting forth from the multiple wounds of the men mixed with the settling gray dust. This vision was imprinted in color on his mind as long as he lived. He doubted if anyone in the hole survived that first blast. It really didn't matter. Succeeding rounds landed close enough to cave their hole in upon them. They had dug their own grave. The man Cottrell knew was Douglas Lamp. Cottrell told me sadly that he could not remember how Douglas spelled his last name, L–A–M–P or L–A–M–P–E. This had always bothered him and haunted his dreams. The answer never came.

After dusk, Cottrell moved to a foxhole on the forward slope, as they had been told to do. He felt secure in his new hole because an old tree trunk gave him some overhead cover. But a mortar round crashed into it and shattered it to splinters. He saw the tail fins of the round stuck in the ground, a few inches from his head. He touched it to test its reality. It was still hot. He felt great pressure in his head between his ears. He felt them with his hands. They were warm, sticky and wet. It was too dark to see but he knew it was blood on his hands. He felt faint. There was no medic around so he used the gauze bandage in his first aid pouch to stop the bleeding. His faintness passed. For the rest of the night he stayed at his position and helped the Third Squad defend their area. At daybreak he was evacuated on a half-track. He never returned to L Company.

Many of the Chinese forces who attacked the Second Platoon that night, came along the left slope of the ridge in front of Baldy. Sergeant McAfee's Third Squad faced them. The machine gun with them was out of order due to the dirt and debris of battle. Corporal Roland Lincke's BAR was out of commission too. Private Herman Bilke's M1 would fire but would not eject the shells and reload semi-automatically, as it was supposed to. So, when a large group of Chinks charged towards them, Bilke lay on his back, his head towards the attackers, so he could kick the bolt back with his foot, as Lincke shot over his prone body at the enemy. As a two-man M1 team they shot a few of the foe. But some of the Chinks got too close for them to shoot them fast enough. With the few grenades they had left Lincke and Bilke destroyed the rest of their attackers. Then they withdrew to a tighter perimeter with their squad.

Throughout the night Sergeant McAfee's squad held their ground. They did not dare to bug out. Private first class Knox had warned them on Eerie of the danger of that. Tonight he repeated his warnings to them. Along with McAfee he encouraged them to stay in their foxholes and fight. Knox, who had been known as an obnoxious loudmouth before the battle on Eerie, was now appreciated for his big mouth and courage in combat.

They had no communications with me or the Company CP. But they knew they were not alone. They knew we were there. They could see machine-gun tracers streaming over the ridge. They could see the Chinks fall.

My platoon had been at only half strength when we went out to Baldy. Now it was down to twelve men. Eight men had been wounded and evacuated. Historical records show that six men were killed that night and sixty-one wounded. So, even though the Second Platoon bore the brunt of the assault, our casualty rate was less than that of others. It was estimated that the Chinese suffered 300 casualties in their battalion-size assault.

Daybreak settled upon a quiet Baldy. The sun did not rise on June 28, 1952 on this hill in the Land of the Morning Calm. The sky was dark and ominous, portending rain and storms. Did it also portend another night of hell and bloodshed?

Not long after dawn, Lieutenant Moroney came to see how we had fared. He greetly me warmly.

"How are you and your men doing, Al?" he asked.

"Okay, I guess," I answered wearily. "I only have a dozen men left. Browne was wounded and had to go back. Cottrell was evacuated also. His radio doesn't work, so we have only the walkie-talkie for communications. We don't have much ammo left. No food or water."

"Okay, Al, I'll try to get some supplies to you," he said. "I have asked Battalion to relieve us, but I don't know yet. They don't think we suffered enough casualties. Do you think you can hold out another night if they don't?"

"I don't know," I replied. "We're spread pretty thin. Most of our weapons don't work. My men are tired, thirsty and hungry. I don't know how much more we can take."

It was eerie. Almost as if we knew the Chinese would hit us again that night. They had no shortage of manpower and seemed to care little for human life.

Moroney returned to his CP. Sometime in the middle of the day, I got word from him to switch positions with Lieutenant Fanjoy's Third Platoon in the middle of the company front. We changed places as ordered. This time I had a real CP, which Fanjoy had had the night before – a small, one-man foxhole with overhead cover behind my platoon on the reverse slope.

Ammunition, rations and water were sent out as promised. My men rested and were partially refreshed. The sun did not shine on Baldy that day. The dark clouds of the morning brought rain before dusk.

Neathery came to me and asked, "What are we going to do about those Chinks we left in the holes down in front of the Third Platoon? I'll go over and blast 'em out if you want me to, sir."

I could not argue against the logic of his offer. It was the fair thing to do for our comrades of the Third Platoon.

"Okay, Jack, but take somebody with you," I told him.

"Sergeant West has already said he'll go with me," he said. "We know where they are."

I marveled at Neathery's boundless energy, combat savvy, dauntless courage and concern for his fellow men.

I arranged for a smoke screen to cover their dangerous daylight mission. They returned before dark – mission accomplished.

I sat alone on an empty ammo box in my little CP. I dozed a little. This served a dual purpose. It helped me regain some strength and moved time along, however slowly. As long as I could sleep and shut out reality, I knew it was safe. The Chinks were not coming yet.

But my nap was short-lived. A repeat of the previous night started shortly after dusk, right on schedule. Artillery and mortars pounded Baldy again. Round after round exploded near my tiny hole in the hill. I huddled with my chest against my knees and the radio in my hand. I could hear bits of conversations between Moroney and his other platoon leaders.

When the barrage subsided somewhat and moved its strike zone to our rear, the Chinese came again, as they had the night before. Only this time they not only struck along the same ridgeline against the Third Platoon, but also against the First Platoon on the right flank.

As the noise of the artillery lessened a bit I tried to doze some more, but was not very successful. I was too scared. I felt trapped and helpless. I thought I should stay where I was because I could hear on the radio what was happening. But how could I fight against artillery and mortars? *War made no sense*, I thought. Combat was a confused mess. It was dirty and painful. After a near miss, a thought stuck in my head. If I ever get through this fucking shit, nothing will ever faze me. I did not pray. I knew no God to pray to. Why pretend? People were getting killed whether they prayed to God or not. Why should I be spared and not others? What good would it do to beg? If there was a God and he was a loving, omnipotent God, how could he allow the cruel, painful suffering of war?

From the information trickling through the radio I learned that both the Third and First Platoons were being overrun.

Lieutenant Moroney called me on the walkie-talkie. I could not understand him. I don't know if it was poor radio reception or because he was so excited he could not talk straight. I thought he wanted me to counter-attack the Chinks on the left flank, but I wasn't sure. His nervous excitement seemed to have a calming effect on me.

"Calm down, Mike," I said in a low, slow voice. "I can't understand you. Get the shit out of your mouth."

Finally he was able to tell me to meet him behind his CP, several yards to the left of my CP.

I grabbed my carbine and went to meet him. Baldy was now dimly lit by flares. The shelling had slackened. Almost as soon as we met, a Chink ran over the crest of the hill towards us. I could tell by his soft cap he was an enemy. I moved a little away from Moroney to divide the Chink's attention. He tossed a grenade at us. It landed midway between us and exploded harmlessly. This was probably his last weapon. He turned and ran. I fired my carbine at him, but it was difficult to line up the sights in the dim light. So I was not sure if I hit him as he ran over the top of the hill and out of our sight.

I returned to Moroney. I gathered from what he said that both the Third and First Platoons had been overrun. It was decided that my platoon should try to hold their ground in the center of our company front.

Moroney returned to his CP. I joined my platoon and urged them to continue their staunch defense. Getting out of my foxhole and engaging in the physical activity of moving among my men on the battlefield seemed to give me a shot of adrenaline and freed me from fear and weariness.

Again my platoon held their ground. Some of the Chinks who

overran the platoons on our left and right filtered through far enough to engage my men in close-in fighting. Much of this happened while I was still in my CP foxhole, so I was not to learn much about it until later.

The Chinese attack petered out towards daybreak. The men of my platoon and what was left of the rest of L Company were worn out. It had rained all night. Now they were not only weary and hungry, but also wet and cold.

Moroney requested relief, food and blankets from Battalion. He was told we must hold Baldy at all cost. Food, water and ammo were sent out, but no blankets. Perhaps battalion staff officers in their warm, dry CP could not understand the needs of battle-weary, fighting men in cold, wet foxholes.

Moroney, I and all the men we had left were highly pissed off about being stranded on Baldy, as if nobody gave a shit about us. I remembered the words I had read in a Latin class at Syracuse University, "This too shall pass." Now they were not much comfort.

But it did pass. We were finally relieved by another company of cannon fodder late in the day of June 29, 1952.

Chapter XLV

Records show there were forty-three casualties on the second night we were on Baldy. Of these, eight were killed. According to estimates, there were 700 Chinese casualties. To accomplish all of that mayhem, people calculated that the Chinese used two battalions and over 4,000 rounds of artillery to try to dislodge L Company from Baldy's barren dome. Surely our artillery output equaled the 4,000 of the Chinese. Add those figures to the numbers of our first night on Baldy and that will give you a rough idea of the cost of real estate in Korea in 1952. And the battle for Baldy on those two nights was only a drop in a bucket in the total Korean conflict.

Lieutenant Moroney led about forty men down the southern slope of Baldy late in the day of June 29, 1952. I shepherded them from the rear. Both Lieutenants Porter and Fanjoy had been severely wounded and evacuated. Moroney and I were the only officers left in the company. Five others had become casualties since I had joined the outfit in late May.

We took refuge in some bunkers on the MLR. After being fed I collapsed on a bunk and slept all night. The next morning, Moroney woke me. He brought me a mess kit full of pancakes and a canteen cup of hot coffee.

"Wake up, Al," he said. "Here's some breakfast. After we eat we're moving back."

"Do I have to get up, Mike?" I asked, still half asleep.

I ate the pancakes and drank the coffee. Moroney brought me some more. With a full stomach, I passed out again into deep sleep.

Vaguely I remember hearing Moroney say, "Let him sleep. He has earned a rest. He can catch up with us when he wakes up."

When I woke up later in the middle of the day, it took me a few minutes to realize where I was. Then I quickly got my gear together, buckled on my cartridge belt, tied the thongs around my legs and moved out of the bunker. It was not hard to find someone and get a ride back to L Company, which was now back in the rest area where I had joined them. Everybody on the line knew about us.

Upon my arrival, Lieutenant Moroney ordered what was left of the company to assemble. As they all stood at attention he ordered me front and center. I wondered what in hell was going on. Was I going to get chewed out for oversleeping?

I stood in front of Moroney. I was dirty and unshaven. My fatigues were soiled, sweaty and smelled. Sweat rings made dark circles under the armpits of my fatigue jacket. I probably looked like a Bill Maudlin WWII GI cartoon.

Moroney stepped forward. He unpinned the silver bar from his own collar and pinned it on mine.

"Sorry," he said. "This is the only first lieutenant's bar in the company. General Smith was here today and promoted you."

I was dumbfounded. I did not know what to say or do. It was an uneasy, though happy, feeling. Moroney helped me by grasping my hand in a strong, warm grip.

All I could think of to say was, "Thanks, Mike."

The next day I met with squad leaders of the Second Platoon. I suppose I was now technically the company executive officer but I still felt like the Second Platoon leader. Moroney had not told me otherwise. We talked about the battles on Baldy. It was decided as to who had earned awards and who would write statements as witnesses. I decided to recommend Bob Browne and Jack Neathery for Distinguished Service Crosses, since their heroism had been much greater than that which they had displayed on Eerie, for which I had put them in for Silver Stars. Others I recommended for Silver or Bronze Stars. I even thought of putting Sergeant Sides in for a Bronze Star. He had finally got enough guts to fire his rifle a few times in the firefight. But I decided against it. He had needed too much urging to be what I considered courageous. Nor did I put Sergeant Amos or Johnson in for anything. In fact, no one knew what Amos had done or where he was during the battles. He had been invisible.

Bob Browne told me that he had been evacuated to a Mash unit somewhere in the rear. They gave him aspirin for his headache and left him in a ward for observation. As he lay on a bunk on the night of June 28, news was coming from a nearby radio that Baldy was under attack again. He thought of his men and his brother Bill. He felt he should be there to take care of them.

When no one was watching him, he grabbed his gear and slipped out of the tent. He hitched rides back towards the front and Baldy. But by time he got to the MLR behind Baldy it was daylight. That night's struggle for Baldy was over. It no longer made sense to him to go on to the outpost. He rejoined L Company during its withdrawal to its rest area.

Soon after his return he learned of his brother's fate. During the barrage of our second night on Baldy, Sergeant Bill Browne had been buried alive in his foxhole. A rescue squad had dug him out and he had been evacuated back through the medical pipeline. Bob Browne was now frantic to learn where his brother was and his condition.

Many days later, Bob was to learn that Bill had been severely wounded and was in a hospital in Japan. Years later, I learned Bill had suffered many shrapnel wounds to his head, arms and legs. He still carries metal souvenirs around in his body. He had been buried and unconscious most of the night. He wasn't sure how he had survived. He speculated that perhaps the rain had washed away an airway in the sand around his head for him to breathe. He also figured being buried may have saved him from the Chinks who overran his platoon area.

I encouraged my men to talk of their personal battle experiences. Private first class Tally told of a Chink who ran up to him at the edge of our platoon area. The Chink's only weapon was a potato masher type grenade. Using it like a club, he hit Tally in the face with it. It chipped one of Tally's upper front teeth and fell to the bottom of his foxhole. The Chink turned and ran. Kentucky shot him. The grenade did not explode. Its pin had not been pulled. Tally kept it as a souvenir to back up his tale of his chipped tooth.

Private first class Knox told of how he saved Sergeant West's life. While West was busy firing at the foe in front of him, a Chink, who had somehow got within our defenses, was about to bayonet him in the back. Somewhere in the confusion of battle, Knox had picked up a Colt .45, one of the most prized souvenirs of war. He shot the Chink in the back of his head. The .45 slug opened a large hole in the Chink's skull and scattered his blood and brains on the battlefield.

The battles on Baldy tightened the already strong bonds between Bob Browne, Jack Neathery and me. Our mutual friendship, respect, loyalty and love were now unbreakable. We started spending a lot of time together, sharing our thoughts and innermost feelings. Bob told me of the Russian made rifle a Chink had tried to kill him with. Bob had beaten him to the punch and had recovered the piece from his dead body. Now he had a treasured, though illegal, souvenir of his hand-to-hand combat on Baldy.

He also told me he had loaned his rifle to Jack when he was evacuated. Jack had broken his against a hard-headed Chink. When Bob rejoined the unit he asked Jack for his rifle. Jack told him he had used it the next night. He ran out of ammunition and slung it at a Chink. Then he couldn't find it.

Both Bob and Jack told me of an episode with Kentucky and Partin. Bob had a headache and was thirsty. He said, "I wish I had a beer."

Jack told him, "I don't think there's any beer around. But maybe Partin and Kentucky have something. They've been acting like they don't feel any pain."

"Let's find out," said Bob. "I'll pull my rank on them and inspect their stuff."

Bob and Jack went to the pup tent shared by Kentucky and Partin.

"I hear you've been drinking again," Bob said with the serious tone of authority. "You know Lieutenant Chamberlin told you drinking's not allowed on the front lines."

"Oh no," Kentucky lied with a sober face. "We don't drink any more. Not after what we went through on Baldy. We saw the light."

"That's right," Partin agreed. "We got religious during that fight. We prayed to the Lord to save us and He did. We promised Him we'd never drink any more. Do you guys have to fight like that very often?"

"Oh, that's just normal," Jack boasted. "We pull that kind of detail about every week."

"Open up your duffel bags," Bob ordered.

"Okay," Kentucky admitted. "We've got a little booze. Don't tell anybody and we'll let you have a drink."

A thorough search of their bags turned up not just a little booze but ten bottles of whiskey carefully wrapped in towels and other items of clothing to hide and protect them.

"Where did you get all this?" Bob demanded.

"Let me tell 'em," Partin said to Kentucky. "You're too dumb."

To Bob and Jack he explained, "You see, Kentucky don't get paid much. Only twenty bucks a month. The rest of his pay is sent to his mother. Well, the Army screwed up and didn't pay him for ten months. Then, when he got paid he bought whiskey in the black market in Pusan."

"What did he do for money all that time?" Bob asked.

"Well, I took care of him," Partin continued, "I promised his mother I'd look after him. Now he's paying me back. Half the whiskey is mine. We were trying to keep it a secret so it would last longer."

They all had a drink and Bob's headache eased. Bob told me later that he and Jack kept the booze a secret. That way they could get more of it. They knew that booze wouldn't last long in a bunch of battle-weary warriors.

Shortly after we came off Baldy, a reporter from the "Stars and Stripes" came to interview some of us. I encouraged my men to tell him what they had done. He asked what role I had played in the battle. I told him about being on a machine gun most of the first night.

"How many Chinese did you kill?" he asked.

"I don't know," "I answered truthfully. "Maybe thirty or forty."

He looked at me askance, as if to say, "Yeah, I bet." He probably had never heard of a platoon leader manning a machine gun.

I really didn't give a shit whether he believed me or not. What non-combatants or cowards thought of me no longer mattered.

He did not ask me any more questions.

A few days into July 1952, both Lieutenant Moroney and our first sergeant, Jim Baker, got orders to rotate back to the States. At a casual parting, Moroney unhooked the Colt .45 from his cartridge belt and handed it to me.

"Al," he said, "as a final token of my deep respect and appreciation for all you've done, I give you this. The company is all yours."

"Thank you, Mike," I replied. "Coming from you that means a lot to me."

I thought of the Colt .45 as a gift from one warrior to another, not as government equipment. I felt it was mine to keep. I made some minor adjustments for it on my cartridge belt and tied it down with a thong. Somewhere along the line I had added a grenade pouch on the left front of my cartridge belt. That carried four grenades and was also tied down with another thong around my left thigh.

In WWII Patton had his pearl-handled pistols. Ridgeway had two grenades on his suspenders. They had their personae. I had mine, more functional than fancy.

We all hated to see Moroney go. Both he and Lieutenant Pierce before him had been good to their men and treated them with respect. I knew of no one in the company who did not think well of them. They had been courageous company commanders.

Now, I guessed, I was the company commander. But before I had time to realize the gravity of that fact, Captain Brown arrived to take over the company.

Chapter XLVI

Captain Brown was a small, short, narrow, thin man. He probably weighed around 130 pounds. His fatigues appeared tailor-made. They were spotless and well starched. His combat boots glistened, as did his captain's bars. He was a sharp contrast to me and the men of L Company whose fatigues were rumpled and often ill fitting and soiled. Our boots did not shine and not many of the men wore their stripes. They didn't need to. They knew who the leaders were.

Brown ordered the troops to be assembled so he could talk to us. He told us about himself. He had been to Officers Candidate School during WWII. His military assignments had included a stint as a general's aide, but no overseas duty until now. I wondered how he had avoided that for so long. He must have been in the Army for at least ten years already and during two wars. He told us about his family, education and other stuff, as if we cared. He told us what he expected of his men. It was the usual garrison type chickenshit: they were to shave every day, keep their area policed and weapons clean, shine their boots, and follow his orders when he led them into battle, which he hoped to do soon. He also wanted the men to sew on their stripes so he could tell who they were. He promised to whip us into the best damned company in the battalion.

The men were angry. They did not like chickenshit. Nor did they want to be led into battle again by anyone, much less a puny little greenhorn. Most of them were short-timers and near rotation. They did not want to defy death again.

Brown turned the company over to me and retreated to his CP tent. Before they were dismissed the men expressed their feelings to me.

Sergeant Sides, who was now the company first sergeant due to Sergeant Baker's rotation, said, "Lieutenant, you'd better straighten him out. None of us want to go back into battle."

"Yeah," spoke up Sergeant Browne, who was now the platoon sergeant of the Second Platoon. "You'd better let him know what in hell is going on. We don't want any damned greenhorn volunteering us for combat missions. They should have let you be our company commander. You know what's going on."

"Yeah, if he thinks I'm going to shine my fucking boots, he's got another think coming," chimed in Sergeant Davidson of the Third Platoon. "He can kiss my royal ass. I don't have any fucking shoe polish or stripes to sew on. If I did I'd throw 'em to hell away. Fuck him."

There was a general rumble of agreement from the ranks of the ragged-looking men. I stood before them and held up my hand to get their attention. I did not scold them for their mutinous voices. They knew I wouldn't. I felt the same way they did.

In a low, soft voice I spoke to them. "Let's wait and see what happens. Captain Brown is new and doesn't understand what you men have been through. He doesn't know what combat is all about. But he is our company commander, whether we like it or not. Maybe he'll turn out okay. In the meantime, I will be talking to him."

The men listened to me silently but intently. There was not much they could do. Whatever else the Army is, it is not a democracy. They may have had a vote with me, but in the end we had to follow orders or suffer the consequences. I remembered well my thirty days in the brig in WWII.

One day Captain Brown, a few others and I were shooting the bull. Brown seemed to want to be accepted and he wanted to talk about combat with us. I guess Sergeant Sides and Corporal Schiefer, our company clerk, had told him a lot about the battles we had been in. Brown was trying hard to be buddy-buddy with me. I was not about to be his buddy, friend or anything else to him until he proved himself under fire.

"I'm a pretty good shot," he bragged. "I shot expert with all weapons in OCS. How'd you do, Chamberlin?"

"Oh, I qualified okay," I answered reluctantly. "But I never went to OCS. I took ROTC in college."

"I bet I'm a better shot than you are," he challenged me. "When we go up on line we can have a contest to see which one of us can shoot the most Chinks. Ten bucks says I can."

"Oh, I wouldn't be surprised," I agreed. "But combat is not a game. I wouldn't want to compete with you. I have nothing to prove. You'd better keep your ten bucks."

"I heard you said it was like shooting ducks on a pond," he continued. "I can't wait to pick off a few."

"Have fun," I said with a skeptical smile.

"How long does it take to get a Combat Infantryman Badge?" Brown asked.

"It took thirty days on the line in WWII," I explained to him, as if he didn't know already. "Probably the same here, unless you're a brown-nose," Brown did not seem to sense my sarcasm.

"Have you got yours yet?" he continued.

"Probably," I answered evasively.

For the few days L Company remained in the rest area after Captain Brown's arrival, he made no attempt to inspect the men or their areas. Quite frankly, I can't remember anything he did. Certainly he did not check on shoeshines or stripes. The men ignored his orders.

Not many days after Brown took over, L Company was ordered back up on the MLR. Brown called me in and asked my opinion of his field order. It was obvious to me he was unsure of himself, nervous and scared.

I remembered vaguely what the manual said about field orders and what I had learned at Infantry School in Fort Benning, Georgia. But Lieutenants Pierce and Moroney had never read a field or combat order to us from a piece of paper. They had just seemed to know what had to be done. I glanced at Brown's writings briefly.

"You seem to have covered everything," I said.

I wasn't really worried about his order. We had made this move before and the men knew what to do.

Brown called the platoon sergeants, mess sergeant, and supply sergeant together and read his orders to them. Now that we were going back to the MLR, he no longer seemed so eager to get within firing range of the enemy. He appeared timid, meek, and above all, small and weak.

But the move was made with no problem. The men, their weapons and gear were transported to the MLR by trucks as they had been many times before. We went to the same area where we had been before, behind Baldy. The men went back to the same bunkers they had lived in earlier. I guess Brown rode up in front of the convoy in the company jeep. I don't think anyone paid much attention to him except his driver, company clerk and Sergeant Sides. I know I didn't. I moved into a bunker with Sergeant Browne, who was now the Second Platoon sergeant, and a few other men from my old platoon. In fact, I still felt like I was the Second Platoon leader. Captain Brown never clarified what my role was in the company.

The first day we were back on line, Captain Brown's true colors began to emerge. It was a hot, humid day. As usual, I was up early and walked over to his CP, in case he wanted to give me any orders. It was a large bunker and he was at one end of it, shaving. Communications Sergeant Spisak came in and reported to him. Spisak was not wearing his fatigue jacket. His white T-shirt looked like he had worn it for a week or so. His face appeared unwashed. His blond, curly hair was disheveled because he had just removed his steel helmet.

"How dare you come into my presence like that?" Brown yelled at him. "Where's your fatigue jacket? Go back to your quarters and clean up. Don't ever come into my CP again out of uniform."

"But sir, I have a message for you—" the startled Spisak started to say.

"Get out!" ordered Brown.

So Spisak left without delivering his message.

I listened with great surprise at Brown's demand for military chickenshit. I followed Spisak outside.

"Sergeant, what was the message you had for Captain Brown?" I asked, thinking it might be important.

"I just wanted to tell him that Battalion called, and said some officers from Battalion were coming up to inspect our positions today," Spisak told me.

"I'll let him know," I said, "Don't worry too much about Captain Brown. Now that we're on the MLR, maybe he'll learn."

When the battalion executive officer, some of his staff, Captain Brown, Sergeant Sides and I were inspecting our positions a little later, a random mortar round landed about a hundred yards away. It was not close enough to be of any great concern. Captain Brown ducked and cowered behind a small bush. None of us showed any fear. Not even Sides. That was the real beginning of my disrespect for Brown.

★

Private White, who had chickened out when we first went on Baldy, was now back with the company. When we got off Baldy, the men of the Second Platoon shunned him completely. Even his buddy, Johnson, refused to share a pup tent with him or speak to him.

Finally, he begged to see me. I felt sorry for him, but could not condone his cowardice. I had decided not to press charges against him. What good would it have done? I saw no danger of my men following his example. Quite the contrary. They were more influenced by the bravery of men like Bob Browne and Jack Neathery.

When he approached me, I asked him, "What do you want?"

"Lieutenant, the men all hate me. I can't stand it any longer. Please give me another chance," he begged.

"Okay, you'll get another chance," I told him. "When we go back up on the line, I'll treat you just like anybody else. But only you can stop the men from hating you. You have to prove yourself to them. My men don't like cowards."

★

Baldy had been secure now for some time. L Company was ordered to relieve the outfit that now occupied it. Brown ordered me to take the Second Platoon and what was left of the other platoons out to man the positions on Baldy. He wanted to maintain his CP in the large, comfortable bunker on the MLR. But Battalion gave him no choice. He was ordered to set up his CP in a bunker on a small knoll between the MLR and Baldy. With him would be Sergeants Sides, Spisak and a couple other headquarters personnel.

We found Baldy in much better shape than when we had left it. Foxholes and gun positions were now well fortified with overhead cover and sandbags. Browne and I set up our CP on the reverse slope. This time nothing much happened. For the time being the Chinese had given up trying to take it back. Occasional artillery rounds and small arms fire broke the monotony as time passed.

However, Captain Brown was indoctrinated to combat. One day enemy mortars zeroed in on his CP. Several rounds landed very close to his bunker. Sergeant Browne answered the phone in our CP.

"Bob, I need help," cried Sergeant Sides on the other end. "Captain Brown is driving us crazy. He's hiding in a corner with a blanket over his head. He wants us to go outside and put more sandbags on our bunker and to build a wall of sandbags inside to protect him. I don't know what the hell to do. He's driving me nuts. Ask Lieutenant Chamberlin what I should do."

Sergeant Browne laughed as he told me what Sides said.

I smiled knowingly. "Tell him to come up here and we'll have our shooting contest. The Chinks are only a couple of hundred yards away."

When Sergeant Sides heard that, he said, "He can't do that. He's scared shitless. I wish I were out there with you guys. I don't know what the hell to do with him."

Browne told Sides, "Tell him not to worry. There's no danger unless they score a direct hit. And even then his blanket might save him."

Hot meals were brought out to us on Baldy by Korean *chogie* crews. We would leave a couple of men in a gun position on the forward slope while the rest went back to the reverse slope to eat. At a noon meal, Privates Mason Bowman and LeRoy White were on guard in the gun positions. Suddenly White came running down the hill yelling, "They shot him! He's dead!"

Neathery and West grabbed their rifles and ran to check on Bowman. White was right. He was dead. A direct-fire weapon had scored a bull's-eye through the gun position's firing aperture. The concussion had killed Bowman. Blood was oozing from his ears, mouth, nose and eyes. Why, I don't know. But White was unhurt. West reported the death to me. I looked at Browne. I tried to control the pain in my guts. I did not want to see a dead Bowman. Not long ago I had held him in my arms. I was afraid of how I would react when faced with the dead body of one of my men. I had not seen Dawes after he was killed on Eerie. I did not want my men see me break down and lose control.

"Bob, would you look after his things?" I asked.

"Sure," he said, I think he understood how I felt.

I sat by myself for a while and thought about Bowman. I knew he was married and had some kids. He had shown pictures of them and his wife to me. He was very proud of them. All the men liked Bowman.

Later Neathery said, "Frenchy knew he was going to get killed. He didn't want to go back on Baldy for that reason. He told me and Bill, he had a dream and saw his dead body. Boy, he had guts. He was a hell of a good soldier."

The Forty-fifth Division got orders to move over to the east central front. L Company was relieved on Baldy. My last job in that area was to set up a listening post out in the valley to the left of Baldy to prevent any sneak attacks during the change over. We had no problems doing this.

Captain Brown and the rest of the company moved off the line, packed the company gear, loaded onto trucks and moved out.

At dawn, I brought my patrol back to the MLR and on down the slopes to where our transportation was. At the foot of the hill Colonel Spottswood was waiting in a jeep. I saw him and went over to report to him.

"Mission accomplished, sir," I said as I saluted him.

"Job well done, Chamberlin," he said. "I knew I could count on you, son."

"Thank you, sir," I answered.

We loaded onto a truck and moved down the road. I leaned back and closed my eyes. I was glad to be leaving. Any place would be better than Baldy, Eerie or Porkchop. We rested as we rode away from hell.

Chapter XLVII

When we arrived at our new rest area in reserve, it was raining hard. It was after dark. The rest of the company was already there. Supply stuff, kitchen equipment and headquarters equipment, along with the three large tents to house them, had been hastily unloaded in the muddy area that was to be our company street. It appeared to me to be a confusing, disorganized mess.

Captain Brown was yelling at a few men to get his headquarter tent set up so they could get his CP gear in out of the rain. There were not enough men available to do his bidding. Apparently, the supply and mess sergeants had grabbed most of the men to put up their tents before Brown got them.

There was little light to work with; only the headlights of a couple of company vehicles and a few random flashlights. Despite his raving, Captain Brown did not seem to know what to do. He appeared small and helpless.

My concern was more for the men than for his CP tent and office equipment. The men were wet, cold and tired. They needed a rest.

"Why don't we cover the office equipment with a tarp and let the men find their duffel bags, pitch their pup tents and get some rest?" I suggested.

The few men available ignored Captain Brown and did as I suggested. Then they quickly set up a tent for the private quarters of Captain Brown, more to get him out of the way than for his comfort. It was large enough to set up two cots for the two company officers, Brown and me.

Like a drunk who escapes reality by the bottle, Brown withdrew from the foul weather by entering his tent and closing the flap. Not unlike Kentucky and Partin, his personal effects contained bottles of liquid courage and sleep medicine. How else could he have tolerated his futile existence in an arena that demanded manhood?

I stayed with the men long enough to see that they all got their duffel bags from where they had been dumped in the middle of the company street, pitched their pup tents and were bedded down on the wet, muddy ground. At least they were finally under cover.

I would have preferred to share a pup tent with one of my men, but I supposed I had to compromise a little with the Army's caste system. So I moved into Captain Brown's tent to spend the rest of that night and the next few nights.

In the next few days' things got organized. The CP tent was set up and it appeared that none of the equipment or supplies had suffered from the rain. My main concern was the morale and well being of the men. The men's main concern, since there were no women around, seemed to be to drink beer. What beer was around was soon gone.

Sergeant Browne approached me. "Jack says he thinks he knows somebody back in Ch'unch'ŏn in a quartermaster outfit. We could probably get some beer there, if we had a jeep to go get it," he said.

I went to our company commander, "Captain Brown, the men are pretty restless and their morale is low," I said. "I think a little beer would make them feel better. Sergeant Browne thinks we could get some beer back in quartermaster. If we could use the company jeep for a few hours. I'd be glad to go with him to see if we can get some beer for the men."

He hesitated for a moment. I didn't think he liked the idea, but so far there had been no open hostility between us and I think he wanted to keep me on his side. "Okay," he agreed.

So Sergeant Browne, Neathery and I hooked a trailer on the jeep and took off for Ch'unch'ŏn, which was about sixty miles south. Our driver whose name I don't remember, was a new replacement. On the way south we passed through a military police checkpoint. I dismounted from the jeep at their request. The two young MPs took a quick look at me with my .45 Colt, twin daggers and grenades all tied down with leather thongs, saluted and told us to pass on.

"Lieutenant, those guys acted like they knew you," our driver said.

"Maybe they know about us," agreed Browne.

"I doubt if they know us by name, but they know we're combat men," said Neathery. "You can always tell a combat man when you see one."

What Neathery said seemed to be true. There did seem to be an unspoken recognition and respect for combat veterans, not only among non-combatants, but among battle-hardened warriors as well. Neathery seemed wise far beyond his education and age.

"How would you guys like to get laid while we're here?" I asked.

"Yeah, I would, sir," our driver said excitedly.

"Not me," said Browne. "All I want is some beer."

"Why don't you drop Bob and me off at quartermaster?" suggested Neathery. "We can get the beer while you two get laid."

"Good. Then we'll pick you guys up later," I agreed.

So that is what happened. While I and our driver found a whorehouse, Browne and Neathery negotiated for beer at quartermaster. We had no trouble finding a house with ladies who made their living satisfying the lust of American GIs. They had no trouble getting beer to satisfy the thirst of their combat comrades.

My woman was warm, soft, cuddly and pleasantly pleasing. She was very friendly and I enjoyed her immensely. She must have been good at her profession. She had an American-style bed in which to work. That was the only bed I had sex in during my stay in Korea. All of my other sexual encounters there took place on mats on the floor, as did most of them in Japan. As I lay there with her in silent serenity, I suddenly felt guilty. I was enjoying myself while my men were suffering in that hellhole from the combat soldier's common ailment, "lackonookie". So, when I was finished, I asked the mama-san if she had any girls who would like to make a lot of money by going up to service my men. She easily found two girls who were eager for a big payday.

Our driver and I took the two girls, picked up Browne and Neathery and a trailer full of beer and headed back to camp.

Browne was a little pissed off at my folly. "What the hell are we going to do at the MP checkpoint?" he asked.

Neathery laughed at his fear, "We'll bluff our fucking way through," he said. "If that doesn't work, just step on the gas and go like hell."

To disguise them we put field jackets on the girls. Then Browne and Neathery separated their steel helmets from their helmet liners and put the steel helmets on the girls. The girls giggled. They squeezed down in the narrow back seat of the jeep. Browne and Neathery rode tall on the wheel housings.

It was dark when we got to the checkpoint. As expected the MPs stopped us. Up until now I had no idea what I would tell them about the girls. I just hoped they wouldn't ask.

I returned their salute. "I'm Lieutenant Chamberlin of the 179th Infantry," I told them, with as much authority as I could muster in my voice.

"Who are your passengers?" one of the MPs inquired.

"Sergeants Bob Browne and Jack Neathery," I replied, as I turned and pointed to them.

"And the other two little guys?" he asked.

As I glanced at them it appeared that the steel helmets almost concealed their whole heads, sort of like a turtle's shell. An idea popped in my head.

"Oh them," I replied. "Listen, we're not supposed to tell anybody about them because it's top secret. But since you're doing such a good job and have caught us, I'll have to share some counter-intelligence information with you. We're part of operation 'Pussy Cat'. They're Korean moles from Division Intelligence. We're taking them up to the MLR so they can slip through enemy lines and gather intelligence information. Remember this is top secret so General Ruffner doesn't want anybody to know about it. So my orders to you from the general are to keep your eyes open and your mouths shut. I will personally let the general know what a good job you men are doing."

"Yes sir," said the MP.

"We're going to be coming back through this checkpoint in a few hours with some returning moles, so let your relief know," I continued to instruct him.

"Yes sir," he said. "Pass on."

The MPs saluted smartly and seemed quite impressed.

Our escort service moved on up the road. When we were out of earshot of the MPs we laughed about our "Pussy Cat" operation.

We entered the camp as silently as possible and set up two pup tents for the girls to work in. Then the word was spread to the Second Platoon. Our plan was to keep it a small operation just among friends. But the word spread rapidly. Soon customers were coming from the whole company and lines formed at the tents.

Business was so heavy that I decided to handle the money myself. I did not want the girls to be cheated. It was two bucks apiece. Jack Tally asked for a little longer time. He said it took him longer. His southern sense of honor made him offer five dollars for his turn. I think he may have done some pimping back in Kentucky. He knew that time was money for the girls.

Word spread to nearby companies. Their men queued up along with L Company men. I became concerned that we might get caught. But we didn't. Much as the battles on Eerie and Baldy had petered out before dawn, this action also tapered off in the wee hours of the morning.

I rounded up my crew and the girls and headed back to Ch'unch'ŏn. The MPs at the checkpoint saluted and waved us on through. I gave the mama-san and the girls over $200 in military scrip. That was equal to 3,000 yen (probably more on the black market), a small fortune to them. I kept nothing for our escort services.

After we returned to camp and slept most of the next day, Captain Brown approached me tentatively. "Al, what's this I hear about some girls being in camp last night?" he asked.

"Captain, I don't know a damned thing about it," I lied. "But I'll take full responsibility."

Captain Brown did not seem able to handle such an illogical, ambiguous response. Apparently he had no concrete evidence. He did not pursue the matter. I doubted that anyone would squeal on us to him.

I think the captain was beginning to sense my complete lack of respect for him. And I sensed that this frightened him.

Chapter XLVIII

The men enjoyed the beer we brought back from quartermaster. Kentucky got so drunk he decided it was time to do away with Captain Brown. Apparently it was his day off, so he could do whatever he wanted to, while Partin had to take care of him. I got word of what was happening so I went to his squad tent (the men were now living in large squad-size tents and sleeping on cots up off the muddy ground) to try to keep his ass out of trouble.

Kentucky was sitting on the side of his cot with a loaded .45 in his hand. Browne, Neathery, West and Partin were blocking his way so he couldn't leave the tent.

"How you doing, Kentucky?" I asked casually, as if everything were normal.

"I'm drunker than a piss pot," he said. "I'm going to blow Captain Brown's fucking brains out."

"I understand how you feel, but you can't do that," I told him.

"You can't stop me. It's my day off and I've got the gun," he said. "I can do anything I want to."

"You want to get Partin in trouble?" I asked.

"Fuck him," he said. "He ain't got guts enough to do it."

"What about your mother?" I asked. "Who's going to take care of her if you end up in the stockade?"

"She gets an allotment from my pay," he explained. "That will take care of her."

"But Kentucky, you won't get any pay in the stockade and your mother won't get her allotment," I informed him. "Didn't you know that?"

"Nobody ever told me that," he said sadly. "Hey Partin, you son of a bitch, why didn't you tell me that? You're supposed to take care of me."

"You're too dumb to listen," Partin retorted.

I sat down on the cot beside Kentucky on his right side so the gun in his right hand was not pointed at me. I put my arm around his shoulders.

"Kentucky, we're asshole buddies, aren't we?" I asked him.

Kentucky's ugly face looked up at me. His eyes filled with moisture. I gently took the .45 from his hands.

"Don't worry about Captain Brown," I assured him. "He'll get what's coming to him."

★

A bulldozer sat idle at the end of our company street. The engineers had not finished their work and had left it there. A day or so after Kentucky had threatened to kill Captain Brown, Sergeant Browne also got very drunk. He decided that Kentucky was right, somebody had to take care of Captain Brown. He climbed up on the bulldozer and got it started. He told Sergeant Neathery he was going to run over Captain Brown's tent, with him in it.

"It will look like an accident," he said.

I was close enough to see what was happening. So I approached the dozer and Browne to keep him out of trouble, the same as I had done for Kentucky.

"Bob, you're not supposed to be operating that dozer," I warned him.

"I'm going to squash Captain Brown," Browne bellowed. "He's a disgrace to our name and the United States Army. I will be a hero. I'll get a medal for it."

"No you won't," I said. "You'll end up in the stockade just like Kentucky would have. Besides, I'll be in trouble too for letting you do it. Don't you care about me?"

"No you won't," he said. "You're a hero too. They're scared of heroes."

As Browne was operating the levers to turn the dozer, the track on Neathery's side stopped. Neathery jumped on the track and grabbed the key from the ignition. The dozer stopped in its tracks. Neathery jumped off.

"You son of a bitch, Jack, come back here with my key," hollered Browne.

Browne jumped off the dozer after Neathery. He fell flat on

his face. Neathery and I helped him up and got him back into his tent and onto his bunk to sleep it off.

Later that same day, Sergeant Davidson approached me in the company street.

"I heard Captain Brown has volunteered the company to go back on line, so he can earn enough time to get his Combat Infantry Badge (CBI)," Davidson said. "Is that true?"

"Well, yes, I know he needs more combat time to earn his CIB," I acknowledged. "He has about two weeks on line and needs thirty days to be eligible. But I haven't heard that he has volunteered us for combat again."

"Well, Lieutenant, you'd better find out," Davidson warned. "Because if it's true, his life won't be worth shit. I'm not going to risk my ass again."

Sergeant Davidson was a short-timer, soon to rotate.

"I'll ask him," I agreed.

A little later I spoke to Captain Brown, "Captain, there's a rumor going around that you have volunteered the company for combat duty so you can get your CIB. Is that true?"

Brown hesitated a moment before he replied. "No, that's not true."

I think he lied. I heard later from other sources, that there was a possible need for a company to go into a blocking position behind the MLR, and that Brown had volunteered our company for that mission once he heard it wasn't very dangerous.

"Good," I said in a low voice meant for his ears only. "Your life wouldn't be worth shit if you did." *Let him figure that one out*, I thought.

Without a word Captain Brown turned and hastened away from me like a scared rabbit.

I knew that he feared me. I reveled in that realization, not fully understanding the consequences of his feelings towards me, should hatred be added to his fear.

I went to bed early that evening in the tent I shared with Captain Brown. I was tired. The last few days had been hectic.

Captain Brown went somewhere that evening. Probably to visit his friend Captain Gatsis, the company commander of K Company. They had joined our outfit together. I had heard they were buddies, which did not make me think much of Gatsis. Later on, however, I was to learn that Gatsis was a fine officer and a gentleman. He was kind to Brown – much like one is kind to dumb animals.

Late in the evening, Captain Brown entered our tent and switched on the light (the company now had power furnished by generators). The light partially woke me. At first, I thought I was on the MLR and a Chink was entering my bunker. I reached out and grabbed Brown's leg just above his knee. He was about the size of most Chinks. Almost immediately I knew it was Brown. But I feigned ignorance. I squeezed his little leg with all my might and reached for one of my nearby daggers with my other hand.

"Al, Al, wake up," Brown whimpered. "It's me, Captain Brown."

I savored the moment for a few seconds while he tried desperately to escape my grip. Then I pretended to wake up suddenly and let go of his leg. I replaced my dagger in its scabbard.

"Sorry," I apologized. "I guess I was having a flashback."

I turned my back to him and smiled as I went back to sleep. I doubt if Captain Brown slept well that night.

The next day, Captain Brown had the company assembled. He appeared to be very angry. He told us that he expected the company to shape up and acts like soldiers. From now on there would be reveille every morning at 0630 hours, followed by police call before breakfast. Boots were to be shined at all times. Living areas were to be inspected every day. Days would be spent either on work details or training classes. Military courtesy would be enforced. The uniform of the day would be posted and was to be adhered to. There would be no more drinking before 1800 hours. I recognized this as standard garrison-type chickenshit, something I had not experienced since I arrived in Korea. It seemed unfair to combat veterans who had been promised rest and relaxation. His get-tough-speech riled the men. As he walked away from the formation, rumblings of discontent rose from the ranks.

Again I felt responsible to calm the men down after Captain Brown had pissed them off. They listened to me as I gently reminded them that Captain Brown was our commanding officer, whether we liked it or not.

Later that day, Captain Brown moved out of the tent we shared. I guess he feared for his life. He moved his cot and personal stuff into one end of his large CP tent. Around this time, our company received two young second lieutenants as replacements. They were assigned to the First and Third Platoons and I continued to act as the Second Platoon leader, in addition to carrying out my executive officer's duties, which Captain Brown never did spell out to me specifically. The new officers moved in with me.

Sergeant Sides rotated home. I arranged for Sergeant Browne to be the first sergeant of the company.

The chickenshit orders of Captain Brown were generally ignored, except for reveille and police call. Not many of the men attempted to shine their boots. I know I didn't. There wasn't much shoe polish available. Daily inspections were a joke. Captain Brown never visited the men's tents. I don't think he dared to. I spent time with my platoon every day, but it was more to fraternize with my men than to inspect them. Nor did I remove my .45 and daggers, with their thongs, from my cartridge belt to conform with the uniform of the day and General Ruffner's Special Order against thongs. I guess I was sort of rebelling against chickenshit and taking orders from a coward. Maybe this was just a way of being a silent spokesman for my men. But in my mind at the time I was just acting and dressing like a combat infantryman.

Battalion scheduled a full field inspection of the troops to make sure all the men had all their equipment and that it was clean and in good shape. Of course, this could not be done while the outfit was on line and had not been done for some time. So the officers were rusty. Orders came down that all officers were to research manuals and memorize how the men were to lay out their equipment and clothing. Everything had to be uniform.

Captain Brown called his three officers into his CP to orient us about the inspection. He told us to hold practice inspections with our platoons until the men got everything perfect. He wanted L Company to look the best. Then he told us that he had noticed a lot of fraternization between certain officers and enlisted men, a remark undoubtedly aimed at me. He wanted this stopped. Fraternization undermined discipline, and discipline was the key to victory in battle.

I leaned back on the bunk I was sitting on, closed my eyes and laughed to myself. What a bunch of shit. I thought of Cottrell and I digging our foxhole together on Eerie and pissing in the same can. I thought of the night on Baldy when I was on the machine gun with Jackson and pissed on Sergeant Sides', rifle to make it work. Real combat officers eat, sleep, shit and piss with their men as far as I was concerned. Piss on what Captain Brown was telling us. The two new lieutenants listened intently to Brown. *Poor devils*, I thought. They know naught of what is in store for them. They had no way of knowing what a coward Brown was.

When he was finished lecturing us (me), Brown asked, "Are there any questions?"

No one spoke.

Brown repeated the question, pointedly. "Lieutenant Chamberlin, do you have any questions?"

I had many questions but realized this was not the place to call chickenshit. I did not want to hang myself. But I didn't want to give in to the little bastard either.

"Captain Brown, you leave me speechless," I said. Perhaps, scorn dripping from my words conveyed my contempt for his message.

When we left, the new officers probably got out their manuals to refresh their memories about full field inspections. I went to the Second Platoon to warn them of the coming inspection and then shot the shit with them in a fraternal fashion.

Chapter XLIX

A day or so later, Captain Brown called me over to him. He was in a small group which included the company clerk, Sergeant Browne and the two new lieutenants.

"Look what I've got for you, Al," he said with a friendly smile, as if we were on good terms.

He gave me a small blue case. I opened it. It was a Silver Star.

"Here's the commendation to go with it," Brown continued.

I must admit my eyes moistened a bit as I read of my actions on Eerie. I did not know what to say.

Finally I looked at Sergeant Browne as my eyes cleared and said, "Thanks. Have any of the other awards come through?"

Captain Brown answered. "No, yours is the first one. The others are being worked on. Maybe I'll get my CIB soon."

The others in the group lowered their eyes, as if embarrassed by Brown's lust for a piece of military glory. From what he said I assumed that the awards I had recommended for my men were being processed.

★

The day of the big inspection arrived. On their shelter halves the men laid out their clothing and equipment. Led by Captain Brown, Major Moore and an entourage of minor officers from Battalion, walked deliberately along, checking the men and their gear. I brought up the rear. When I came to Kentucky he was being chewed out by a captain about his boots. Kentucky had on a pair of non-government-issue combat boots. They were made of glossy leather that could be shined and they laced all the way up. They were well shined and looked especially nice. Kentucky had a decorative way of lacing them, unlike the normal Army way. I was proud of Kentucky. He looked so nice.

The captain asked Kentucky, "Soldier, is that the way to lace your boots?"

"Yes, sir," Kentucky replied.

"But that's not the Army way to lace boots," continued the captain. "Who told you, you could lace them that way?"

"Nobody, sir, I figured it out myself," Kentucky answered proudly.

The captain turned to me. I thought I recognized him as the company commander of I Company who had called in friendly artillery on his own positions when they were being overrun on T-Bone, a tactic I did not agree with. I don't remember his name.

"Lieutenant, make sure he corrects those shoelaces," he said.

"No sweat," I told him. "He only wears them for inspections and parades."

The captain looked at me and did not seem to know what to say. I'm sure he noticed that I was much more out of uniform than Kentucky, with my twin daggers, .45 and leather thongs. But he did not seem to want to confront me. Brown had probably told him how I pulled a dagger on him.

We moved on and came to Neathery's shelter-half. The captain pointed to the display of knife, fork and spoon.

"Is that the correct way to lay out eating utensils, Lieutenant?" he asked me.

"Beats the hell out of me," I replied, truthfully. I had not reviewed the manual and did not think it mattered much.

"You'd better check your manual, Lieutenant," the captain snapped at me.

As we moved on, the captain picked up his pace to catch up with the other officers, as if he did not want to be left back alone with me.

After the inspection, the inspectors retreated to Captain Brown's CP to discuss the results. I did not join them. I felt much more kinship with my men than I did with my fellow officers. So I joined my platoon as they put away their stuff. We talked and joked about the chickenshit of the day.

The next day Captain Brown summoned me, Bob Brown and Jack Neathery to go with him to see Colonel Spottswood. *Maybe it's about the Silver Stars and Distinguished Service Crosses I had recommended them for*, I thought, as we followed him up the slight slope to the colonel's CP.

When we were seated the colonel offered us drinks. Captain Brown accepted a shot of Scotch. Browne and Neathery looked at me for a lead.

"No thanks, sir," I said. I don't drink on duty."

"So Captain Brown, you asked to see me?" Spottswood opened the meeting.

Captain Brown looked at a piece of paper on his clipboard as if he were going to read something. Instead, he handed the paper to the colonel. Spottswood read the paper carefully. His countenance became very serious.

"This is a list of very serious charges against you, Chamberlin," he said. "What do you have to say for yourself?"

"I don't know," I said. "What are the charges?"

"Didn't you explain the charges against him, Captain?" Spottswood asked.

"Well, no sir," said Brown. "I didn't have a chance to."

Probably didn't dare to, I thought. For some reason I was very calm. I had no fear of what Captain Brown might say about me. I wondered why he had brought Browne and Neathery along. He never explained, nor did Spottswood ask. I was glad he did. I felt secure in their presence.

"Lieutenant, Captain Brown accuses you of being uncooperative and disobedient," Spottswood said. "Why can't you work things out and get along with each other?"

After a moment of heavy silence, I spoke the truth. "Because I have no respect for him."

Brown looked at me and whined meekly, "But why, Al?"

"You know damned well why," I continued. "You're a coward and I can't stand your lack of guts."

I stopped briefly. Nobody said anything. Browne and Neathery exchanged glances. Then they lowered their eyes as if startled at my bluntness. Captain Brown looked at Colonel Spottswood beseechingly as if to say, "There, see what I mean?" Spottswood kept his eyes glued on me and waited.

I figured I'd better explain further. "You've treated the men like dirt since you took over the company. You expect combat men to act like garrison soldiers. Before we went on line you bragged about what you were going to do in combat. Then when we did go on the MLR you were scared shitless. I can understand a person being scared in combat, but when that person treats others like dirt and expects to be obeyed and respected – well, I can't stand that."

Again I paused.

Finally Spottswood asked, "What's this about drinking beer with the enlisted men?"

"Yes, sir, I've had a beer with some of my men once in a while," I admitted. "But I don't see anything wrong with that. We fought together. We saved each other's lives. We shared foxholes. What's wrong with sharing a beer? We shared a lot on Eerie and Baldy. But I don't drink much."

"Captain Brown reports that you are turning his men against him," Spottswood continued. "Is that true?"

"I've never tried to turn the men against him," I denied. "I never had to. In fact, I've reminded them many times that he is their commanding officer, even if they don't like it. Also, on at least three occasions, I have prevented men from trying to kill him."

"That's a serious situation," the colonel said. "Who are those men?"

There was another long, tense silence. They all waited for my response.

I answered slowly and carefully. "It does not matter who they are. They are all men of great courage."

The colonel did not press me for their names. He looked at the charges again while we waited for his decision. Captain Brown kept his eyes lowered. I expect he was more scared than ever, now that he knew some of his men wanted to kill him.

Spottswood made his decision. He folded Brown's paper in half and tore it to pieces. Then he spoke. "I want all of you to go back to your company and settle your differences."

Captain Brown jumped up and led the exodus from the tent as fast as he could. I followed Sergeants Browne and Neathery slowly. I was in no rush to settle anything with Brown.

When I was only a few feet away from the tent, Spottswood stuck his head out of the flap and said in a low voice,

"Chamberlin, can I see you for a minute?"

Reassured by the tone of his request, I returned to his CP.

"I'm going to have another drink," Spottswood said. "Sure you don't need one?"

"Maybe I'll have a beer, sir," I agreed.

"I'm disappointed in you, Chamberlin," the colonel said somewhat sternly. "You were such a good officer in combat that I had great expectations of you."

"I'm sorry, sir," I replied, sensing that he was on my side. "But I can't respect a coward who treats his men like dirt. I have great respect for my men after what we went through together. He has no respect for his men."

Spottswood pondered for a moment. Then he said, "How would you like to be transferred to I Company? They lost a lot of officers on T-Bone and their commander could use a combat-tested veteran to help break in his new replacements."

As far as I knew, I Company was still being commanded by the captain under whose command it was on T-Bone and the one who had words with me at the recent inspection. "I don't think so, sir," I said. "I didn't think too much of his calling in artillery on his own men on T-Bone. I doubt if we would get along."

"How about K Company?" he offered. "They're short of officers too."

"Well, I know that Captain Brown is a close friend of Captain Gatsis," I said, feeling relieved now that Spottswood didn't seem to want to lose me, "so I'm not sure that would work out either. I wouldn't mind going to M Company though. I was in a machine-gun platoon in WWII. I guess I told you that before."

"Yes, I remember you told me that when I first met you," he said. "And I heard all about what you did with a machine gun on Baldy. Unfortunately, M Company has no openings for officers right now. But there are a couple of other possibilities. A new general has joined our division and is looking for an aide. With your combat record you would have a good chance of getting it if you wanted the position. Your chance of promotion would be good too."

I had never thought of being a general's aide. I didn't think I was cut out for the spit and polish chickenshit that such a position would require. Could I kiss a general's ass if I didn't like him? I probably could, but I knew I wouldn't want to. By now, I had concluded that I would probably not stay in the Army after my three years were up. I would put in my time in Korea, finish my three years and go back to civilian life where I would not have to take orders from some military prick like Captain Brown. If I didn't like my boss, I could always quit. I couldn't do that in the Army. Besides, I was not sure I was smart enough to be a general's aide.

"Sir, I don't think I'm cut out to be a general's aide," I said. "What's the other possibility?"

"They're looking for instructors back at the School of Standards," he said.

I had never heard of the School of Standards, but I had been an instructor at Fort Dix so I guessed that would be no sweat. And that might keep me out of combat. I'd had all the horrors of combat I wanted, on Eerie and Baldy.

"I wouldn't mind being an instructor, sir," I said.

"Okay, Chamberlin, I'll see what I can do," he said.

"Thank you, sir," I said. "Is that all, sir?"

"Yes, that's all," Spottswood said. "Good luck, son."

We exchanged salutes and I left. My orders came through the very next day. I was to report to the School of Standards in Wŏnju, on detached duty.

Chapter L

The School of Standards was a short stopover for new replacements to review vital parts of their basic training – those having to do with killing or being killed. General Ruffner's operation "Counter" had created many casualties. These had to be replaced by more young bodies. During their brief stay at the school, the new men would review what they had learned about how to kill from veteran combat men, like myself, most of whom had had some part in the slaughter of the communist foe.

I arrived at the school decked out in my full combat gear; colt .45, twin daggers and leather thongs. No one else wore daggers or leather thongs. Few wore .45s. At least not lieutenants. But that did not bother me, I felt comfortable with my warrior persona.

Soon after my arrival, I reported to the school's commanding officer. I have forgotten his name, but he was a captain of nondescript appearance. If I remember correctly, he was a little pudgy around the waist.

His first matter-of-fact question was, "Lieutenant, what is your TO&E weapon?"

"An M2 carbine, sir," I replied. "But on the line company commanders and executive officers carry .45s."

"You're not on the line here," he reminded me. "And you're not a company commander or an executive officer. You are an instructor. I will expect you to carry your TO&E weapon and adhere to the uniform of the day. Is that clear?"

I had no ready argument. "Yes, sir," I said. "Is that all, sir?"

"One more thing," he continued. "Get rid of those daggers and thongs. General Ruffner doesn't like them."

When I returned to my quarters, I did as I was ordered. I was not about to mess up an easy, safe assignment during this ugly war. I stowed my .45, daggers and thongs in my duffel bag, along with another contraband weapon.

Before I had left L Company on this assignment, Sergeant Browne had asked a favor of me. "I don't think I can get my Russian rifle through customs," he had said. "Being an officer, do you think you could get it through?"

"I don't know, but I'll try," I had offered. I would have done anything for him.

So his souvenir of combat was already in my duffle bag, broken down into its two major components, the barrel and stock/receiver groups. If it had not been taken apart, it would not have fit into my duffel bag.

I got along well with the other lieutenants at the school. There were a few captains there too, but they lived in their own tent. Another example of the Army caste system, not that it mattered to me. I taught mostly bayonet and unarmed combat. I had learned these skills well at Fort Dix, New Jersey.

When I taught a class the simple system of flat-blade bayonet, a murmur went up from the class, "Why didn't they teach us this before?"

I did my best to convey to my classes the importance of courage under fire and commitment to caring for their comrades. My lessons were well received by my students. During most of my free time, I played volleyball or exercised to stay in fighting fitness in case this easy duty didn't last.

But a lot of my free time was taken up by a pursuit of a different nature – sex. Wŏnju was a fairly large city with lots of shops and other attractions for U.S. servicemen, i.e., bars and whorehouses. As I was walking along one of the narrow streets near the school one afternoon, I saw a very beautiful Korean girl in a small shop. She was selling some wares. I had seen many pretty girls in Korea, but few of them had such gorgeous, large breasts as this one. Immediately I wanted her.

I entered her shop. She spoke enough English to communicate with me. I asked if I could see her later when she was off duty. She agreed and told me to come back that night. With great anticipation, I returned after dark. There was no pretense. She led me back into her sleeping space. She demanded payment up front. Her price was five dollars, higher than the norm of two dollars, but I expected it would be worth it. After I paid her we stripped for action. She insisted I wear a rubber, which she furnished. I didn't care for rubbers. To me, they diluted the warm pleasant feeling of flesh against flesh. But I went along with her demand. Then I wanted to play with her nice tits a bit to warm her up and for my own pleasure as well. But she was completely unresponsive, as if it were a waste of time.

"Come on, let's go," she urged.

So I entered her without further ado. She was dry and not as adept as her tits had led me to expect. I never went back for seconds.

One of the duties the lieutenants at the school had to pull, was Officer of the Day. Among other things the OD had to make the rounds of several places near the school to look for GIs who were looking for pussy. It was against Army regulations for Americans soldiers to be in these places.

My turn to be OD came soon after my arrival at the school. With a driver and my authoritative OD band on my left bicep, I set out in a jeep on my mission of morality to keep GIs from getting laid by local ladies. Our first stop was down by the large river that ran past the school. A lot of camp followers lived there.

When I dismounted from the jeep to look for fellow-sinners, I was quickly surrounded by Korean kids begging for candy, soap, cigarettes, money – or whatever they thought I might have. They didn't bother the driver. Maybe they thought an officer had more to offer.

Before I realized what was happening, a young Korean girl wearing glasses squeezed close to my front and looked up into my eyes. She was not very attractive. She was rather plain and looked like a smart kid who would sit in the front of a class and know all the answers. Certainly she was not my idea of a sex object. But with nimble fingers she opened my fly and put her little fingers around my little soldier. He rose to attention instantaneously.

"*Sucha hachi*?" she asked. "Me number one *sucha hachi* girl."

Her mouth was just about the right height. She was eager and confident. She asked for no reward. We were in a public place with many looking on. This was, to me, perverted, abnormal behavior. All those facts seemed to add excitement to my cock. However, I quickly, though gently, rescued my throbbing member from her tantalizing fingers and closed my fly.

"No, no," I spoke to her softly. "Not here. Not now."

The implication was surely there in my words, tone and gentle touch that I would not be averse to her advances under different circumstances.

As I finished my twenty-four hours of OD duty, thoughts of the little girl's fingers fondling my privates would not leave my mind. As soon as I was off duty, I returned to the riverside shantytown to look for her. I didn't worry about being caught. I was an officer and could bluff my way as I had done before, I figured. To me, there was a certain thrill to sneaking around in off-limit areas and breaking chickenshit rules and social mores. As a private first class, I had enjoyed doing it in Japan after WWII and now I was enjoying doing it in Korea, as an officer and gentleman. Ever since I was a kid being made to do things by my mean old father, I had not liked being told what I could or could not do.

She was not hard to find. She was outside, as if she were waiting for me, as if she knew I would come. Actually, she was probably just on duty waiting for any customer who came along. Silently she led me into the small hut she shared with her parents. She removed my boots at the door. Her parents grinned as she led me past them into a small room where the family slept and she worked on mats on the straw floor. She steered me to the mat we would use. She unbuckled my belt, opened my fly and removed my pants and shorts. She folded them neatly and placed them on the floor near by. I was ready. I lay on my back on the mat. From her knees she bent forward and plied her trade on my prideless prick.

I had had oral sex before, but never anything equal to this. Her tiny fingers, lips and tongue tantalized and caressed my joystick tenderly and gently, as if it were to be adored, loved and cherished, like a child getting pleasure from licking and sucking on an ice-cream cone. She seemed happy also when she brought me to a wild climax. I held her head tenderly and caressed her dark hair affectionately for a few moments as we relaxed. Then she washed me and I put my clothes back on. I gave her two dollars. Her parents grinned again as I departed.

During my stay at the school, I visited my little number one *sucha hachi* girl many times. I brought her gifts of candy, soap and other goodies and always paid her two dollars. I expect she was a vital support for her family.

One day I was taking a leak by the river. The urine burned a little. I milked it down as we had been taught for short-arm inspections. A drop of pus oozed from my urethral canal. *Son of a bitch*, I thought. *I've got the clap.*

I rushed back to camp to see the sick-call doctor, a young first lieutenant. He gave me a shot of penicillin in my ass. It cured the clap. I had no more urinary burning or discharge. Unlike most things in the Army, treatment for venereal disease was not put in your record, at least not for officers. So it was my secret and the doctor's.

From what I had been told the incubation period for gonorrhea was two weeks, so I could not figure out who I had got it from. Was it the girl I had had sex with around three weeks before I came to the school, or the one I had screwed about a week ago? I was puzzled. Surely it could not have been my little *sucha hachi* lover.

I did not let my short scare with the clap bother me. I continued with my duties as an instructor. I became friends with Corporal Tom Ryan. He was from the 120th Engineers and had helped build bunkers on Baldy, in between the two times I was there. So we had some things in common to talk about. We taught some classes together. In the course of our conversations I learned that he, too, enjoyed the pleasures of forbidden fruit. So we visited a Korean hut a few times together and partook of the favors of the two ladies living there.

The officers at the school had a club where they drank and socialized. I did not care to drink much, so I never went to the club of my own volition.

However, I did feel obligated to attend a birthday dinner party for the commanding officer. It was a command performance and all the officers were expected to be there. I felt it was in my best interest to go. I didn't want to be sent back to my unit. There was no telling when they might be sent back to the front lines. Several of the officers had Korean girls with them. I wasn't the only gentleman who enjoyed Korean camp followers. One of the captains had an extraordinarily beautiful girl with him. Her body was even more gorgeous than the lady from whom I might have got the clap. Her face was as pretty as a doll's. Her features and rosy cheeks were perfectly proportioned. I noted her beauty and envied the captain she was with. But after the party I forgot about her.

On one tour of duty as OD, I patrolled to the outskirts of a community of camp followers. Officially, I was looking for GIs who were not supposed to be there. Those I found I sent back to camp with the admonition, "Go, son, and sin no more." Far be it from me to "cast the first stone" by pressing charges against a fellow-sinner. That was the way I would have wanted to be treated, if I were caught. Unofficially, I was looking for potential places for my own pleasures. As I peered into a small, dimly lit shack, I saw the beautiful girl who had been with the captain at the recent party. She had another young girl with her.

I took note of the location of the dwelling. It would be easy to remember. It was the last hut in the community. The next evening I returned with my friend, Tom Ryan. We decided before we got there to treat the girls like ladies, not prostitutes. We would try to make love to them and seduce them like we would American girls. Ryan was willing to pursue the other girl while I tried to make out with the more beautiful one.

Our plan did not work out. The beautiful girl was a pro. She demanded money up front.

"No, no," I lied. "We just want to be friends and talk to you."

The girls were not pleased with my proposal. They resisted our advances. Nothing happened in the short time we were there.

And it was a very short time. As if just in the nick of time to rescue the poor maidens from the foreign aggressors, a jeep pulled up outside. It was a guard patrol led by the Sergeant-of-the-Guard. The sergeant took our names and told us we were in an off-limits area and should go back to camp. I told him that I was just trying to make an innocent date with the girl I had seen at the party. He still insisted we were off-limits, so we went back to camp, mission unaccomplished.

I was disappointed, but forgot about it until a few days later. Then I received a letter from a Captain W. C. Kusener, by command of General Ruffner, stating that I had solicited an enlisted man to accompany me to an off-limits Korean house. General Ruffner proposed to impose punishment pursuant to Article 15, unless I demanded a trial by court martial. I was ordered to reply by endorsement stating whether I demanded a trial. I was also permitted to submit any matter in mitigation, extenuation, or defense.

That son of a bitch had turned us in, I realized.

Chapter LI

I replied by endorsement as ordered. I did not ask for a court martial. I lied about why I was in a Korean off-limits house. I said I was there to invite a Korean lady to a party at the officers' club and that I had taken an enlisted man with me for protection.

In the next endorsement, General Ruffner doled out his punishment under Article 15. I was fined $135 – the highest price I ever paid for a piece of ass I didn't get. I was also reprimanded for deliberately transgressing the standing orders of the Army commander and setting a deplorable example for my subordinates. My conduct was considered to have been extremely prejudicial to good order and military discipline. My solicitation of an enlisted man to accompany me upon this illegal venture, constituted an intolerable aggravation of my offense. It was expected that my future conduct would set an example of decorum worthy of emulation by my associates in the service.

I wondered how the captain had got away with taking that lovely Korean lady to the officers' club. One might say I was only following the example of a superior officer, I also wondered if General Ruffner was getting any Korean pussy.

A few days later, I was ordered back to my unit. While I was gone I had been transferred to M Company. I reported to Captain White, the new company commander of M Company. It was now early November.

But even before reporting to Captain White, I donned my combat garb. My .45 and twin daggers were reattached to my cartridge belt and stabilized by thongs tied around my thighs. I was again ready for battle.

Captain White was very cordial, polite and well spoken. His graying hair indicated that he was probably in his late thirties or early forties. He had a nice-looking face, with fair skin and pale blue eyes. He was of average size.

"Lieutenant, welcome to our company," he greeted me. "I've

heard a lot about you. They say you're a good man with a machine gun. That's good. I want you to take over my machine-gun platoon. While we're still in reserve you can teach them how to best use machine guns in combat. That will give you a chance to get acquainted with your men. I think you'll find that M Company has a fine group of officers. Lieutenant Black has the Recoilless Rifle Platoon and Lieutenant Brownly has the Mortar Platoon. They are both fine young officers."

"Yes, sir, I know Lieutenant Brownly," I said. "We were at Fort Dix and Fort Benning together."

"They're out in the field with their men today, but you'll have a chance to meet them at dinner tonight. We all eat together," White continued. "By the way, Lieutenant, only company commanders are permitted to carry .45s."

"Well, this .45 was given to me by Lieutenant Moroney when he rotated. It has a lot of sentimental value to me," I said.

"But it really wasn't his to give to you, was it?" White said.

I realized he was right. The Army has no room for sentiment. "No, I guess you're right," I agreed. "What should I do with it? It's not on anybody's books."

"It should be turned in to supply," said White. "Also those leather thongs. General Ruffner doesn't like them."

Reluctantly, I did as I was ordered. *Another chickenshit superior*, I thought bitterly.

That evening, I met Lieutenants Black and Brownly. Black was a black man. He appeared to be a quiet, polite man who did not question anything White said. Brownly acted very much the proper gentleman who followed White's lead in behavior and conversation.

At chow that evening, I learned a new way to harass and try to control the enlisted men. The food was prepared in a large mess tent. The men lined up outside the tent and filed through the tent to get their food. Cooks and KP personnel ladled out the food from a serving line. After getting their food, the men passed through the other end of the tent into the open to eat. They sat on the ground, logs, stones or whatever. They were not allowed to sit on their steel helmets.

In all my training I had been taught that if officers and enlisted men share the same mess facilities, the men eat first and the officers last. But not here. In the corner of the mess tent was a table for four with chairs set up for us officers. It was located near the entrance, where the men had to pass within inches of the officers just before they got to the serving line. Anything the men said or did was within the sight and hearing of the officers. This arrangement stymied any cussing or horsing around. And, of course, the officers were served first.

I started off on the wrong foot, "Pretty fucking crowded in here, isn't it?" I asked, pointedly.

White gave me a paternal look. "We don't use vulgarity here. We try to set a good example for our men," he moralized. "I believe vulgarity is the sign of a poor vocabulary."

When our food was served and before the men were allowed to be served, Captain White asked us to bow our heads while he said grace. I did not bow my head. I ate my meal in silent contemplation of how stupid this fucking setup was. White told tea-party jokes. Black and Brownly smiled and laughed appropriately. In the course of the conversation it came out that White had been a professor of English at some college and in the Army Reserves. He had volunteered for active duty because the pay and benefits were better. He had been in WWII, but never left the States.

That night in their quarters, Black, Brownly and White had some more polite, decent conversation. I did some push-ups and sit-ups, ignored them and turned in early.

The next morning, I did not join the other officers at their breakfast table. Instead I stood at the end of the line of enlisted men and ate outside. I found a spot a little apart from the men and ate alone. I didn't give a shit whether White liked it or not. If he said anything about it, I could tell him what officers were supposed to do, as he had told me the day before.

Maybe White felt obligated to appease me. For when the company lined up to march to the field, he asked me to march at the head of the column and set the cadence. White marched the troops as one would in basic training or on parade. "Hut, two, three, four," he shouted.

I had not marched in such a fashion for a long time, but it was not difficult to stay in step with White's cadence counting. However, White had trouble matching his counting with my stride.

"Keep it at 120 steps per minute," he hollered at me. "Hut, two, three, four."

This is ridiculous, I thought, *making the men march in step.* In combat you don't march men in step. You spread them out and have them move at rout step. They should be practicing how to move in combat, not on a parade field. Besides, I didn't know the difference between 120 and 100 steps a minute. Nor did I give a shit.

I turned towards Captain White and said, "Let somebody else lead."

I moved to the side of the column and Lieutenant Black replaced me in the lead spot. Black had rhythm and knew how to march to White's cadence.

When I was alone with my platoon in the field, I decided to teach them how to fire a free-swinging machine gun, as I had done on Baldy. I demonstrated it to them by firing a few bursts into a bank.

Almost immediately, Captain White was on the radio. "What's going on over there?" he demanded to know. He sounded a bit upset.

"I'm showing my men how to fire a machine gun in a combat situation," I informed him calmly.

"Well, teach them without wasting all that ammunition," White ordered.

So the rest of the day, I taught my men unarmed combat and how to use knives and bayonets in hand-to-hand combat.

Before Captain White could scold me for my maverick behavior the next day (if he had intended to), the regimental commander, Colonel Jefferson Irvin, called all his officers together for a pre-combat pep talk. Irvin was a redheaded bird colonel. He looked very young for his rank. He told us we must maintain discipline at all cost in combat. Officers must not fraternize with their men. Familiarity breeds contempt, which in turn undermines discipline. Even on the front lines or outposts, officers should be careful not to share the same latrines or foxholes with enlisted men. Military courtesy and non-fraternization build respect, the sine qua non for success in battle.

I thought about the colonel's words. What would have happened on Eerie and Baldy if I had not shared a foxhole with Harry Cottrell? What if I had not manned the machine gun with Cecil Jackson on Baldy, or cleaned Sergeant Sides' rifle by pissing on it in front of the men I was sharing the foxhole with? I wondered. *Familiarity can breed contempt*, I thought, *but not necessarily so*. It can also breed respect. Non-familiarity can also breed alienation, disrespect, poor communications and loathing. What officers needed was courage. That was the sine qua non for victory in combat. And sometimes that was not enough. Contrary to the cliché, bullets did not have their intended victims' names written on them. Both the brave and the coward were vulnerable to the random whims of war. Except that the brave were more apt to expose themselves to danger, in attempts to protect their comrades and their own ass. I knew of no prescription to prevent death in battle. Of course, success in battle and casualties were two different things to rear echelon military leaders like Colonel Irvin. But to the individual warrior success was coming out alive. Death was defeat. Thus my thoughts drifted as we listened to the colonel's lecture, as if he knew what he was talking about.

The next day we were ordered back up to the MLR.

Chapter LII

My machine-gun platoon was made up of four squads. Each squad had a heavy 0.30-caliber, water-cooled machine gun. It was just like the machine-gun platoon I had been in during WWII. One section, made up of two squads, was attached to I Company on the right side of the battalion sector. The other section was attached to K Company, which was now in reserve. None of my men were attached to L Company. Perhaps someone – the new battalion commander, Major Anderson, or even Captain Brown himself – was trying to avoid a renewal of the conflict between Brown and me. It didn't matter to me. I could not have cared less.

As if fearing more problems with me, Captain White expressly ordered me to stay with the section attached to K Company under the command of Captain Gatsis. I followed his orders, but only after I had made a trip to my machine guns with I Company to make sure I knew exactly where they were, what their targets were and how my men were doing. In the K Company sector I moved into a bunker with some of my men and did what our regimental commander had warned us not to do – fraternized with my men.

Upon arrival on the MLR, I dug out my daggers, grenade pouch and thongs and attached them to my cartridge belt. To hell with General Ruffner's ban.

Captain Gatsis invited me to attend daily morning meetings in his CP with his other officers. These were informal gatherings where we all had a cup of coffee and said whatever we wanted to. They were mostly for communications so that we would all know what was going on. I found Captain Gatsis to be a very pleasant, quiet, unobtrusive person. He was not at all the kind of person I would expect a friend of Captain Brown to be. But then, when I thought about it, he was the kind of person Brown would cozy up to because he was so tolerant. Captain Gatsis made no mention of my combat gear.

Shortly after returning to the MLR I got a call from Captain White. "I'm going on R and R for four days," he informed me. "I just learned that you have seniority over Black and Brownly." (R and R meant Rest and Relaxation. Under this program soldiers who had been in Korea for a while were rewarded with a trip back to Japan. Originally it was meant to give battle-weary GIs a short break to recuperate from the rigors of war. I had gone on R and R myself while at the School of Standards. I had spent a couple of nights in Tokyo with a couple of lovely geisha girls. Also while there I met my old roommate, Fats. Remember him? He had got married and taken his new bride to Fort Benning, where she ended up screwing his friend while he lay drunk on the couch. Fats had been sent to Hokkaidō instead of Korea. Now he was down in the dumps. His wife wanted a divorce. We met in a nightclub where I was checking out which geisha to share my bed with that night. With no pretense of modesty I was proudly wearing my Silver Star and first lieutenant's bars. My short-puckered friend was still a very obese second lieutenant.)

"Yes, I know," I said.

"So that means I have to leave you in charge of the company while I'm gone," White continued.

"You don't have to if you don't want to," I told him. "It doesn't matter to me."

"Yes I do," said White. "It's only proper."

"Okay," I agreed. "Anything special you want me to do?"

"No, just report to my CP each morning to sign the morning report," White said. "My clerk will tell you what to do."

I went over to M Company's CP the next morning as ordered. The clerk had the morning report ready for me to sign.

"We have a problem," the clerk said.

"What is it?" I asked.

"Corporal Hardy didn't shave this morning," explained the clerk. "He was driving a staff officer from battalion this morning and the officer told me he has to be court-martialed. You have to recommend it."

I knew Hardy. He was a jeep driver and a good soldier. I also knew he was married and had some kids. If he were court-martialed he would probably be demoted to private and lose pay, a loss that would be hard on his family.

"Have him report to me," I told the clerk.

Hardy admitted to me he had not shaved that morning. The detail to drive the officer had come up so quickly he had not had time.

I knew there was a silly special order from General Ruffner that an unshaven GI, even on the front lines, had to be court-martialed. I not only did not agree with Ruffner's special order, I also did not think it was fair that Hardy and his family should suffer because of it.

So I got out the manual on Military Justice and turned to the section on Article 15, the one with which General Ruffner had punished me. As company commander, I did not have the rank or authority to conduct a court martial. But I could administer company punishment under Article 15, and thereby control the punishment. With due process and seriousness, I gave Hardy company punishment. He was to report to the mess tent each evening and squash cans for a half hour for one week. Now they could not court martial him. That would be double jeopardy.

I ordered the company clerk to type up the papers for company punishment for Hardy for me to sign.

"But sir, you can't do that," the clerk warned me. "He has to be court-martialed. You'll get in trouble."

"I can do it," I told him. "I did it. Now get the papers ready."

Soon after the papers were finished, signed and forwarded through proper channels, the phone rang. It was Major Moore.

"Lieutenant, one of your men was found unshaven by Major Ross this morning when he reported as a driver," reported Moore.

"I know," I replied. "It's already been taken care of."

"Then you've recommended that he be court-martialed," Moore assumed.

"No, I gave him company punishment under Article 15," I explained.

"But you can't do that," Moore countered. "He has to be court-martialed."

"I don't think he deserved to be court-martialed," I argued.

"But its Division policy," Moore insisted.

"I know, but did anybody ever think of challenging that policy?" I counter-punched.

As though floored, Moore hung up.

Later, I learned that Captain White's R and R had been canceled before he even got out of Korea and he was ordered to return to his company. But it was too late to court-martial Corporal Hardy.

★

In early December 1952, K Company relieved the company occupying Christmas Tree Ridge. My machine-gun squads attached to K Company also made the move. The move was made at night. It was very dark. The route of march was down a steep slope made slippery by a light covering of snow and frozen ground, then up a narrow road to the Christmas tree-shaped ridge. No lights were allowed. It was nearly impossible to see where one was going and to maintain one's footing going down the treacherous slope. Many of the men slid down on their asses. It was a difficult move and took most of the night. We had to wait to follow K Company. When my men got to the gun positions vacated by the outfit we were relieving, I checked on each gun squad. I told them to set up their guns, keep two men on each gun and have the rest of the men rest as much as possible. Then I retired to my new CP and rested myself.

As a matter of fact, I was still resting when Captain White called me on the phone.

"Chamberlin, Major Anderson inspected your area this morning and he told me the gun positions and men were filthy," White scolded me. "He said the area was not policed up and the men were dirty and unshaven."

"What time was the major here?" I asked. "He didn't bother to stop to see me."

"Around 0800 hours, just after dawn," White continued.

"Well, what did he expect?" I asked. "At that time my men did not have any water to clean up with, except what they had in their canteens and the gun jackets," I argued.

"That's no excuse," White said. "Major Anderson wants to see you in his CP at 1800 hours. I'll send a jeep over for you."

"I don't need a jeep," I told White. "I can walk. I know where his CP is."

I had never been in the battalion CP before but I knew where it was. It was about a half mile east of my new CP. It was a short distance behind L Company's CP. The quickest way to get there was to walk through the trenches that L Company occupied. I was not afraid of walking the trenches at night. Many of L Company's men knew me or had heard of me. They knew my silhouette and I knew the password if I needed it. I didn't worry about soldiers with nervous trigger fingers. Most soldiers feared drawing attention to themselves by firing their weapons anyhow. A few spoke to me as I passed. I returned their greetings politely.

Major Anderson's CP was warm and well lit. The major's desk was near the entrance. Farther back in the large field tent were staff officers busy with various tasks of battle business. Captain White and Lieutenant Brownly were also there. Whether plotting mortar targets or to see me get my ass chewed out, I didn't know, nor did I care. I paid no attention to anyone in the tent except Major Anderson. But I did notice that all was quiet as soon as I entered.

I saluted Major Anderson. "Lieutenant Chamberlin reporting as ordered, sir," I said.

After returning my salute from his chair behind his desk, the major said, "Take off your jacket and sit down, Chamberlin."

I leaned my carbine in a corner and slowly, methodically, untied my thongs so I could remove my cartridge belt and field jacket. Then I sat.

"Chamberlin, I was in your area this morning and the place was a mess," the major bellowed at me in sharp contrast to his initial pleasant greeting. "Some of your men hadn't shaved for a week." His voice was loud and scolding for all to hear.

I knew he was lying about my men not shaving for a week. So I jumped to my feet and answered in an equally loud, confident tone. "That's not true, sir."

I guess it surprised him that I stood up to him so boldly. Anyhow, I was not about to be intimidated by him.

"Sit down, Chamberlin," Anderson said in a much less

threatening voice. "Don't get excited."

I sat. Silence resonated throughout the tent. Tension mounted.

Finally the major broke the spell. "What did you inspect your men for, after they moved last night?"

"I checked to see they all made it, to see that their guns were operating, that they had plenty of ammo and were ready to fight," I answered.

Apparently the major forgot about the rest of his complaints. He suddenly changed the subject. "We're having trouble capturing prisoners," he said in a low voice, as he leaned forward in his chair towards me. "Do you have any ideas on how we can capture some prisoners?"

"I don't know, sir," I answered less defensively. "Send out some contact patrols, I guess."

Maybe the major wasn't so bad after all, I thought. At least he's asking for advice from a subordinate.

"You want to take out some patrols for me?" the major asked eagerly.

"Hell, no," I answered.

I had already applied for an Inter-FECOM (Far East Command) transfer. My punishment by General Ruffner under Article 15, had been the final straw that made me decide not to stay in the Army after my three years were up. I had two more months to do in Korea before I would be eligible for transfer. I hoped to be able to ride out those two months in M Company. Officers of a heavy weapons company were not usually asked to take out patrols.

"You've had enough of patrol duty already, huh?" Major Anderson asked.

"That's right, sir," I agreed.

"Say, while you're here, you want to show me where your guns are and their primary targets?" the major asked. "Here, show me on our war map."

Anderson got up and led me to the center of the tent where a large war map was located. I wondered if I was being tested.

I picked up a pointer and showed the major exactly what he had asked me.

Major Anderson thanked me. The other officers in the tent remained silent. I put my field jacket and cartridge belt back on. When I bent forward to tie my thongs carefully around my thighs, I faced the entrance to the tent. My ass was towards the other officers as if to say, "Kiss it." I picked up my carbine, with its 120-round clip hanging awkwardly from its receiver, saluted Major Anderson and walked out of the battalion CP into the darkness. I felt smugly pleased with myself and my performance. I smiled to myself as I walked back through the trenches. In low tones I spoke to the men on guard in the trenches in a friendly, fraternal manner. I encountered no officers in the trenches.

Chapter LIII

My new CP was a bunker with overhead cover. It was located a few yards south of Captain Gatsis' CP, which was a larger bunker at the base of Christmas Tree Ridge. A narrow dirt road came to an end between our CPs. At the top of Christmas Tree Ridge was Bethlehem Point. Beyond that, across about 300 yards of no man's land, was Luke's Castle, which was the foremost Chinese position. A good marksman could hit a six-inch bull's-eye at that distance. Therefore we had to be careful not to expose ourselves to direct view of Luke's Castle, because enemy snipers were there.

I found that out one day. A jeep drove up the road and stopped between our CPs. The driver asked me for directions to some rear echelon outfit. He was lost. I decided to impress him with the danger of his mistake.

"Want to see where you are?" I asked him. "Come on, I'll show you."

He followed me to a spot from which we could see Luke's Castle. The top parts of our bodies were also visible to the enemy. I pointed to the sheer rock face of Luke's Castle.

"See how close you are to the Chinks?" I informed him. "That's Luke's Castle. Chinese snipers are over there. This is a dangerous place."

As if to prove my point, a bullet snapped as it passed between our heads. I ducked and led the frightened lad back out of sight of the sniper.

"See what I mean?" I said.

"Yes, sir," the young driver said. He jumped into his jeep, turned it around and sped down the road to safer places.

I smiled. *That will give him something to tell the folks back home*, I thought.

The American and Chinese forces would exchange mortar rounds occasionally, just to let each other know they were there. Normally these random shillings did little damage. But soldiers were warned to wear their armored vests and steel helmets when they were outside their bunkers.

One of my squads was set up on a finger ridge running off the main ridge to the left, like a branch from the trunk of a tree. From there they had a good shot at Luke's Castle. While outside his bunker using his steel helmet to shave in, a common practice, one of my men was hit in the head by shrapnel from one of those random mortar rounds. It was a foggy morning so he could not be seen from Luke's Castle. I guess he figured it was safe. I would have felt the same. They told me he died instantly. In that sense, he was lucky. I wrote a letter to his mother, who, I'm sure, did not feel so lucky. He was a young, handsome, well-liked lad, a good soldier. I'm afraid I can't recall his name.

I got along well with Captain Gatsis. I liked and respected him. I think he liked me. One night there was a heavy snowfall. While at the morning meeting (which now included an artillery forward observer, a young second lieutenant), I noticed the snow was so deep it had covered the observer's porthole.

"What are you going to do if you need to direct some artillery fire?" I asked the observer.

"I don't know," he replied.

"Why don't you go out and shovel it out?" I asked.

"Not me," he replied. "I'm not going out there and expose myself to sniper fire."

Perhaps to show off my courage and disdain for cowardice, I said, "I'll do it for you."

I picked up a shovel, went outside and wallowed through the knee-deep snow up around the bunker to the observation porthole. I was in direct sight of Luke's Castle, from where a sniper had shot at me only a few days before. My olive-drab parka stood out vividly against the white snow. Quickly, I shoveled out the porthole. Nothing happened. The initial exciting feeling of fear left me. *Things had been boring lately*, I thought. I stood up to my full height and looked straight at Luke's Castle defiantly, as if to challenge the Chinese sniper to take his best shot at me. Was I crazy? Did I need bullets flying around me to prove how courageous I was? Didn't I have enough medals already? In one of my mother's letters (after I had told her about Eerie), she had told me, "Stop showing off." She used to say that to me when I was little, if I showed off trying to get attention. If she were here now she would say the same thing. And I would probably ignore her as I did then. But if she were here now she would be the one to show the courage to do what needed to be done. Whatever courage I had I got from my mother, not from my father. He was a cowardly bastard.

Speaking of medals, the Distinguished Service Cross I had been put in for after the battle on Baldy had been disapproved. It had been approved all the way up through Division. General David L. Ruffner had approved it on November 20, fourteen days after he had signed the papers for my punishment under Article 15. I wondered if he had remembered. His approval was vetoed by Lieutenant General Paul W. Kendall, by command of General Van Fleet, the Eighth Army Commander. It was recommended that it be lowered to another Silver Star.

One night K Company sent out a contact patrol from Bethlehem Point. Even though I had no gun there, I went up to the point to be near the action. Why, I don't know. I could have easily stayed in the safety of my CP. K Company had an air-cooled machine gun located at the point for support fire if needed.

Soon after it set out towards Luke's Castle, the patrol was ambushed by a Chink patrol. Support fire was called in. Artillery and mortar rounds were exchanged. Shrapnel filled the air with its deadly mission. K Company's machine gun opened fire to help out.

From where I was standing near the machine gun, I saw the gunner was firing in short bursts from a fixed mount as he had been taught to do in basic training. The gun jammed. Something was wrong. The young gunner could get it to fire only one round at a time. He didn't seem to know what to do. *Acts like too much head space*, I thought.

"Here, let me help you," I volunteered.

I quickly unscrewed the barrel, tightened it back up and backed it off two clicks for head space adjustment. Then I reloaded and fired it. It worked perfectly. I loosened the clamps and sent streams of support fire out, in front of where the patrol was supposed to be. *This was exciting*, I thought. Not as dangerous as Eerie or Baldy had been, but exciting. I fired many long bursts while one of the willing crew members fed the belt of bullets into the receiver. Soon the stream of tracers started to bend too quickly towards the ground, a telltale sign that I had fired the gun so fast I had burned out the barrel. I had heard this could happen, but it had never happened to me before.

"Got another barrel?" I asked.

The gunner had a spare barrel and I replaced the burned out one with it for him. Then I turned the gun back over to him.

None of the crew questioned what I had done even though I did not tell them who I was. On the front lines I wore no evidence of my rank, though some officers did. But perhaps they had heard of the lieutenant with the leather thongs, the one who had brought the girls up to the men for their pleasure.

I moved back to where the patrol had set out from. They had suffered casualties and a litter team was there to go out to bring them back. The patrol leader said there was still a wounded man out there. He needed three men and a stretcher to go with him to bring him back. The litter team seemed to be short a man. Several K Company men were standing around but none of them volunteered to help go get their fallen comrade.

"I'll go," I said simply.

We went out into no man's land and found the wounded man. The other three men proceeded to load him onto the stretcher. Suddenly I had to take a leak. I watched for the foe while I pissed. Then I noticed that one of my thongs was untied. I bent over to tie it.

"Come on, let's go," the patrol leader whispered urgently.

"Don't get your piss hot," I whispered back calmly.

We each took a corner of the stretcher and moved slowly and laboriously back along the slippery trail to the safety of friendly trenches. Once, one guy slipped and our casualty nearly rolled off the stretcher, but we caught him just in time. He didn't complain. We handled him as carefully as we could. No one had taken the time to check if he was alive. We did not know he was dead. Nor did the men of K Company know that an officer from M Company had helped them, unless they recognized the man with the thongs. I never told them.

During the days after my meeting with Major Anderson, I wondered if he thought I was a coward, afraid to go on patrols. That bothered me. Sure, I was afraid. Everybody with any sense was afraid in combat. But I was no coward. I could not stand the idea of people thinking of me the way I thought of Captain Brown. I heard that Brown now had a personal bodyguard, an ex-boxer, who was stationed at the entrance of his well-fortified bunker. I wasn't that scared and I didn't want others to think I was.

Maybe taking a patrol out and capturing some prisoners was not such a bad idea. At least it would show Major Anderson, General Ruffner, Captain White and other military pricks what kind of a combat man I was. I wished some men like Bob Browne and Jack Neathery were with me again. They would go with me and capture some Chinks.

Come to think of it, I thought, *some of my men from the second platoon – Partin, Tally and Kentucky – were still over there in L Company. I bet they would go with me.* So I went over and asked them.

"Sure," said Kentucky. "We have to go on patrols anyway. I'd rather go with you than the dumb officers in our company."

All three of them were willing. Before I left their area, others volunteered to go with us, more men than I needed. Thanks to my buddies, my reputation and renown in L Company was greater than I had expected.

I returned to my CP and thought about how I would take out a patrol. First I would do some reconnoitering. Maybe I would even sneak out alone under cover of darkness, get close to enemy lines, and spend a day or two listening and observing from a hiding place. I would want it to be secret – time, route, place, everything. I wouldn't even want S2 to be in on it. Patrols sent out by battalion intelligence were frequently ambushed or ran into minefields. I thought that this was because they were predictable. They always took the same routes and at the same time of night. The enemy knew their pattern.

The more I thought about it, the more intrigued I became by the idea. I spent some time at Bethlehem Point with field glasses observing Luke's Castle and no man's land between us. I looked for enemy activity, studied the terrain for routes of movement and hiding places. I tried to figure where the Chinks might place listening posts of a few soldiers who could be easily overcome and captured. I thought if I was out there hiding close to their lines I could learn even more of their routines. They would become as predictable to me as we were to them. Maybe they had soldiers hiding close to our lines to figure us out also. I wouldn't mind running into one out there alone. I was confident I could out-fight any Chink in hand-to-hand combat. With my full automatic carbine I could take on quite a bunch of them.

I spent some more time on the right flank of K Company, studying the slope down towards a small stream, where I had heard the Chinks often set up a small listening post. I decided that might be more favorable for my secret operation than up closer to Luke's Castle. This was further away from the main enemy forces, so we would be less apt to run into large numbers of Chinks.

Then I spent more time in L Company's trenches talking with Kentucky, Partin and Tally. We selected a couple of other guys to go with us, if and when we went.

It was time to put my plan into action. I called Major Anderson.

"Sir, this is Lieutenant Chamberlin," I said. "I've been thinking about your asking me if I wanted to take out a patrol for you, I'd like to talk to you about it."

"Good, Lieutenant," Anderson replied. "I'm coming over to see Captain Gatsis at 1400 hours today. Meet me in his CP."

Major Anderson listened to my proposal to take out a patrol of volunteers. I told him how I planned to do it. The major heard me out without interrupting. The others in the CP also listened silently. This was all news to them. I had not told anyone except my volunteers. Probably they were surprised to hear anyone offer to take out a patrol. I think the major was impressed.

"But I will do this only on one condition," I said. "No one is to know the details of my plan, not even S2."

"Lieutenant, I can't agree to that," the major said. "My staff would have to know."

"Okay," I said. "But that is the only way I will do it."

After the meeting I had mixed feelings. I was both relieved and disappointed. Relieved that I would not have to take out a dangerous patrol after all, disappointed that I would not have a chance to be a real hero without having it forced on me like it was on Eerie and Baldy. I wanted to be recognized for something I didn't have to do, like going out to help bring back that dead man. There was something in me that prevented me from bragging about hero stuff like that, even though I wanted to. How I missed Bob Browne and Jack Neathery. We could talk, even joke, about things like that and understand one another. Maybe it was because they, too, had been equally heroic and perhaps equally crazy.

Still, I was again a little smug about how I had talked to the major. I had shown him I was no coward like some of his other officers.

But Major Anderson was not dumb. The next day, I was transferred to K Company. Now I would have to take out patrols when my turn came, without conditions, whether I wanted to or not.

Chapter LIV

Captain Gatsis assigned me to the Third Platoon. Sergeant Gunther had been the acting platoon leader. He had been recommended for a battlefield commission and a Silver Star for leading a very successful attack patrol against the Chinks behind Luke's Castle. They had sneaked up on a large group of Chinks in some sort of group meeting. He had positioned his men skillfully. Then they opened fire and mowed down many of the surprised enemy.

Captain Gatsis filled me in on all this background. I expect he thought two war heroes would relate well to each other. We may well have, but we were not together long enough to really get acquainted.

The Third Platoon was located on a ridge line southwest of Christmas Tree Ridge. There was a greater distance between us and the Chinese lines. We did not think an enemy attack was probable there. We were somewhat isolated from the rest of the company.

I introduced myself to Sergeant Gunther. I told him to carry on as he had been doing. I did not expect to be there long. I hoped to be transferred to Japan soon, so I did not want to usurp any of his authority over the men.

Gunther's CP was a bunker large enough to house about a half-dozen men. It had overhead cover and an oil stove inside to ward off the Korean winter cold. There were no other bunkers in the platoon area for the rest of the men. They had to sleep in foxholes or the trench running along the ridge line. In this CP bunker there was a wooden platform about a foot off the ground on which the men slept and kept their gear. It had been built by and for Korean soldiers who averaged about a foot shorter than Americans. A six-footer would have had difficulty stretching out on it. There was an unplatformed area of about four by eight feet at one end of the bunker. It seemed to be unoccupied.

Gunther offered me space on the platform. I did not want to take anybody's spot, so I declined. I put my things on the dirt floor at the end of the bunker.

I was pretty pissed off that I had been transferred to a rifle platoon. I was not in a friendly or talkative mood. I did not say much to Gunther or his men.

After looking around the bunker for a few minutes, I borrowed a hatchet from one of the men. I went outside and cut down some hard wood saplings and cut them into poles of the right length. Then I scrounged up some discarded commo wire (there was lots of it on most battlefields in Korea) and wired together a frame about seven by three feet. I took it inside and hung it from the log ceiling with more wire. Then I wove more wire between the poles to make a sturdy bunk bed upon which I put my air mattress and sleeping bag. Soon all my stuff was organized. I had all the comforts of combat on the MLR.

The men in the bunker watched me in silence as I worked. I asked for no help. None was offered. They appeared surprised at what I did, as if unused to seeing officers work. The next day they all followed my example. They built double-deck bunk beds along the back wall of the bunker. Now they could sleep more comfortably and have more room to organize their things.

Even though I was not happy with my new assignment, I could not be angry or neglectful of the men for whom I was responsible. The second day I was there, I inspected the ridge line my platoon was responsible to defend. The South Koreans not only slept on short beds, they also did not dig very deep trenches. The platoon had been ordered to dig deeper and better defensive positions. They were to rest during the day and stand guard and dig at night. It was now winter and very cold. There were no bunkers other than the CP bunker. The men had no overhead cover. They slept in their sleeping bags on the hard, frozen ground. Some of the men did not even have air mattresses that would hold air. The mummy sleeping bags were good, much better than what we had had in WWII, but they were not warm enough for sub-zero weather. The men appeared numb and slowed down by the cold. *How in hell did they expect half-frozen zombies to be able to fight, if they had to, or to dig trenches in hard frozen ground*, I wondered. As far as I could see they had not dug much yet.

My heart went out to the poor, cold bastards of my new platoon. But I did not criticize Gunther for their plight. It was not his fault. He was doing what he was told. But they were now my men. I had to figure out how to take care of them, so they could take care of me if need be. I had planned on just putting in my time without making waves until my transfer came through. But now I had to do something.

A few yards east of our CP, somebody had started digging a hole into the bank before the ground froze. I tested it with a pickaxe to see if it could be dug out more. It was frozen too solid. I remembered how the frozen ground would thaw around a campfire when we helped our father in the woods in the cold Vermont winters. So I gathered some firewood and built a fire near the hole in the bank.

"We're not allowed to build fires," Gunther warned me. "We can't even cut any trees without the permission of the South Korean government."

"I know," I said. "But a fire doesn't show up much in the daylight, so nobody will know, will they? Tell the men they can come and get warm by shifts. Then they can work better at night."

Gunther was a soldier of few words. He did not argue with me. He did as I told him. The men got warm. Gradually the ground thawed. That night we kept the fire burning. A crew of men dug into the bank in preparation to build a bunker. For the next day or two we dug and filled sandbags. Soon we had the walls up for a squad-size bunker.

I requisitioned picks, shovels and axes from supply. No one questioned why we needed them. No one from Battalion or even Company Headquarters came to see what we were up to.

Gunther got his commission and was transferred.

I cut trees for logs for the roof of our new bunker. When it was completed the men built bunk beds, as they had learned from my example, and a squad moved in.

Things went so well with the first bunker that I stopped the men from trying to dig the trenches deeper. They were not accomplishing much anyhow. We picked out places for two more bunkers, enough to get all my men up off the ground and under cover. I requested new air mattresses for all the men who needed them. I stationed lookouts at key places along the ridge, to warn of any enemy approach, while most of the men worked on the new bunkers by the light and warmth of fires. The KATUSAs (Korean Army Troops attached to U.S. forces) preferred standing guard to working. So I gave them that choice. It worked out well.

One night, a call came from Captain Gatsis. "Battalion reports sighting fires in your area," he said. "Are you doing that, Al?"

"Yes, sir," I admitted. "We have a small fire going to keep the men warm while they work. It's on the rear slope, so I don't think the Chinks can see it."

"Well, you have to put it out," Gatsis ordered. "Battalion is very upset."

I thought about the Turks. They were some of the fiercest fighting men of the United Nations forces in this silly, stalemated war. I had heard they built large bonfires around which they sang and partied at night, as if defying the enemy to attack them. The Chinese usually avoided them because of their fighting spirit. But I did what Gatsis ordered. We put out the fires.

But it didn't matter much now. The fires had served their purpose. We had two bunkers with oil stoves in them for heat and the ground thawed for two more bunkers. The men worked on these for a while and then went inside the finished bunkers to get warm. The KATUSA sentries did the same with big smiles on their faces. My men finished building the last two bunkers. Then all of the men of my platoon had bunk beds up off the ground and a warm place to sleep.

The men and their clothes were very dirty when I arrived. There had not been much water for them to wash with. What there was had to be kept in the CP to keep it from freezing. From there it had been rationed out sparingly. The numbing cold had made the men neglect their personal hygiene. It did not bother me that the men were dirty, but I did not want them to get sick.

I knew about field showers about a mile behind the MLR. These showers were inside large heated tents. Soldiers could shower and swap their dirty uniforms for clean ones there. I don't know why Gunther had never taken the men back to use these facilities. Maybe he was waiting for permission. I neither waited nor asked for permission. I took some of the men for showers. No one asked any questions, so I set up a shower schedule. Half the men went back one day and the other half the next day. Probably it was not permissible for half of my men to leave the MLR at one time. But I didn't care if it was or not. The Chinese never attacked during the daytime. I doubt if any other outfit on the MLR allowed their men to go back and shower every other day. I was glad I had the balls to do it. I think my men were too. In less than three weeks I had the best housed, warmest and cleanest platoon in the battalion.

No one from Battalion visited our positions to see our good work, I invited Captain Gatsis over, but he did not come either. However, I was very pleased with what we had accomplished.

★

Soon after my transfer to K Company my turn came to take out a patrol. Captain Gatsis was apologetic when he told me about it.

"I'm sorry, Al, but it's only fair to my other officers," he said. "I know you've been through a lot already."

"That's okay," I told him. "I don't expect any special treatment."

In order not to leave any area unguarded by pulling out an entire unit – squad or platoon – men were picked from different units to make up a patrol. The disadvantage of this system was that the men often did not know each other.

I did not really care to take a bunch of strangers on a dangerous mission where the men might have to depend on each other. So I took my small group into a bunker on Christmas

Tree Ridge and from the roster I learned each person's name – not necessarily their real names, but what they wanted to be called. I had each patrol member memorize the names also. Then I told them the order we would move out in and had each one carefully memorize the names of the men in front and at the back of him. I explained our mission to them. It was simply to set up a listening post, a few hundred yards in front of Bethlehem Point.

"Whatever you do," I told them, "stay in that order. If we get hit don't panic and run. It's safer to stay together in the dark. Then you can help each other out."

We moved out after dark. It was very cold. We were dressed warmly in long johns, wool uniforms, heavy, fur-hooded parkas and insulated Mickey Mouse boots. Mittens with trigger fingers kept our hands warm. Fresh snow covered the frozen ground. The moon and stars were bright. We could easily see where we were going. There was no trouble maintaining contact. We set up the listening post with no difficulty.

The night was long and silent. Time passed slowly. After huddling in the snow for a few hours, I became bored and restless. I almost wished some Chinks would show up so we could shoot at them. Maybe we could kill a few or even capture some. I wondered if there were any Chinks near by. Luke's Castle was not far from us. I made a snowball and threw it down the hill into some trees to see if I could stir up some action. Nothing happened. I threw a few more. It didn't scare up any enemy, but my recklessness probably scared hell out of the other members of the patrol. Nobody said anything though. Just before daylight we returned to the MLR.

★

The Chinese would often use loudspeakers from various points along the front to broadcast propaganda to the American troops. Sometimes they played melancholy music to remind our men of home and their loved ones, trying to make them homesick. Sweet songs were sung by Chinese girls with beautiful voices in perfect English. They would tell our lonely lads that fat, rich, capitalist businessmen were taking care of our wives and sweethearts back home, while we were in Korea fighting a war for their profit.

A few days before Christmas the loudspeakers from Luke's Castle began broadcasting to the men on Christmas Tree Ridge. They boasted that the Chinese were going to attack on Christmas Eve and that they would bring back many GI dog tags.

True to their word, the Chinese did attack Bethlehem Point on Christmas Eve, 1952. They did not warn us with the usual artillery barrage. At dusk, before our listening posts were in position, many Chinks silently and swiftly swarmed across no man's land and poured into the trenches, throwing grenades, firing their rifles and bayoneting the men at Bethlehem Point. There was mass confusion. Chinks mixed with Americans in hard-fought, hand-to-hand combat. Some GIs hid in their bunkers only to be blown up by grenades tossed into their hiding place. Others bravely struggled with the foe in the open trenches. There were so many Chinks the Americans were forced to fall back. When he heard that his men were being pushed back, Captain Gatsis left the safety of his CP and moved into the thick of the fight. He rallied his retreating men. Following his example of courage, his men fought valiantly until the Chinese withdrew. Many men, including the platoon leader of the platoon guarding Bethlehem Point, were killed that night.

On Christmas Day, my platoon relieved the remainder of the platoon at Bethlehem Point. We were apprehensive. Had the Chinese promised to attack again on Christmas Day? I could not remember. Was my luck running out? I had heard of many men who had been killed or badly wounded just before they were due to rotate home. But we were not attacked that night, nor on succeeding nights. A few days later the battalion was pulled off the line and moved back into a reserve position. Lady Luck was still with me.

One day, I was talking to K Company's first sergeant about Captain Gatsis' courageous action on Christmas Eve.

"We've put him in for a medal," the sergeant said.

I was interested in learning the extent of Gatsis' heroism. "What medal did you put him in for?" I asked.

"The Medal of Honor," replied the sergeant.

I was surprised and envious, but those feelings did not detract from my admiration for my company commander. I wondered if they would lower his award as they had done my Distinguished Service Cross.

Many years later I learned they did exactly that. They lowered it to a DSC.

Chapter LV

Not long after moving off the MLR, orders came through for me to report to Company B, 8069th Replacement Battalion, Camp Drake Replacement Depot, Sasebo, Japan on January 13, 1953.

Captain Gatsis shared the good news with me and thanked me for my service with K Company.

One evening, Captain Brown came to visit Captain Gatsis. All of K Company's officers were quartered in the same tent. My bunk was just inside the flap of the tent, so to see Gatsis, Brown had to pass me.

"Hi, Al," Brown greeted me in a low, meek voice.

"What the hell are you doing here?" I challenged him, sarcastically. "Where's your bodyguard? Aren't you afraid somebody might hurt you?"

"Let's have a drink and let bygones be bygones," Brown offered.

"I don't drink with cowards," I replied, with anger and hostility dripping from my tongue.

Everyone in the tent pricked up their ears and listened silently to our exchange. I did not pretend to hide my hatred of Brown. No one came to his defense, or chided me for my blunt honesty. I don't know if it was for fear of me or lack of respect for Brown. I expect it was the latter.

Brown moved by me timidly towards Captain Gatsis, whose bunk was in the back of the tent. I turned my back to him.

★

On the train trip south to Taegu where I was scheduled to board a flight to Sasebo, I met Lieutenant Mello who was going to Japan on R and R.

Mello had joined L Company after I left. I had met him briefly after we had returned to the line in the fall of 1952. But I didn't know much about him, except that he had taken over my Second Platoon.

But apparently he had heard a lot about me. When he saw me he rushed up to me and held out his hand.

"Chamberlin, can I shake your hand?" he asked, excitedly. "I've always wanted to talk to you. My name is Mello. My friends call me Mel. I met you once on the MLR, but you probably don't remember me."

"Yes, I remember you," I replied. I was not sure I wanted to be very friendly with anyone connected to Captain Brown. My former men in L Company's Second Platoon had not said much about Mello when I had talked to them.

"Can I sit with you?" Mello asked eagerly.

"Sure, why not?" I replied non-committally.

After he sat down next to me Mello continued the conversation. "Do you remember Kentucky, Partin and Tally? They were always talking about you. You were a difficult act to follow."

"Of course I remember them," I said. "They were damned good combat men. How could I forget them?"

"They sure are," Mello agreed. "They were on patrol with me when we captured a couple of Chinks down by the river."

"I heard something about that," I said. "I didn't know you were on that patrol."

"Yes, I was," Mello said. "But those men deserve all the credit. I learned a lot from them. They had a lot of guts."

I began to feel better about Mello. He could not be too bad if he gave his men the credit they deserved. He was certainly not like Captain Brown.

"Say, is it true what they said about you?" Mello asked.

"I don't know," I said. "What did they say?"

"They said you brought a couple of geisha girls up to camp for the boys," Mello said. "Is that true?"

"I've never known those boys to lie," I answered evasively, wondering what Mello was up to.

After a few moments of silence, Mello asked, "Do geisha girls give blow jobs?"

I was surprised by his question and naiveté. Maybe he could

be trusted.

"Some do, some don't," I informed him, like a pro to a rookie.

"I'd love to get a good blow job," Mello continued to express his sexual desire.

"Well, while we're in Taegu overnight, why don't you get one?" I told him.

"How would I go about it?" Mello asked.

"Just go to a geisha house and ask for one," I said.

"How would I find a geisha house?" Mello asked.

"Oh, just ask any little kid," I told him. "They're all over the place. Want me to find you one? I wouldn't mind getting laid myself."

"Would you?" Mello asked, gratefully. "That's great. I guess everything they said about you was true. You're my kind of guy. Say, can I call you Al?"

"Sure," I assured him.

Mello continued his questioning. "What if they don't want to give you a blow job? Do you just make 'em do it?"

"No, I wouldn't," I told him. "Just let the mama-san know what you want and she'll find a girl that will give you a blow job. I'll ask her for you if you want me to."

"Boy, you're great," Mello exclaimed. "No wonder the men thought so much of you. You're my hero."

"Thank you, but I doubt if Captain Brown said anything good about me," I replied.

"Oh that puny little coward," Mello said. "Did you know that he had a personal bodyguard and never left his bunker while on the MLR? He's a real prick."

"Yeah, I heard," I said.

"I heard you tried to kill him," Mello said. "Is that true?"

"No," I answered. "I just scared him a little."

"That's not what Neathery told me," countered Mello.

"Did you know Neathery?" I asked. "I thought he rotated."

"He did," said Mello. "But he was the Second Platoon sergeant when I joined the company in August. He left a little after we went on line in November."

"He was one of the best combat men I ever met," I said. "He was my hero. I learned a lot from him. Did he ever get the medals

I put him in for?"

"Yes, he got one of them," Mello said, "the Silver Star. I heard he had a DSC coming. I don't know if he ever got that."

"Did any of the other men I put in for medals ever get them?" I asked.

"Not that I know of," Mello said. "Probably Brown screwed 'em out of them."

"Yeah, he would," I agreed. "The son of a bitch."

"I put Kentucky, Partin and Tally in for medals for capturing those prisoners," Mello said. "I hope Brown doesn't screw 'em out of those too."

"Did Neathery ever mention Bob Browne?" I asked. "He was another damned good combat man. He and Jack were buddies. I put him in for the same medals as Neathery, a Silver Star and DSC. He wrote me that he hasn't got them yet."

"Yeah, the men were always telling stories about you, Browne and Neathery," Mello said.

Mello and I had at least three things in common: admiration for courage, loathing for Captain Brown and horniness.

In Taegu, we checked in at where we were supposed to spend the night, dropped off our gear, had a bite to eat and set out in search of sex. It did not take long to find a whorehouse. As I had promised, I asked the mama-san if she had a girl who would give my new friend a blow job. None of the girls in her house were willing, so she sent out for one that would. I picked the prettiest of her girls for my pleasure. We paid a few extra bucks and spent the night. In the morning Mello appeared happy but pretty well drained.

We returned to our billets and picked up our gear. Mello boarded a plane for Tokyo in quest of his sexual desires. I boarded one for Sasebo, for mine. Thus my tour of duty in Korea ended, on a sexual note, as it had started some eight months before.

On the plane, I relaxed and my thoughts drifted. I certainly had been lucky. I had seen combat in two wars and never been hit. The thought that I had had on Baldy, "If I get through this shit, nothing will ever faze me," kept popping into my head. I no longer planned to stay in the Army. After my three years were up I would return to freedom. I now realized that whatever rank one obtained in the military there would always be some prick like Captain Brown or Captain White one would have to take orders from.

Despite my bitterness towards the military, I was proud of what I had done as a leader in combat. I was proud of the courage I had found within me. I was proud that I had lost only three men in the fierce fighting we had been through. I was proud that most of my men had fought bravely for me, and prouder yet that they held me in such high esteem. The fact that I had killed many enemy soldiers was also a source of pride, not guilt, for me. I knew that pride was some sort of sin according to the Bible and was also frowned on by most. But I would have been a hypocrite had I tried to be humble. Besides, the Bible was not my guide for living.

Now I knew why I had had to come to Korea. It was to test my courage under fire. It had been tested in WWII, but the only answer I had received then was that I was scared like all the rest. But in Korea the results were more definite. Sure, I had been scared, but I had passed the test of courage and had the medals to prove it.

But I did feel guilty about one thing. Had I done all I could to make sure my men got the medals they deserved for their heroism? I tried to rationalize that I had, but maybe I had put my own selfish interest first. Perhaps if I had stayed in L Company longer, I could have seen to it that my recommendations were processed out of the company. Maybe I should have hung around the CP more and got on the clerk's ass to get the paper work done, maybe even helped him do it. I could type. Maybe I could have even done more while I was there if I had kissed up to Captain Brown a little. That thought repulsed me. How I hated that cowardly little bastard!

Chapter LVI

Everyone was very friendly with me when I arrived at my new assignment in Sasebo. One of the first officers I was introduced to was First Lieutenant Studman. He was the company commander of a company in our battalion. For some reason my new company commander, Captain Mostrum, was not on duty the day I arrived.

Lieutenant Studman had also earned a Silver Star in Korea, so we had something in common from the start. He seemed to like me. He invited me to go with him that first evening to a rather exclusive nightclub. Only officers were allowed there. It was a place where one could drink, buy drinks for the lovely Japanese ladies who were there and buy tickets to dance with them. Then, if one wanted to, for twenty bucks he could spend the night with the lady of his choice in one of the rooms at the establishment.

Soon after we entered the club, Lieutenant Studman spotted Captain Mostrum dancing with one of the ladies. He introduced me to him. I noticed that Captain Mostrum was also sporting a Silver Star on his Ike jacket. It was also obvious that he was very well lubricated and his hands were holding his sexy partner by her buttocks, pressing her close to his love muscle. He did not pay me much mind. The next day he had forgotten he had already met me.

Studman and I sat in a booth and were joined by a lady who could have passed for a mama-san. She appeared to have more years on her than most geisha girls. She sat with my new friend. At least two other young ladies came and sat next to me. Studman was drinking Scotch and water, so I followed his example. The ladies ordered expensive drinks too, but I think they were pretty well watered down. The girls did not seem to be affected by them.

I was naive about how to act in such a high-class environment until Studman said, "Pick one."

So, out of some vague consideration for my wife, I picked one with her name, Josephine. She was quite pretty and had a nice figure.

After a few more drinks of Scotch we retired to the ladies work areas to have sex and sleep. I was pretty drunk, but I was still able to enjoy Josephine's soft, warm, willing body at least three times before daybreak. A painful hangover greeted me in the morning. I vowed never to drink Scotch again.

Lieutenant Studman and I returned to camp. I was introduced to Captain Mostrum again and the other officer in our company, Lieutenant Littleton, who was also to be my roommate at the officers' quarters. My main assignment was mess officer and Littleton was to be the supply officer.

The company's mission was to process replacements going to Korea and troops rotating from Korea back to the States. Company personnel consisted of us three officers, a mess sergeant and some cooks, a supply sergeant and his assistant, a first sergeant and clerk and a few non-COMS (non-commissioned officers, corporals and sergeants) to help process the troops as they moved to and from Korea through our company. The main things we had to do were feed them, house them, outfit them with uniforms and equipment appropriate for where they were going, take care of whatever clothing and gear they turned in and change their money from U.S. currency to military scrip or vice versa.

When I arrived, there were no troops in the company to be processed so there was actually little or nothing to do except sit around and drink coffee and be available when needed.

So Studman and I planned another trip to town. I had asked Josephine what she liked. She said she loved chocolate bars. So I bought a whole box of them at the PX (Post Exchange) for her.

As we stood waiting for the bus into town, Studman asked me, "Could you loan me ten bucks? I'm a little short."

I didn't have a lot of money myself, but I reluctantly said, "Sure."

For some reason we didn't say much after that. Our mutual admiration seemed to have run its course. I wondered if he was using me or if he just wanted to get rid of me. It really didn't matter to me. Somehow I sensed that was the last I would see of that ten dollars. If he could be bought for ten bucks he was no great bargain. I needed him like a hole in my head.

I gave the candy to Josephine in anticipation that she would be available for another night in the sack with me. She took the gift with great glee and eagerness, but, unfortunately, her dancing time and company had already been purchased for the evening by some other sex-hungry military gentleman. So I was temporarily stranded. Studman went his way with his mama-san.

But I was not alone for long. A cute little chick caught my eye. Her name was Chico. I bought her a drink and some tickets to dance with her. As Japanese go, she was quite short, with a round face and pleasantly curved body. She felt good moving to the music against my warm belly, with her head leaning against my chest about a foot and a half below mine.

I chose not to drink that night and Chico probably drank less than usual also. But she smoked, as did most of the other geishas there. Some of my money was spent on her smokes and drinks as well as the tickets to dance with her. Staying sober that night helped me realize that I was not getting as much screwing for my bucks as I would going to lower class whorehouses at two bucks a crack.

But Chico was sweet, attractive and nice, so I stayed the night with her. Her warm, soft body accepted my eager hardness with a warm welcome and squeezed snugly around me. In a short time an explosive orgasm shook my body. She pushed hard up against me, as if with pleasure. I pushed down deep into the very bowels of her innermost being. She began to cry; I know not whether from pain or joy. She did not tell me. Tears rolled down her lovely cheeks in the dark. I felt them with my hand. I caressed her face and hair gently and whispered to her softly. Her tears inspired me to make her happy, so I stayed joined to her and moved slowly and tenderly so as to ease her pain or enhance her pleasure, whichever. As she moaned softly and my heart softened towards her, my erection did not fail me. It remained stiff and hard. Soon it was again caressing the inner walls of her love canal with slower but equally powerful strokes. She responded with equal cooperation. When we were spent, she snuggled close to me

330

and sobbed silently on. Not knowing anything better to do I cried with her. Our tears mingled as they trickled down our cheeks onto our pillows. I hated to pay that extra ten bucks for a room for the night but I decided she was well worth seeing again.

I think that was the last time I saw Lieutenant Studman at the club. His wife came from the States to live with him. Nor did I see Captain Mostrum there again for the same reason. I also applied for my wife, Judy, Rocky and my 1947 Packard to join me during my tour of duty in Japan. We were eligible for this privilege as long as we had more than a year left to serve.

A batch of troops from the States came to our company on their way to Korea. Our mess hall became a very busy place. We were warned that a Major Wright was coming to inspect our mess operation. I was told that he was very chickenshit, that he went strictly by the books. He came during a midday meal. As mess officer it was my duty to follow him around as he made his inspection. True to my vow made during the height of horror on Baldy, this didn't faze me. Our mess sergeant followed me as I followed the major. The major watched as the food was being dished out to the men by the cooks and KPs on the serving line. To me everything seemed fine.

Major Wright looked at me and said, "Lieutenant, what would you suggest to make this food more attractive and palatable?"

I had no ready reply for him, so I said, "I don't know, sir. I'll ask my mess sergeant."

"I asked you, not your mess sergeant," Wright said. "You're the mess officer, aren't you?"

"Yes, sir," I replied. "What would you suggest, sir?"

"Perhaps the individual servings of food could be separated more by the use of more china," he suggested.

I looked at the mess sergeant. He nodded.

"Yes, sir," I agreed. "We can do that."

"Good," the major said.

After walking around checking refrigerators, stoves and stuff in the kitchen, the major remarked about the dining hall. "The windows are awfully bare. Wouldn't it be nice to have some drapes to make it more homey for the men?"

"Yes, sir," I agreed. "I suppose it would." But, I thought to myself, what the hell difference does it make to them, where they're going.

As a result of Major Wright's inspection the company came up with some funds. The mess sergeant bought some pretty green material and had drapes made for the dining hall windows. Later on Major Wright complimented our company for them and gave me the credit, but I really had little to do with it, I think we got the mess-hall-of-the-month award, or something like that.

When Captain Mostrum's wife came from the States, he took a few days off to help her settle into their housing off base. That left me as the company commander.

The first morning in my new capacity, Corporal Dudley reported to me. He had been on night duty. That night he had made the usual eleven o'clock bed check. First Sergeant Sharp had been missing.

My first thoughts were that I could not let things get out of hand. If others were expected to be in bed by eleven o'clock, so should the first sergeant. He should set a good example. So I called him into the office.

"Sergeant," I addressed him, "Corporal Dudley reports that you missed bed check last night. Is that true?"

"Yes, sir," Sharp admitted. "I was a little late."

"Well, you can't expect your men to follow the rules if you don't," I told him. "So I'm going to restrict you for the weekend."

"Sir, that's not fair," Sharp snapped back angrily. "Saturday is my birthday and I plan to celebrate with some friends. Besides, lots of the cadre miss bed check and nobody ever did anything about it before."

A moment of chilly silence came between us. Sharp broke it by asking, "May I have your permission to ask for a transfer?"

"Sure," I said.

"Is that all, sir?" Sharp asked.

"Yes, that's all," I said. Second thoughts sped through my head. I had not always obeyed chickenshit rules. Maybe I was being too hasty. "No, wait a minute, Sergeant. You say the eleven o'clock curfew is not enforced?"

"That's right, sir," Sharp said. "As long as the men are on duty when needed, nobody ever complained before. I think Dudley is a little bit of a troublemaker. He is not well-liked by the other staff."

"Okay, Sergeant," I said. "I guess you're right. As long as you do your job, forget about the restriction. I never liked chickenshit rules myself."

"Thank you, sir," Sharp said.

Sergeant Sharp saluted me and left. After I returned his salute, I sat behind Captain Mostrum's desk deep in thought. I had nearly been trapped in a power struggle over silly rules made up by some soft staff officer sitting on his ass behind a desk, far removed from the realities of a lonely soldier's life. The urge to see Chico again flowed through my veins. But I decided it was best to wait until Captain Mostrum returned to duty before continuing my pursuit.

Chapter LVII

We had two typewriters in our offices. One was used by the clerk in the orderly room. The other was in the captain's office at the disposal of the officers. I used it occasionally to type letters on it. I also typed copies of my citations for my Silver Stars to send to my brother Willard and my mother. As I have said, I was not humble about my courage in combat. Like a diploma or a college degree, no one could ever take that away from me. I was a proud warrior.

One day as I was typing one of my citations, Lieutenant Littleton looked over my shoulder and noticed what I was doing.

"Why are you doing that?" he asked.

"To send to my mother," I replied. "What's wrong with that?"

"Oh, I don't know," he answered. "Somehow it doesn't seem appropriate. It's not something I would do."

His judgment upset me a little but not enough to stop me. After all, who was he to judge? He had no medals for heroism to brag about. He could not walk in my shoes.

While Captain Mostrum was still on leave, Captain Blowhard, the S4 (supply officer) from Battalion, paid us a visit. It seemed they were behind in their typing at Battalion and they needed another typewriter. Blowhard had heard we had an extra one. He came to get it. The company clerk was about to hand it over to him with no questions asked.

I told the clerk, "Get the serial number off it and have the captain sign a requisition form so we can take it off our books."

"Lieutenant, who the hell do you think you are," Blowhard yelled at me, "telling me what to do?"

"I'm Lieutenant Chamberlin, sir," I answered. "Acting company commander. I'm responsible for the company's property while Captain Mostrum is gone."

Captain Blowhard was a big man, much larger than me.

"Stand at attention when I talk to you," he said loudly as he pulled rank on me.

"Yes, sir," I answered. I snapped the heels of my well worn, unshined combat boots together. They made a dull, unimpressive thud. I squared my shoulders and sucked in my gut.

"Don't ever tell a superior officer what to do," Blowhard bellowed. "I could have you court-martialed for insubordination. You hear me?"

"Yes, sir," I said. "I hear you, but I will keep track of where our typewriter goes."

While we were confronting each other, the company clerk prepared the paper work to remove the typewriter from our inventory. Still in a huff, Captain Blowhard took our typewriter and left.

A day or two later at a staff meeting, which I was obligated to attend as a company commander, Captain Blowhard extended his hand to me and said, "Still friends?"

I took his hand and answered non-committally, "Sure, whatever you say, sir."

I never had anything more to do with him. Fortunately, our paths never crossed again.

Captain Mostrum returned to duty. I went back to see Chico. We danced and whiled away the evening. I tried to talk her into going to her place so I could save the price of a room at the club. She resisted at first, saying it was against the rules to leave the club with a client. But she finally agreed to tell me where she lived, to leave separately and meet at her place.

When we made love this time she cried even harder, perhaps because she was breaking the rules. Again I cried along with her. For me, they were tears of joy for I was enjoying my full measure of sexual fulfillment. I gave her ten dollars for the night.

We did the same thing one more time before she decided it was not right to break the house rules.

There was a beer garden on post where the enlisted men passing through our depot would often spend their free time. At times things would get rowdy and in need of a sober figure of authority to maintain control. Therefore officers were assigned to be there for two-hour shifts during busy hours.

One day, Captain Mostrum was assigned there from 1500 hours to 1700 hours. I was to follow him from 1700 hours to 1900 hours. When I arrived a few minutes before 1700 hours, I found that Captain Mostrum was not there. But a little, short major was. Apparently he was from Battalion and was checking up on us. But I didn't know him from Adam.

"Where have you been?" he demanded to know. "How come you left your post?"

"I didn't leave my post, sir," I explained. "I'm supposed to be here at five o'clock. Someone else was scheduled to be here until five o'clock."

"Don't talk back to me," the major snapped. "You're not supposed to leave your post."

Apparently my explanation did not register with him, or he didn't believe me. People shooting off their mouths don't usually hear what others have to say. He sure had a bug up his ass. He looked me over from my unshined combat boots to the top of my cunt cap.

"Look at you," he continued sarcastically. "You're the worst-looking officer I ever saw. What do you say about that?" He seemed to be almost daring me to challenge his authority.

"That's your opinion, sir," I replied.

I didn't give a shit what he thought. I expect he saw my Silver Star with Oak Leaf Cluster and my Combat Infantry Badge awards for WWII and Korea, as he looked me over. I don't know if my medals saved my ass from further chewing or if they maddened him with envy. He had no combat medals on his chest. And he had no grounds to belittle me.

As a parting shot, he said, "See to it, Lieutenant, you don't leave your post again."

I was fast learning that the percentage of military pricks in Sasebo was as great as they had been in Korea, perhaps even greater. But at least in Sasebo I could leave camp and get laid on a regular basis. More often even than at home. That made the stupid Army caste system a little easier to tolerate. I was now convinced more than ever not to stay in the Army any longer than I had to.

I returned to the sex club to see Chico. She did not want to break the rules again with me. Her excuse was that she was already spoken for that evening.

I asked a female hostess if she had a girl who did not smoke or drink. She introduced me to Tomeko. Tomeko was not as beautiful as many of the other geishas, but she was attractive. She used less make-up than most. She seemed more homespun, the kind of Japanese lady I would have wanted to bring back to the States as a wife, if I had been free to do so. It was refreshing that she did not smoke or drink. It also saved me some money. We danced and stayed at the club until closing time so she would not get in trouble. She had no objections to meeting me at her place to spend the night.

In bed she was excellent. Her smoke-free kisses were much sweeter than those of a smoker. Our tongues met and caressed each other. Our passions rose. Her breasts were soft and warm to my touch. I took time and kissed them. Her nipples became hard with excitement. When we joined we were a nice fit. She was damp with the lubricant of desire. Slowly and rhythmically our bodies moved to a lusty climax. I could have sworn she came with me. At least she appeared as satisfied as I was.

As usual I stayed in her, resting my weight on my elbows so as not to burden her. I kissed her eyelids, her neck and her sweet lips. Our passions were rejuvenated and we moved on towards another great climax. Then we lay locked in each other's arms. Serene sleep swept over us. In the morning, before it was time for me to return to camp to face a warring world, we enjoyed another piece in our own little peaceful world. I paid her ten dollars and promised to return.

As on any Army post, officers in our battalion were assigned to be Officer of the Day. My turn came up. As luck would have it, Major Wright was the OD of the whole camp. He came to inspect us. My role was to lead him around to our guard posts as he checked each one, like an escort in waiting.

He asked one of our guards, "What is the eighth general order?"

The guard stood stiffly at attention with his rifle at port arms and rattled off a general order loud and clear.

The major turned to me and asked, "Is that right, Lieutenant?"

I had no idea whether the guard had recited the right general order or not. I had memorized them long ago as a private at Fort

Bliss, Texas, during WWII. But I had long forgotten them. I suspected (and hoped) that the major had also forgotten them. If not, I hoped the guard was right.

"I believe so, sir," I replied, as if it mattered.

Apparently the major was satisfied. He made no criticism of the guard or me. I wondered if the major perhaps appreciated someone who was not quite so cocksure of himself as he was of himself.

I did not wait long to return to see Tomeko. She was now my favorite lady of the night. On my twenty-eighth birthday on February 27, 1953, I went to the club again in anticipation of a pleasant evening with her. In the beginning it was anything but pleasant.

When I arrived, Tomeko was already in the arms of an elderly Navy officer. I did not want anyone else, so I sat, waited and watched. Perhaps she would be dancing with the old man for only a little while. But he did not let her go. When they finished dancing to one tune he took her to a table and drank. She could not leave him. She was a slave to the house rules. He bought more tickets and they danced some more. He became quite intoxicated and amorous. His large, horny hands squeezed her buttocks and pulled her tight against him as they danced.

Tomeko knew I was there. Over the old man's shoulder she looked at me with wistful eyes. They told me she was sorry. She had to be with him because he had paid for her. But she wished she could be with me. It was a pleasant pain, knowing she wanted me but I could not have her. So I waited as the hours slipped slowly by, hoping he would pass out drunk or would leave the club without taking her to bed. He was so old and so drunk he probably couldn't get it up anyhow. I hated the thought of him pawing her in bed and trying to make love to her with a limp dick.

Chapter LVIII

I don't know what happened to the poor old Navy officer that night, but he did not bed down with Tomeko. Probably he was too drunk to worry about where he slept or who he slept with. I never saw him again.

Tomeko slipped away from him somehow. Perhaps when he went to the head to piss or puke.

She rushed up to me and said, "Thanks for waiting."

"Can I see you at your place?" I asked.

"Yes, I be there soon," she agreed.

When we were in her bed again, slowly making up for our long, torturous wait to be together, I told her it was my birthday.

"I give you birthday present," she said. "You no pay tonight."

"Thank you," I said. "You're my sweetheart."

Again we made love much as we had the first time. But this time it was more caring. It was what we both wanted. It was a great climax after the dreadful first half of the evening. Beneath her warm covers our naked bodies held each other close. Knowing that she had preferred me over the old sailor was a great boost to my ego and little soldier. She was loving me for free. He could have given her great gifts. She may have been a prostitute but she was not all out for money. I had a tender spot in my heart for all geishas. They were always so nice to me. But Tomeko was the most special of all. It was as if she were not a prostitute. Sex with her was not just to get my rocks off. I wanted her to be as satisfied as I was. Therefore I engaged in foreplay with her until I knew she was ready for my entrance. I kissed her, fondled her breasts and caressed her inner thighs until she warmed to my touch and became wet with want. We joined and stayed connected for a long time. I loved every minute of it so I tried to make it last as long as possible. My theory was that the longer it lasted the greater the rewarding climax for me, and the greater the pleasure for her. Again we spent the night sleeping in a loving embrace. In the morning I let her get on top of me so she could be in control. That seemed to please her. Then I donned the uniform of a military slave and returned to camp.

Lieutenant Littleton and I got along well as roommates. We shared a large room, so space was no problem. We did not do much together except our duties at the company. Sometimes we played pool in the day room. For the first few weeks we were together he never seemed to be interested in screwing around with the natives. He knew that I was spending a night or two a week off base pursuing the pleasures of the flesh. I made no secret of it. He was not openly critical of my promiscuous adultery. But I had the impression he did not think it was right. He knew I was married. One evening he surprised me. He did not sleep in his bed. When he returned to duty the next day, he had a big smile on his face, like a well-satisfied tomcat.

"Where were you last night?" I asked out of curiosity.

"I went out," he said. "I went to this officers' club and met this fabulous girl. She really liked me and let me spend the night with her."

"You had to pay for it, didn't you?" I asked.

"Yeah, I had to pay for the dance tickets and the room but I didn't have to pay her," he said. "She really liked me. She wants to see me again. We have a date this weekend."

"That's good," I said. "I'm glad you found somebody you like."

That Saturday Littleton got all spruced up for his date and left for town. A little later that evening I also left camp, hoping to see Tomeko again.

When I arrived at the club, lo and behold, there was Littleton dancing cheek to cheek with my latest lover. They were about the same height, she being tall for a Japanese lady and he being short for an American man.

I sat at a table and watched them dance. I was not happy that my lady was again taken for the evening. But, thinking rationally, I realized she was making her living as a paid prostitute, even though she had seemed to enjoy sex with me and had given me some free. Perhaps Littleton was right. Maybe she had acted like she enjoyed his peter too. Acting was part of a geisha's job.

When they spotted me, they joined me. Littleton seemed eager to introduce me to his date.

"Al. I'd like you to meet Tomeko," he said, proudly. "Tomeko, Al is in the same company as I am and we are roommates."

"I'm very pleased," I said.

I instinctively reached out to touch her. She bowed, as was the Japanese custom, and took my hand in hers. I put my other hand on her forearm seductively.

"You two seem to know each other," Littleton said.

"Yes, I've seen Tomeko when I was here before," I admitted, without divulging the full extent of our relationship.

But Tomeko was not the actress I suspected her to be. Her face became very flushed at the sight of me. She could not pretend she wanted to be with Littleton when she wanted to be with me.

Out of loyalty to the rules of the club, she remained at the side of Littleton. He had more tickets to dance with her. But she could not take her eyes off me. It became very obvious she was uncomfortable with Littleton while I was there.

After they danced some more Tomeko excused herself to go to the ladies' room. Littleton returned to my table.

He said, "She seems to want to be with you. Have you been together before?"

"Yes, I've been with her a couple of times," I admitted. "She does seem to like me. But you've paid for her. I have no claim on her."

"That's very gentlemanly of you," he said. "But I don't want to stand in her way if she wants you."

Soon he left the club, and Tomeko and I were together again for another night of lust and caring. Later as we lay naked under the covers of her bed in contented comfort, I asked her about Littleton.

"Oh, he's a nice little fellow," she said. "But I like you best. You make me happy."

"You make me very happy too," I told her.

After another night of long, lovely fornicating with my favorite paramour, I paid her ten bucks and went back to camp.

Lieutenant Littleton had nothing to say to me about being bested in the battle of sexual prowess. Nor did I rub it in to him. We carried on with our duties much as before.

Though I cared a great deal for Tomeko, I could not afford to spend ten dollars every night to be with her on my meager first lieutenant's pay. A couple of nights a week would be the most I could afford.

I was still sending my wife eighty dollars a month. That wasn't much but she also had the money from the roomers to live on. So she was managing pretty well. I still had not got completely over the power struggle we had had over money in our marriage. So I felt entitled to keep or spend most of my check for myself, I rationalized that I was saving for our future. I did not try to rationalize my adultery. I just felt sex was good for me and the natural quest of men. I wasn't trying to hurt anyone. I did not plan to confess to my wife. She could have been cheating on me too, with one of the roomers or whoever. If I had thought she was cheating, I'm not sure how I would have felt about it. I never thought about it.

I missed my little Judy. I was anxious to see my son, Rocky. But I did not really miss Josephine an awful lot, now that I was in Japan where I could have sex even more often than she allowed me at home with her once-a-week schedule.

But, getting back to Tomeko, since I could not be with her every night, she was not really my girl. No geisha could ever be the exclusive sex partner of one GI. The nights I would not be with her she would, by the nature of her profession, be with some other gentleman. That reality sort of diluted the strength of our relationship.

What I really wanted was a Japanese lady who would always be there for me when I wanted her, one who was not putting out just for money. For such a one, I would gladly give her enough money to live on, five or ten dollars a week. I was not a total cheapskate.

One day, I was having coffee in the dining room with a couple of guys in our company. One of them, Corporal Giftman, was about to return to the States. We were talking about pussy. While most officers felt it inappropriate to discuss such an intimate subject with enlisted men, I had no qualms about it.

Giftman said he had a problem. "I have this girl I've been seeing for a long time and taking care of. I hate to leave her stranded. I'm her only means of support. I'm going to see her tonight and tell her I'm going home. I only wish I knew somebody who would take care of her."

"What's her name?" I asked.

"Midori," he answered. "Hey, Lieutenant, would you be interested? You like women."

"What kind of a girl is she?" I asked.

"Oh, she's beautiful and smart too," he replied. "She speaks perfect English. And she's the best piece of ass I ever had. And I've had lots of it. Why don't you come with me tonight and I'll fix you up with her?"

"Okay," I agreed. "I'm looking for something more steady and less expensive."

So that night Giftman and I met Midori in a small cafe in town. As he had said, she was a very nice-looking Japanese girl. She was quite petite and attractive. She wore little, if any, make-up and plain clothing. Her appearance was much different than a geisha girl's. And she did speak English fluently. But she spoke very little to me. After the introduction she practically ignored me for the rest of the evening while she and Giftman conversed intimately. I felt left out and a little peeved. I could have been spending the night with Tomeko. Midori didn't seem to give a shit about me. *If that's the way she is, to hell with her*, I thought.

Then, as we were about to depart, Midori turned to me and said, "Take me home."

Chapter LIX

Midori and I traveled by public transportation to some remote residential part of Sasebo. It was late at night and very dark. I had no idea where we were, but I was not afraid. I trusted her. It would take a lot more uncertain danger than this to keep me from my pursuit of sex. She had not told me what we were going to do. But when she squatted down to take off my boots outside a house, I was pretty sure I was in. Then she took me by my hand and led me into the dark interior.

When we were inside, she pressed a little index finger against my lips for silence. In almost total darkness she led me carefully into the corner of a room, using the wall as a guide. At the allotted spot she stopped me and started taking off my clothes. I was most cooperative. She folded them neatly and silently placed them carefully next to a sleeping pad. Then she directed me with her little hands where to lie down. No words were even whispered. This was all done by body language and hand signals. I lay as she ordered and she covered my almost naked body with a light quilt. In a short time her naked body was beside mine. I drew her close to me and kissed her, making sure to make no noise. I was not sure why we had to be so quiet. I knew no way to ask her quietly. I assumed there was somebody near by whom she did not want us to be heard by, perhaps her parents. But it didn't matter to me. I had made love under similar restrictions before. I could do it again. The danger of being caught made it more exciting. I put my hand on her breasts. They were small and pleasing to my touch. She quickly took my hand away. I wondered. Was she saying "no?" But no, she was not saying "no." For when I rolled on top of her, she wrapped her slim legs around me with the litheness of a gymnast. She knew exactly how to maneuver her body to align our passion parts. She pulled me all the way into her. My penetration was complete. I was on top, in the position of control. But I could barely move. Her strong little legs kept me pinned close and deep inside her. She was warm, moist and snug. Her muscles tightened around me. This was a nice entrapment. Not moving made it last longer. But the coming was no less glorious. Out of deference to her wishes, I did not whimper, moan, or groan with ecstasy, as I was wont to do. We remained silent. My little soldier stayed at attention. He did not relax until after the third coming. Even after that, her legs remained around my waist as I rolled onto my right side. They were so slender that her left one fit underneath me in the hollow between my hip and chest with no pressure on it. We slept joined as one.

In the morning, I awoke to see other people sleeping on mats in the room. We dressed silently and left. I tried to make a date to see her again soon. She said she would call me. She did not explain with whom we shared the room that night, nor did I ask. She asked for no money. I offered none.

I cannot remember precisely the chronological dates and sequence of events that happened to me at Sasebo. Most of the first part of my duty there was not bad, except for the few pricks I ran into. And even they did not faze me much. A lot of troops passed through our company. Some poor bastards going to Korea. Some lucky ones rotating back home. I personally handled thousands of dollars and military scrip while changing their cash from one to the other. This was a tedious task, but not unpleasant. Most other duties were just routine stuff that required the presence or signature of an officer.

Somewhere about the end of March 1953, I was assigned to be a legal officer for special court martials. I did not want the job but I had no choice. I was given the position of prosecuting officer. Even though I had done very well in Military Justice in ROTC, I had no idea how to handle this new task.

First Lieutenant Lawson, who was in charge of this detail, said it was simple. "All you have to do is read certain paragraphs from the Manual of Military Justice and then question the plaintiff, defendant and witnesses to bring out the facts of the case."

He showed me the parts I would have to read. "Memorize them if you can, but if you can't, it's okay."

He made it sound easy and not all that important.

All the cases I remember handling were Korean War veterans

on their way home from the horrors of war. They were usually cases of insubordination, often the result of drinking to celebrate their good fortune of getting out of Korea alive.

For me it was no fun standing in front of a panel of five captains and majors and prosecuting some poor enlisted man for something I could well have been guilty of myself, if I were in his shoes. I remembered well my own court martial in WWII and my punishment under Article 15 in Korea. I easily identified with the defendant. But invariably I won the cases I tried, and the victims were sentenced to six months of hard labor, demotion to private and loss of two-thirds pay. I did not enjoy winning.

After two or three cases as prosecuting officer, I spoke to Lieutenant Lawson of my feelings.

"Perhaps you'd be happier as a defense officer," he suggested.

"Yes, that would be better," I agreed.

But being the defense officer was even worse for me than being the prosecutor. I lost all of the two or three cases I tried to defend. I felt frustrated and guilty that I was unable to help the poor devils. It seemed so senseless to me that men who had gone through the hell of Korea should be treated so harshly.

Several days passed with no word from Midori. I was about ready to give up on her and go back to see Tomeko, or to visit a less expensive whorehouse.

Then one day the phone rang as we officers were meeting in the office of Captain Mostrum. Mostrum took the call. He handed the phone to me.

"Some woman wants to talk to you," he announced with a touch of annoyance. It was Midori. She asked me to meet her at a hotel in Sasebo.

"Okay," I said.

Captain Mostrum gave me a look that seemed to say that I should not have women calling me on his phone during duty hours. Perhaps he did not say anything because his wife often called him during the day, now that she was with him in Sasebo.

Midori met me at the designated hotel. We had a bite to eat and retired to a room. This time I tried to engage in foreplay. I felt that women wanted and appreciated it. It was the best way for them to warm up and get ready for an orgasm and be as satisfied with sex as men were. So I kissed her little lips, caressed her long, straight, black hair and put my hand on her bare bosom. Everything was fine until I touched her tits. She giggled and quickly removed my hand, as she had done the first time, except she had not giggled then.

"Don't do that," she commanded. "I'm very ticklish there. I can't stand to have anyone touch my breasts."

"What about when my body touches them when I hold you?" I asked.

"Oh, that's okay," she said. "I like the feel of your body on me. You have a nice warm body. Sex with you is good. You make it last a long time. That pleases me."

So I forewent the foreplay. This time we did it on our sides after she had maneuvered her left leg under my waist and the right one around me. As she locked them behind my back in a scissors-like grip, her playpen engulfed my baby maker. But this time we could move and make noise as we wished. Even so, our movements were not swift or jerky, but slow and steady, orchestrated as much, or more, by her than me. After multiple orgasms, at least by me, and probably by her, we again drifted off into slumberland. Corporal Giftman had been right. Midori was the best.

In the morning, when I was about ready to get up, I had a piss hard on. Midori mounted me before I was able to leave our bed. She lowered herself down around me and sat on me resting on her knees. At first she moved slowly up and down on me. Thoughts of having to pee lessened. Suddenly she shifted gears and went into overdrive. She moved up and down faster than a buck rabbit on a doe. Once she went up too high and we disengaged. As she plunged back down, her perineum slammed against my bonehead with great force. It hurt like hell! However it felt to her, it did not stop her. She realigned our tools and continued with her jackhammer moves. Finally she crashed down upon me. I exploded up into her. We were spent.

When we parted she again said, "I'll call you."

Chapter LX

One day around the start of spring, 1953, a few of us young lieutenants were playing pool in the day room of our quarters. A short, stout black captain walked in on us.

"Don't you young men have anything better to do with your time than play pool?" he asked.

"What's wrong with shooting a little pool when our work is done?" I asked.

"Well, you could try to better yourselves by trying out for my track team," he challenged. "Can any of you run?"

"Sure, I can run," I said, thinking of all the miles I had run to get into shape for the paratroopers. "What would I have to do?"

"Meet me at the track tomorrow at four o'clock," he said. "By the way, my name is Captain Robinson."

"I'm Lieutenant Chamberlin," I said. "I'll give it a try."

So the next day was the start of about three months of training for track. We met almost every day at around four o'clock and worked out for about an hour. We were a small group of only five or six men.

Captain Robinson was a good coach. He took each of us from where we were and built us up gradually. In my case, he started me off jogging slowly for about three miles a day, on the quarter mile oval. Right off, Robinson noticed my underdeveloped, flat chest.

"You need to develop some pectoral muscles," he informed me.

So he told me to extend my arms straight out to the side and swing them in small circles.

"Do as many as you can clockwise and then as many as you can the other way," he instructed me. "Do these every day until you can do a hundred each way."

"Okay," I agreed, thinking it would be easy.

However, it wasn't as easy as I thought. After about ten or

fifteen swings my shoulders started to burn with fatigue. But I refused to give up. I kept at it religiously and eventually, after a few weeks, I reached the goal Robinson had set for me. Arm swings became a part of my life from then on.

The jogging was not hard. I had previously gone down to the parade ground by myself, where the track was located and jogged a few miles once in a while just to stay in relatively good shape, even though I no longer needed to get in shape for the paratroopers or for combat. My combat days were over and becoming a trooper was not now in my plans.

After about a month of training in heavy canvas sneakers, Coach Robinson got us some track spikes. Running in them gave me a painful case of shin splints. Again I did not give up. Robinson wouldn't let me. He made me jog through them.

I was no sprinter. So I trained for distances of a half-mile or more.

Finally sometime in June, Coach Robinson entered some of us in a meet against Japanese runners. He entered me in events of 800 meters (about a half-mile) and 5,000 meters (about three miles).

I knew nothing of track etiquette, something that Robinson had neglected to teach us. I was later to learn that it is polite to give the better starting positions to the favored runners, up front and on the inside. So I should have allowed another member of our team, who was much faster than I was, to have the inside position up front in the 800 meter race. But I took it. He lined up outside of me. He was polite enough not to remind me of my error.

Seconds into the race, I was boxed in. *I couldn't run in such a tight spot*, I thought. So I let them all pass me and went outside where there was room to run. Then I raced by the whole pack. There were several Japanese runners and us two Americans in the race. As soon as I was in the lead, my legs went into oxygen debt, something I had never experienced before and knew not of. I was reduced to a slow jog and the pack quickly passed me. By the time my strength returned, it was too late. I finished dead last.

My teammate finished second and might have won had I let him have the inside position.

After that humiliating defeat, I wanted to redeem myself by staying to run in the 5,000 meters, which was scheduled for a couple of hours later. I'm sure Coach Robinson knew I was a lost cause, but he waited patiently there with me long after the other members of the team had completed their competition and left. Robinson himself ran in the 100 meters sprint and won.

In the 5,000 meters I did no better than in the 800 meters, except that I did pace myself. I finished last in that event also, after being lapped by most of the other runners, and probably twice by the winner.

Training for track did not interfere with my main interest in life – sex. As promised, Midori called me again. We arranged to meet again at a hotel.

When I arrived at the hotel Midori was already there and so were three or four other American soldiers. It was a small party atmosphere. It was not something I had expected or wanted. Everyone there was very cordial and friendly. But no one seemed open about why we were all there. I knew why I was there – to make love to Midori. Were they all there for the same purpose? It was a mystery to me why Midori would want them there. Food and drinks were there, I partook of some of the food but did not drink any of the beer or sake they had because I was now in training for track.

As the evening wore on cards were brought out for a game of poker. I declined their invitation to play. I was there for only one thing, which was not card playing. I watched for a while, hoping the game would break up and Midori would be ready to go to bed with me. The game went on and on. Midori and her companions seemed to be enjoying themselves. I remained cool, calm and silent outwardly, but inside me dark anger was simmering gradually to a boiling point.

Somewhere around ten o'clock I said to myself, "Fuck this shit. Midori can go fuck herself and her friends too, if she wants to. She can kiss my ass. I'm going to bed."

I was not angry at the other men. I could not blame them for wanting a piece of the action. They had no moral obligation to me. Nor did Midori, for that matter. Neither did I to her.

Two rooms had been rented for the night. Why, I don't know.

Perhaps her plan had been to service each of us men privately in one of the rooms. If so, I thwarted her plan. I went into the other room and went to bed on the mat there. It took a while, but I finally went to sleep after my anger had subsided somewhat. After all, I had to get some rest for track practice the next day.

Suddenly, to my surprise, I was awakened by Midori quietly crawling under the covers with me. There was no sound from the other room. Apparently the other men had left. All was darkness.

"Love me," she ordered in a soft, serene whisper.

Her naked body pressed against mine was all I needed to be aroused. I was already sleeping with a hard on. My anger towards her turned to lust. What she had done previously that evening was no longer an issue for me. She was already damp with desire. I was ready for business at the touch of her warm little body. I rolled on top of her and penetrated her playpen completely.

This time it was different. She did not wrap her legs around me as before. She seemed totally relaxed, almost sedated. Her movements were slow and gentle like a calm sea stroking the sands of the shore. It did not take long for my first orgasm of the night. Her mellow moans signaled her pleasure for my warm sperm shooting up into her.

"*Hi, hi,*" she whispered. "Give it to me."

As usual, I continued a slow motion up and down on her for a little while. Then I stopped to relax and rest.

"*Dami, dami.*" she commanded. "Don't stop."

So I started my engine again in low gear and she lay there under me idling in peaceful bliss. For a long time my little soldier played in her playground. Inevitably, a second orgasm shook my body.

"*Hi, hi,*" she repeated the Japanese word for yes. "*Joto,* that's good."

Again I tried to stop and rest.

Again she said, "*Dami, dami,* don't stop."

So again I complied with her wishes. The snugness and warmth of her love canal demanded that my tool remain hard. After a long period of rear-end push-ups, I tried again to pause for a break. She appeared to have fallen asleep underneath me.

But as soon *as* I stopped she whispered, "Don't stop. It feels so good."

So I continued on with our sex marathon. Finally I came again. With each of my comings she moved softly against me and cooed with blissful contentment. She seemed to lack the energy for vigorous movement.

It had been a long time. I guessed we had started around two or three in the morning. Surely it was now time to rest and recuperate. So I stopped again, fully expecting my peter-to-peter out.

But she would not let me rest. She wiggled a bit up against me and said, "Please, don't stop. Love me."

So love her I did, on into the morning. Her inner muscles seemed to have some sort of magical control over my organ to keep it erect. Whenever I tried to rest she demanded that I continue.

I lost track of how many times I came that night. Certainly more times than I ever had before on one bone and more than I ever did afterward. How long we were joined together is hard to tell. My estimate is about four hours.

I had no idea what Midori and the soldiers who were with her did between the time I left them and Midori came to bed with me. She never told me and I did not ask her. Did she become mellow on liquor? Were they using drugs? Did they give her some Spanish Fly? I had heard that Spanish Fly made a woman crave sex. I wondered what it did to men. Had they slipped me some too? I didn't know and, now that the night was over, I didn't care.

When we parted that morning, she again said, "I'll call you."

Chapter LXI

Midori called me much sooner this time. We met in Sasebo and she took me to where she lived. It was in another hard-to-find residential area of the city. I took careful note of how to get there, for future reference.

She lived in a humble abode with an elderly lady. She did not tell me their relationship, but I guessed the lady was someone Midori was taking care of, and not her mother.

This time everything was normal. Nobody shared the room with us. There was no preliminary party. And Midori was her natural self. She seemed to have developed a genuine affection for me, perhaps because of my stamina.

We made beautiful love that night and slept securely in each other's arms.

From then on Midori was my girl. I went to her place almost every night. She was always there waiting for me. So I guess she was loyal to me, at least at night. I never asked her.

But Midori was not completely normal. She had another eerie quirk about her that astonished and almost frightened me. One evening, when I joined her for a night of peaceful togetherness, she told me of her exciting day and secret passion.

"I saw a big fire today," she said. "A big warehouse burned down. It was beautiful. The flames were so bright and beautiful. I love to see fires. They are so warm and pretty."

I was shocked that an intelligent person would take pleasure in seeing another's pain and loss.

"But what about the damage and destruction, loss of property or even lives?" I asked, incredulously. "Doesn't that bother you?"

"That doesn't matter," she continued. "Fires are so beautiful. I love to watch them burn. They make me feel so warm and happy."

I did not argue further with her. She was only a sex object to me. I took advantage of her warm, happy excitement. Her body was especially warm and exciting that night.

From then on, however, I was conscious of how to exit her room quickly in case of fire. I must say Midori was like no other.

I was not overly generous to her, but I did give her enough money to live on – about twenty dollars a month. The cost of living was much less in Japan at that time than in the United States. And she could have traded the military scrip for much more in the black market. At least that's the way I rationalized my stinginess. Midori was a great savings for me. My wife would have appreciated that aspect of my adultery.

Speaking of my wife, she wrote me that they were already packed and ready to join me in Sasebo. She sounded eager to be with me again.

At about this time, I learned of a new directive from the Pentagon allowing for the "early out" of officers like me (who had signed up for three years) at the end of two years. Some requirements had to be met, like having been in Korea and in combat a certain amount of time. I was eligible to get out of the damned Army by the end of June! I was overjoyed. Immediately I notified my wife to unpack without any explanation. If I came home early, I would surprise her.

A good friend of mine, Lieutenant Goodman, was also eligible for "early out". So we got together and filled out the necessary papers to request our "early out" and sent them to Battalion. From there they were supposed to go on up through military channels to be approved in Washington. Then we waited in happy anticipation of becoming free men again.

While we were waiting May Day came. May first was a communist holiday. It was supposed to be dangerous to be on the streets of Sasebo on that day. Therefore all military personnel were restricted to camp, except those who lived off base in military housing, like Captain Mostrum and others whose wives were now in Japan with them.

But I was not about to be told I could not go into Sasebo to see Midori. So I boarded the bus which took us through the main gate and on into town. An MP entered the bus at the gate and asked me why I was going to town. I lied that I was living off post. He asked me the name of the housing complex. I remembered one and told him. He asked me the address. I told him we had just moved in and I had forgotten. I think he knew I was lying but he let me go. Probably because he wasn't too sure how to kick an officer off the bus. Or maybe he just didn't give a shit.

Anyhow, I went on into Sasebo and walked boldly through the narrow streets to Midori's place. No big, bad, anti-American communist accosted me. Something about breaking the rules and facing possible danger gave me an adrenaline high, somewhat like (though to a lesser degree) the ones I had experienced on Baldy and Eerie in the heat of battle.

Cuddling with Midori that night was especially sweet. Being May Day she had not expected me. So perhaps it was special for her too.

Lieutenant Goodman and I waited patiently for our applications to be approved. Meanwhile, I continued my new hobby of training for track. I'm not sure my constant lovemaking with Midori was conducive to good running performances, but I was not willing to give up either one.

Our applications came back sooner than expected. They had not gone far. Captain Rednek, the personnel officer at Battalion had disapproved them. According to him, we were not eligible.

Goodman and I were madder than hell! We knew we were eligible. We steamed and plotted for a few days. Then we resubmitted our applications through channels as we had done before, with further arguments for our cases.

Again, after a little longer wait this time, our applications were returned disapproved by the same Captain Rednek. Each time he had not forwarded them on to the next higher command.

Goodman and I stewed about it some more. Then Goodman came up with a new idea.

"Let's send them in again," he said. "Only this time we'll send an 'information copy' to the adjutant general in Washington. On our applications we'll write that an 'information copy' has been sent to the adjutant general. That will scare the shit out of him and he'll have to forward them through channels."

"That's a good idea," I said. "Where did you learn about that?"

"Oh, I read about it in Army Regulations," Goodman said.

So that's what we did. We submitted our applications for the third time through channels and an "information copy" to the adjutant general.

All of this correspondence back and forth and the waiting periods between took up most of May. But, after the third submission, we got some action. I was ordered to report to Colonel Dumkoft in his office in downtown Sasebo. I did as ordered.

"Lieutenant Chamberlin reporting as ordered, sir," I said, as I saluted smartly.

The colonel returned my salute and said, "At ease, Lieutenant. I have your application here for an 'early out' under the directive put out by President Eisenhower. Unfortunately, I have to disapprove your application. You are not eligible."

"I think I am, sir," I disagreed with the Colonel.

"No, you're not," he replied bluntly. "But I can understand why you would want to get out of the service. You have a wife and two children to support. Being in the service must be a tremendous hardship for you and your family. I think you are eligible for a hardship discharge. So I recommend that you put in for a hardship discharge. But you have to withdraw this application first."

I knew what his game was. If I withdrew this application and applied for a hardship discharge, the chances were that one would be turned down also. And I would have a hard time reapplying for "early out". In the meantime the Army could put the screws to me as a malcontent. Maybe even send me back to Korea.

So I spoke up to the colonel. "Being in the Army is no hardship for me or my family. I don't think I would be eligible for a hardship discharge. So I'm not going to withdraw this application."

The colonel's demeanor quickly changed. I guess he was not used to having lowly lieutenants disagree with him. He glowered at me for a moment and then said, "Okay, Chamberlin, that's all. Get out of my office."

Three days later orders came from Headquarters Camp Sasebo that I be sent back to the States to be released from active duty. Lieutenant Goodman's idea had paid off.

To my knowledge Colonel Dumkoft did not order Goodman

Printed in the United States
5265

9 781930 493957